BARBARISM AND ITS DISCONTENTS

Cultural Memory
in
the
Present

Mieke Bal and Hent de Vries, Editors

BARBARISM AND ITS DISCONTENTS

Maria Boletsi

STANFORD UNIVERSITY PRESS

STANFORD, CALIFORNIA

Stanford University Press
Stanford, California

Printed in the United States of America on acid-free, archival-quality paper

Library of Congress Cataloging-in-Publication Data

Boletsi, Maria, author.
  Barbarism and its discontents / Maria Boletsi.
  pages cm. — (Cultural memory in the present)
  Includes bibliographical references and index.
  ISBN 978-0-8047-8276-0 (cloth : alk. paper)
  1. Civilization. I. Title. II. Series: Cultural memory in the present.
CB19.B575   2013
909—dc23

                                                        2012020741

For my parents,
Spyros Boletsis and Anastasia Giouleka

Contents

Preface

Barbarism and Its Discontents is an inquiry into the operations of the concept of "barbarism" and the figure of the "barbarian" in modern and contemporary works of literature, art, and theory. Although barbarism is traditionally viewed as the negative offshoot of "civilization," it can be recast as a creative and critical concept in cultural theory: it can unsettle binary oppositions, imbue authoritative discourses with foreign, erratic elements, and trigger alternative modes of knowing and relating to others. This study situates barbarism in a broad context: it touches on theory, politics, history, literature, and visual art and brings together cultural objects from several national contexts, including Argentinean, Czech, German, Greek, Mexican, North American, and South African. Staging encounters among diverse objects, media, and discourses pluralizes barbarism and charts its complex operations.

"Barbarism" and the "barbarian" are not only treated here as objects of analysis but are also cast as theoretical and methodological concepts, which help me reflect on *how* I do what I do. This study therefore contains bits and pieces of what I imagine as a barbarian mode of theorizing. The premises of this theorizing, which inform and guide my approach, can be sought in certain ongoing theoretical conversations. In the last three decades, theory in the fields of comparative literature, postcolonial studies, and cultural studies has been accompanied by metaphors of travel and mobility. Edward Said's (1983) "travelling theory," Mieke Bal's (2002) "travelling concepts," and Deleuze's (2004) "nomadic thought" are cases in point. Said's concept of "travelling theory" unsettles the tendency of theory to seek stability and abstract generalization and draws emphasis to specific "sites of production, reception, transmission and resistance to specific theories" (Clifford 1989). Bal proposes a concept-based interdisciplinary methodology for cultural analysis based on the possibilities that unravel as concepts travel from one discipline to another. Deleuze introduces the notion of nomadic thought as producing a mode of writing that creates something uncodable in theory, traverses the frame of the text, and connects thought to the outside (2004, 255). Such tropes mark the attempt to conceptualize theory as an open and unfinished process and prevent it from becoming "monolingual, presentist, narcissistic" (Spivak 2003, 20).

Nevertheless, as Peter Hallward (2001) argues with regard to postcolonial theory, while theory aspires to create a nongeneralizable discourse that privileges difference, indeterminacy, and contextual specificity, it often ends up masking a self-regulating and self-authenticating discourse. Concepts invested with a revolutionary potential often turn into dogmatic, saturated versions of their initial forms, deprived of rigor and specificity. Moreover, theoretical concepts often lose their transformative potential by being entangled in a web of limitations, which make scholars overly cautious when employing them. Being alert to our blind spots and to the risk of excluding others from our discourses; the demands of political correctness; the catachrestic nature of available terms; the complicity of the critic in the discourses she employs and questions; and the demands of self-reflexive scholarship: such considerations are indispensable for practicing responsible scholarship, but they can sometimes also operate as a straitjacket, which strips theoretical discourses and concepts of their transgressive potential and controversiality, making them too "civilized."

This study is an attempt to dislodge barbarism from its conventional contexts and rekindle the critical and transgressive potential of this concept, not despite but *through* its controversiality. Instead of reinforcing a discourse that divides the world into civilized and barbarian, barbarism can also challenge this discourse and engage in constructive operations. This critical potential in barbarism can take the form of a "barbarian theorizing"—a term I borrow from Walter Mignolo (1998).

Some of the tentative premises of such barbarian theorizing, which also function as implicit guidelines in this book, are the following. The theorizing I call barbarian is not a disavowal of method but constructs tentative methodologies in practice, using tools from different disciplinary fields. It invites unlikely juxtapositions that may push our thinking, shift our theoretical presuppositions, expose their shortcomings, and make our theories more relational and less narcissistic. Barbarian theorizing welcomes instances whereby theoretical discourses stumble, stutter, or lose some of their confidence vis-à-vis their objects.

Barbarian theorizing focuses on dissensus or miscommunication not as problems to be resolved but, in line with Chantal Mouffe (2005) and Jacques Rancière (1999), as constitutive of "the political." It accommodates nonconsensual speech in order to counter the semblance of congruity in culture, interrogate the premises of established theoretical and academic discourses, and determine which voices are excluded from the social or even perceived as "barbarian noise" and why.

Barbarian theorizing invites experimentation with playful expressive modes, which break with the formal conventions of "serious" theory. Annexing literary strategies in theoretical or philosophical discourses—for example, by imagining literary modes of reading or doing theory—would be one of the many forms this experimentation may take.

Barbarian theorizing is never fully present, complete, or identical to itself. It knows only provisional moments of realization and simultaneously points to not-yet-existing modes of knowing: it promises a future "barbarian" epistemology. This promise, even if it can never be fully realized, enables theory to constantly renew itself.

Although "barbarism" is an overdetermined and historically charged term, this book makes a case for its critical thrust—its "edge"—in cultural theory. If we do not take this concept for granted, relying on its conventional meanings and functions in discourse, we are more alert to the shifts and fissures it may create in the categories of this discourse. Through these fissures, new grammars, new relations, and new modes of speaking and knowing could emerge.

Acknowledgments

This book is the product of a long intellectual journey that started in 2005, during which I benefited from the insights, commentary, and support of several colleagues and friends.

I owe a great debt of gratitude to Ernst van Alphen and Mieke Bal for their rigorous readings of my work, their constructive and insightful criticism, and their guidance. Their work has been a continuing source of inspiration to me.

I also want to thank my colleagues at the Film and Comparative Literature Department of Leiden University, Yasco Horsman, Isabel Hoving, Madeleine Kasten, Frans-Willem Korsten, Liesbeth Minnaard, and Peter Verstraten, for their advice, stimulating conversation, and helpful feedback. The theory seminars at the Leiden University Centre for the Arts in Society (LUCAS), the Amsterdam School for Cultural Analysis (ASCA), and the OSL Research School for Literary Studies in Utrecht were hubs of intellectual labor. I wish to thank the seminar organizers as well as my colleagues for the exchange of ideas and productive collaborations.

I am also grateful to the LUCAS, with which I have been affiliated since 2005. Their financial assistance made it possible for me to present parts of this study in several conferences and seminars abroad and gave me the opportunity to take part in the School of Criticism and Theory (SCT) at Cornell University in the summer of 2006 and to spend a semester at Columbia University in 2008–9 to work on this project. I also owe a big thank you to Eduardo Cadava, Vangelis Calotychos, and Stathis Gourgouris for their personal conversations and insightful commentary, which enriched this book and my stay at Columbia University. In the past few years, I also had the privilege of discussing this material with a number of scholars. Derek Attridge, Vassilis Lambropoulos, and Christian Moser were among these invaluable interlocutors.

I would like to thank the artists Kendell Geers and Graciela Sacco for their generous permission to reprint images of their works in this book. The images *Piedad postcolonial* (2005) and *Abu Ghraib Reenactment* (2006) by Guillermo Gómez-Peña in collaboration with photographers Javier Caballero (first image) and Teresa Correa (second image) are reprinted here courtesy of BRH-LEON editions. The images *Generic Terrorist, Hybrid Gang Banger*, and *Islamic Immigrant* by Guillermo Gómez-Peña in collaboration with photographers James McCaffrey (first two images) and Ramon Treves (third image) have appeared in *The Journal of Visual Culture* 5.1 (2006) as part of "The New Barbarians: A Photo-Performance Portfolio." They are reprinted here by permission of Sage Publications. The English translation of C. P. Cavafy's poem "Waiting for the Barbarians" by Edmund Keeley and Philip Sherrard is reprinted by permission of Princeton University Press (Keeley, Edmund; *C.P. Cavafy*. © 1975, revised 1992 by Edmund Keeley and Philip Sherrard). The parts of the performance texts by Guillermo Gómez-Peña cited in Chapter 7 have been published in *Ethno-Techno: Writings on Performance, Activism, and Pedagogy* (2005) and are reprinted here by permission of Routledge, part of the Taylor & Francis Group.

A different, earlier version of Chapter 5 appeared in *Comparative Literature Studies* 44.2 (2007): 67–96, and is reproduced by permission of Pennsylvania State University Press. Some portions of Chapter 5 also appear in my article "Barbarism as a Mode of (Not) Knowing," in *Inside Knowledge: (Un)doing Ways of Knowing in the Humanities* (Cambridge Scholars Press, 2009), edited by Carolyn Birdsall, Maria Boletsi, Itay Sapir, and Pieter Verstraete. Some portions of Chapter 6 have appeared in the online *Cavafy Forum* of the University of Michigan.

BARBARISM AND ITS DISCONTENTS

Introduction

Rien de plus compliqué qu'un Barbare.
—Gustave Flaubert, "Lettre à Sainte-Beuve"

The words *barbarism, barbaric,* or *barbarians* figure prominently in political rhetoric at the dawn of the new millennium. While the rhetoric of "civilization versus barbarism" seemed to partly recede with decolonization, after the end of the Cold War and the fall of communism in the Soviet Union and Eastern-bloc Europe, and especially after the terrorist attacks on September 11, 2001, it has made a comeback in Western politics, the media, historiography, political and cultural theory, and everyday speech. Although different things are being written and said these days about barbarism and civilization, more often than not the meaning of these terms remains uncontested. Especially in Western political rhetoric, there appears to be a silent consensus on what "barbarism" means, what constitutes "barbaric" behavior, and who a "barbarian" is. This book contends that there is nothing natural or self-evident about these categories and their uses. Despite their standardized deployment in contemporary rhetoric, these categories are mobile, complex, and versatile. They assume a variety of meanings and operations in language and other media, which can contest their deep-rooted uses in Western discourses.

By charting diverse significations, functions, and effects of barbarism and the barbarian, this study contests the seeming historical rigidity of these categories by centering on their performativity. To this end, I propose a shift from an essentialist to a performative approach to these categories. The central question is not "who (or where) are the barbarians?" but "what kinds of critical operations can barbarism and the barbarian be involved in"? This shift aims at dislodging the notion of the barbarian from a metaphysics of presence and exploring what it could mean to *perform* a critical and perhaps even productive kind of barbarism rather than *be* a barbarian in any absolute sense.

This book proposes barbarism as a theoretical concept in cultural critique by laying out some of the epistemological and comparative operations it can trigger from within or from the margins of dominant discourses and modes of representation. It develops an affirmative approach to this notion, not despite but *through* an engagement with its negative meanings and injurious effects in speech and in social life. Revisiting underexposed aspects of barbarism unravels its potential operations in language and other media without circumventing its violent history in Western discourses and without rendering it "harmless." In the gaps and tensions between its various meanings, between its history and present uses, and between its formal meanings in language and its effects in speech, one can trace possibilities for doing different things with this concept in the space of literature, art, and theory.[1]

This study does not wish to replace the negative associations of barbarism and the barbarian with a brand-new positive meaning. Instead, it probes the (sometimes hidden) critical potential of their existing meanings and pushes it toward small resignifications while charting new sets of relations and contexts for barbarism and the barbarian within literature, art, and theory. In a Foucauldian vein, I take barbarism and the barbarian as objects produced by discourse rather than as preexisting essences waiting to be linguistically and conceptually acknowledged and named. Small modifications in the discursive constellations that form these objects in specific ways could help us envision a different connotative space for them. To borrow Stuart Hall's words, this book aims to help "disarticulate a signifier from one, preferred or dominant meaning-system, and rearticulate it within another, different chain of connotations" (1982, 80).

Barbarism is not an inherent quality of a human subject, language, medium, or cultural object. Rather, it is here revisited *through* and *as* a series of operations, taking effect at sites of encounter between different subjectivities, languages, discourses, or systems of reference. The term "(barbarian) operations" here refers to a form of agency, not (necessarily) person- or intention-bound, that manifests itself in critical interventions often produced in the contact zones between heterogeneous discourses, narratives, or knowledge regimes. My use of the term "operations" is based on Michel Foucault's use of the term in the context of discursive operations and operations of power/knowledge.[2] In this framework, the following questions are posed: How can the operations of barbarism in literature, art, and theory expose and unsettle the uses and violent effects of this category in current and historical Western discourses? Can the concept of barbarism perform critical interventions in our discursive frameworks and even inspire new modes of knowing, comparing, and theorizing? Can this concept help us imagine ways of relating to others that are not fully dependent on essentialist binary schemes?

Rather than support a discourse that prescribes what is good and evil, this book contends that barbarism and the barbarian also carry a performative force with a transgressive potential. This potential is already implicitly registered in the definitions of these terms. If we look up the word "barbarism" in major English dictionaries, among the definitions we find are the following:

—uncivilized nature or condition; uncultured ignorance; absence of culture; barbaric style (in art etc.), unrestrainedness (*Shorter Oxford English Dictionary on Historical Principles*, 2002)

—the absence of culture and civilized standards (*Oxford American Dictionary and Thesaurus*, 2003)

—ignorance of arts, learning, and literature; barbarousness (*Webster's New International Dictionary*, 1913)

In all these definitions, barbarism is captured through negative categories and through a grammar that signifies lack or absence. The same experiment with the word "barbarian" yields similar results:

—a foreigner; a person with a different language or different customs; spec. a non-Hellene, a non-Roman; also, a pagan, non-Christian

—savage, wild, or uncivilized person

—an uncultured person; a person without sympathy for literary or artistic culture (*Shorter Oxford English Dictionary on Historical Principles*, 2002)

These definitions set the barbarian against a positive standard of civilization, whether this standard is defined by one's language or customs, ethnicity or culture (Hellene, Roman), religion (Christianity) or behavior (good manners and sophistication). In all definitions, the barbarian is situated outside the borders of civilization, as a being who does not speak the language or share the culture of the civilized and, by extension, as incomprehensible, unfamiliar, uncanny, improper.

Both "barbarism" and the "barbarian" are thus accompanied by a seemingly inescapable negativity. This negativity resides not only in the terms' semantic content—the connotations of violence, brutality, exploitation, and destruction—but also in their opposition to the positive notions of culture, humanism, and particularly civilization. Barbarism operates as the negative standard, against which civilization measures its virtue, humanity, or level of sophistication. From a high standing, civilization constructs its abjects—those barbarian others who function as its "constitutive outside."[3] Within this oppositional scheme, the barbarian and the civilized are interdependent notions. The "civilized we" can be sophisticated, mature, superior, and humane, because the barbarians are simple, infantile, inferior, and savage.

The term "barbarism" is associated with unintelligibility, lack of understanding, and mis- or noncommunication. These associations can also be extracted from the etymology of barbarian: in ancient Greek, the word *barbaros* imitates the incomprehensible sounds of the language of foreign peoples, sounding like "bar bar." The foreign sound of the other is dismissed as noise and therefore as not worth engaging. Consequently, the *barbarization* of others—their construction as barbarians—disempowers them. Those tagged as "barbarians" cannot speak out and question their barbarian status because their language is not even understood or deemed worthy of understanding. In certain ways, the "barbarian" is a nonconcept because it tries to signify and capture the unsignifiable, the unintelligible, the unknowable. But the fact that by definition a barbarian cannot be "known" or "understood" enables the term's function in language as a generic appellation. Naming someone "barbarian" denies this person an actual face, subjectivity, and singularity. The other is treated as a hollow vessel, filled by the discourse of civilization in ways that reinforce the civilized identity.

The aforementioned meanings of barbarism do not cover the entire scope of its lexicographical definitions. Barbarism is also used as a countable noun in another, primarily linguistic, sense, denoting "an offensive word or action, especially a mistake in the use of language" (*Longman Dictionary of Contemporary English*, 2003) or "something that breaks rules of convention or good taste" (*Encarta Webster's Dictionary of the English Language*, 2004).

A more extensive definition of this second meaning captures barbarism as

the intermixture of foreign terms in writing or speaking a standard, orig. a classical, language; a foreignism so used; also, the use of any of various types of expression not accepted as part of the current standard, such as neologisms, hybrid derivatives, obsolete or provincial expressions, and technical terms, or any such expression used in discourse. (*Webster's New International Dictionary*, 1913)

Although this second meaning is again mainly expressed through negative formulations, it simultaneously invests barbarism with a quality I am tempted to call *insurgent*. Barbarism is an element that deviates from (linguistic or other) norms and conventions; it is an insertion of "foreign terms" and elements that do not fit or are "not accepted as part of the current standard"; it can be an element that strikes a discordant note in conventions of "good taste." Based on the previous definition, "barbarisms" signal encounters between heterogeneous spatial or temporal frames, linguistic registers, and discursive orders. They bring the familiar in contact with the foreign by introducing "foreignisms" in classical idioms. They confront the new with the old and the past with the present through "neologisms" but also "obsolete . . . expressions." They disrupt elevated speech with "provincial expressions." They bring heterogeneous elements together in "hybrid derivatives."

It follows from these definitions that foreign or erratic elements, inconsistencies, disruptions, and unlikely encounters or comparisons are included in barbarism's connotative range. If we push these definitions a bit further, barbarism could denote an invasion by foreign, disruptive elements into dominant, normative discourses and modes of reading, writing, viewing, or knowing. Barbarisms could be elements that break with traditional rules, cross cultural or disciplinary boundaries, and delve into new, unexpected combinations—elements that cause confusion and misunderstandings and invite counterintuitive modes of reading. Barbarisms appear in a zone of error ("a mistake"), as well as of hybridization and syncretism ("intermixture of foreign terms"). They thus take effect at moments when two (or more) discourses, systems, or subjectivities meet. By staging encounters between diverse objects, this book shows how the concept of barbarism can trigger alternative ways of knowing, comparing, and theorizing that accommodate strangeness, reversals, bewilderment, and other such phenomena that arise at border zones between "languages" in the broadest sense of the word.

Thus, instead of dismissing barbarism as noise not worth engaging (the "bar bar" of the other), I argue that this noise has the potential to unsettle the supposedly harmonious, elevated speech of the "civilized self" by confronting it with its own cacophonies and foreign elements—its internal barbarisms. The mumbling of the barbarian—the confused speech, the stuttering, the noise—can turn into a force that interrupts the workings of language and incites a rethinking of the premises of the discourse of the self.

Barbarism, then, oscillates between two main functions: it reinforces the discourse of civilization that needs it as its antipode but it also nurtures a disruptive potential, through which it can interrupt the workings of the very same discourse that constructs the category of the barbarian for the sake of civilization's self-definition. As Brett Neilson remarks, barbarism oscillates "between two poles":

The first represents the persistence of binary thought (master/slave, white/black, male/female, voice/writing, etc.) and of the material processes of domination that support this dichotomous logic. The second stands for the ambivalent processes of discursive slippage, the repetitions and doublings, that the articulation of binaries can never completely close up. (1999, 92)

While the pervasive use of "barbarism" in Western discourses testifies to the "overwhelming power of the binary," the notion also registers "the openings, ambivalences and dislocations that problematize this inexorable logic of overcoding" (92). This double potential of barbarism makes its workings in language far from stable and predictable. Even as it is implicated in one of the most steadfast hierarchical oppositions in Western history, a part of the name "barbarism" remains unmasterable by binary logic and can thus debunk the opposition to which it is attached. In other words, the opposition between barbarism and civilization, rigid as it may be, cannot achieve closure: its apparent fixity is constantly challenged by the otherness and exteriority of the same barbarism it tries to repress, subdue, and expel.[4]

The term's instability and transformability are not only a result of the tensions within its formal meanings. Barbarism is not (only) a formal linguistic unit but also an unpredictable event, co-shaped by a constellation of factors that constitute its performativity: the term's formal meanings; the tension between its accumulated historical meanings and its signifying force in the present; the intentions of the speaker that uses the term; the way the listeners or readers perceive it; the contexts in which it appears; and the multiple contexts it evokes. The performativity of barbarism—the way the word functions in the here and now of its every use—is not a by-product of the formal unit called "barbarism" but is just as constituent of barbarism as its formal dictionary meanings.

Because barbarism may function differently every time it is iterated, it does not always fulfill the intention implicit in its conventional, long-standing meanings—that is, it does not always end up *meaning* what *it means to*.[5] Consequently, its use could yield meanings or effects that do not coincide with, and may even run contrary to, the speaker's intentions. Precisely in the disjunction between the term's intentions, meanings, and effects, possibilities open up for a creative recasting of barbarism.[6]

The breach between meaning and intention also has consequences for what barbarism and the barbarian end up doing: their effects in our realities. Barbarians do not exist independently of discourse but are produced in the act of an utterance. Naming someone "barbarian" creates him or her as a threatening, foreign, savage being. But what an utterance says—what it wants to say—is not always what it ends up saying. An utterance, Shoshana Felman argues, is always "*in excess* over its statement," and thus its effects cannot be reduced to its constative aspect (its meaning). The performative force of an utterance can be seen as "a sort of energizing 'residue,'" the residue of meaning (2003, 52). Thus, the act of naming someone "barbarian" constitutes a "dynamic movement of modification of reality" because it can turn a person into a less-than-human enemy (51).

But between the formal meaning of the barbarian and the production of barbarians as effects of naming, there is excess, a residue of meaning, which allows "barbarism" and the "barbarian" to perform operations with unexpected effects. These operations may result in new modifications of reality but also in a resignification of the terms themselves.

While a resignification of a violent, injurious term may try to redirect the term's negativity and violence toward affirmative and productive operations, such a move, as Judith Butler argues, runs the risk of reiterating the abusive logic of the term's past (1997a, 14). This is a risk this book also takes with "barbarism." Nevertheless, casting "barbarism" and the "barbarian" *otherwise* also creates a future context for these categories—a context that is open. Thus, while an affirmative appropriation of the term "barbarian" in new discursive constellations may end up restaging the violence of its past uses, the term does not necessarily have to perform that violence each time it is used. The space of discursive performativity, Butler contends, makes it possible for words to "become disjoined from their power to injure and recontextualized in more affirmative modes" (15).

Thus, this book tests barbarism and the barbarian in discursive relations and contexts that do not always bind these concepts in a hierarchical opposition to civilization, or, when they do, they leave small fissures for questioning the terms of this hierarchy. In this venture, barbarism not only is an object of study but becomes a theorizing agent: it is recast as a theoretical and methodological concept.[7] "Barbarism" and "the barbarian" are thus involved not only in *what* I explore but also in *how* I explore it. As the main objects of this study are implicated in the methodological and theoretical problematics that frame it, they become interlocutors in the close readings that unfold in the following chapters.

This book's aim is to tease out the critical thrust of barbarism in order to propose it as a useful concept in cultural critique, operating on its own right and not just as civilization's offshoot. Deep-rooted and overcharged concepts such as "barbarism" and "civilization" cannot be banned from our discourses. Notions of otherness can offer a positive contribution to the identity construction of the self. The distinction between "self and other" or "we and they" and the antagonisms it contains can be seen as constitutive of any identity, and thus essential components of social life. However, there are different ways to conceptualize this distinction.

According to Chantal Mouffe, "The constitution of a specific 'we' always depends on the type of 'they' from which it is differentiated" (2005, 19). Therefore, based on the way the other is constructed, we can "envisage the possibility of different types of we/they relation" instead of trying to overcome the "we/they" distinction altogether (19). The distinction between self and other can thus be envisioned differently—in ways that do not construct the other as threatening, inferior, or illegitimate, and thus seek its destruction, but turn the barbarian *enemy* into an *adversary*, and "the Other" into *an* other.

Exposing the Objects

The works of literature, art, and theory that take center stage in this book are not viewed as embodiments of "high culture" or as the quintessential sites of civilization but, counterintuitively perhaps, as fertile sites of barbarism—sites in which different conceptions of barbarism can be developed and barbarian operations can be performed. Most of these cultural objects are recent or contemporary. Some date from the first half of the twentieth century, but the issues they bring forth place them at the heart of the present, inviting comparisons with the contemporary works discussed in this book. Although these objects are spread across various geographical sites, they all share a critical engagement with the *Western* discourse on barbarism and barbarians, which they challenge, whether they address it from within or from its margins.

The case studies situate barbarism in a broad, comparative context: pluralizing barbarism and its operations can be best accomplished through "barbarian encounters" among diverse objects, media, contexts, and discourses. The connecting thread of the objects is neither a particular national context nor a specific genre but a concept and the questions to which it gives rise. There are several valuable historical studies of "the barbarian" in particular periods or cultures. There are, however, few comparative and interdisciplinary approaches to barbarism, and even fewer attempts to chart it as a theoretically, methodologically, and epistemologically productive concept. This book makes a contribution to such approaches.

The objects analyzed explicitly thematize barbarians and barbarism. Nevertheless, the "barbarian operations" I introduce here are not the prerogative of objects in which either the terms "barbarism" and "barbarian" or visual representations of barbarians make their appearance. Barbarian operations can take effect in various cultural objects, regardless of their thematic connection to barbarism, as well as in different kinds of discourses: artistic, literary, philosophical, scholarly, nonscholarly, and so on. This study scrutinizes barbarian operations mainly in works of literature and art, because literary works and artworks tend to be more receptive to the ambivalences and stuttering of barbarism than, for example, the standardized rhetoric of politics, which tends to neutralize signs of ambiguity and confusion. Thus, the objects that figure in this book invite readings that allow the creative potential of this concept to unfold.

Selecting objects wherein barbarians are thematically foregrounded enables me to explore issues related to barbarism and the barbarian, while probing the methodological potential of barbarism. Thus, each chapter has a thematic and a methodological or theoretical component, as it deals with (1) an issue that emerges from a different aspect of barbarism or the barbarian and (2) a different methodological or theoretical aspect of the concept, that is, a different "barbarian operation."

Chapter 1 offers a preview of the main operations of barbarism at play throughout this book through a close reading of Franz Kafka's short story "The Great Wall of China" (1931). This reading probes the critical thrust of barbarism, its relation to civilization, the intertwinement of its positive and negative aspects, and its relation to epistemological and comparative questions. Revolving around an unfinished wall, Kafka's story functions as a scale model through which the structuring principles of this book are presented.

Chapter 2 situates this study within contemporary debates. It sketches the current discursive landscape around culture, civilization, and barbarism in the turn it took after the Cold War and the collapse of communist regimes in Europe, and especially after the events of September 11, 2001. The chapter presents examples from recent Western political rhetoric, especially the rhetoric of the US administration after what became nicknamed "9/11," and scrutinizes some critical responses to this rhetoric, which depart from various theoretical premises, including conservative, liberal, humanist, left-wing, relativist, and deconstructionist perspectives. By delineating the ways in which "barbarism" and "civilization" are deployed in them, I position my own approach through and against these perspectives.

Chapter 3 looks into the uses of the "barbarian" in Western history. Most historical studies of the barbarian focus on a specific era and culture, and a few others adopt a genealogical approach. Instead of providing a chronologically ordered historical overview of the barbarian, this chapter is structured thematically around a series of criteria that have determined what constitutes "civilization" in the West from Greek antiquity to the present. In order to map out the complex discursive space of the barbarian in the West, this chapter relates its significations and uses in different eras to normative standards that have determined what counts as "civilized."

To that end, this chapter lays out a provisional typology of what I call "civilizational standards." These include language, culture, political system, morality, religion, ethnicity, class, gender, race, progress, and the psyche. Through this structuring principle, the history of the barbarian does not emerge as a linear succession of significations but as a narrative of discontinuities, repetitions, and unexpected intersections, unraveling through a web of cultural, social, political, ideological, religious, and scientific discursive strands. Thus, Chapter 3 prepares the ground for the pluralization of barbarism and the barbarian and for the disruption of conventional uses of these concepts in the succeeding chapters.

After the diachronic travels of the barbarian as the negative pole of civilization, Chapter 4 delves into the notion of "positive barbarism" by zooming in on Walter Benjamin's essay "Experience and Poverty" (1933), in which "positive barbarism" is introduced, and juxtaposes this notion to other uses of "barbarism" in Benjamin's writings. The issue is how Benjamin's positive barbarism breaks with the genealogy of barbarism and articulates a new project without dissociating itself from the destructive, violent aspects of this concept.

This chapter has a parallel methodological objective: it experiments with a kind of reading that activates the "barbarian" qualities of Benjamin's writing—a reading that combines philosophical with literary perspectives. By means of a microscopic approach, I look for odd, deviant details as an entrance to the text and treat these details as latent "barbarisms" in

Benjamin's writing, activated by the reader. Through these linguistic barbarisms the chapter explores how Benjamin's project of positive barbarism is put to work in his own writing as a textual strategy.

Whereas Chapter 4 follows Benjamin's prefigurations of the kind of barbarians that could actualize positive barbarism, Chapter 5 foregrounds the critical potential of the barbarians' absence. Here, I center on the topos of "waiting for the barbarians" through a comparative reading of C. P. Cavafy's poem "Waiting for the Barbarians" (1904) and J. M. Coetzee's homonymous novel (1980). Thematically, this chapter probes the implications of the barbarians' nonarrival in Cavafy's and Coetzee's works. Theoretically, it addresses *repetition* as a barbarian operation. If the previous chapter examines barbarism through a microscopic lens—as an operation unleashed by textual details—this chapter uses a multiplying, kaleidoscopic lens: it highlights barbarism *in* repetition and *as* repetition and explores the ways in which the overdetermined name "barbarian" can be repeated into new senses in the space of literature.

In the previous chapters the question of barbarism is located in—and limited by—language (either that of history, literature, philosophy, or cultural critique). Chapters 6 and 7 transpose barbarism from its purported "natural habitat" into an extralinguistic, barbaric realm: the visual. Chapter 6 turns to visual stagings of the topos of "waiting for the barbarians," whereas Chapter 7 focuses on artistic embodiments of "new barbarians." These chapters show how the "barbarian theorizing" this book puts forward does not necessarily rest on linguistic practices but also takes form through the visual, as well as in the interstices of the visual and the textual.

Chapter 6 explores possible alternatives to the state of waiting for the barbarians. The artworks that take center stage here—South African artist Kendell Geers's labyrinthine installation *Waiting for the Barbarians* (2001) and Argentinian artist Graciela Sacco's billboard-type installation *Esperando a los bárbaros* (1996)—flirt with two different answers to the aporia of a civilization trapped in a passive state as it awaits the barbarians in vain. These works transpose the topos of waiting for the barbarians into a visual medium, into sites of enunciation outside or in the margins of the West, and into a contemporary context. Through these artworks, I ponder what waiting for the barbarians might mean today and how the predicament this topos captures may be overcome in art.

Chapter 7 centers on a number of photo-performances belonging to "The New Barbarians" project (2004–6) by Mexican-born performance artist Guillermo Gómez-Peña and his troupe. While Sacco's and Geers's installations play with the theme of waiting, Gómez-Peña's constructed barbarian personas appear to materialize the promise of the barbarians' arrival. However, these materializations fall far from the expectations of the civilized imagination. The barbarians in these photo-performances overwhelm the viewer through an overload of cultural references that play with Western stereotypes of barbarian others in new, subversive constellations. Gómez-Peña's project addresses barbarism and the figure of the new barbarian by means of a *barbarian aesthetic*, taking shape through a visual grammar of "barbarisms." Through their barbarian operations, the artworks discussed in Chapters 6 and 7 intervene in contemporary discussions about barbarism, comparison, and cultural translation and perform a kind of "barbarian theorizing" from the West's periphery.

1

Piecework

Something there is that doesn't love a wall,
That sends the frozen-ground-swell under it,
And spills the upper boulders in the sun
And makes gaps even two can pass abreast.
—Robert Frost, from "Mending Wall"

Through Franz Kafka's "The Great Wall of China" (Beim Bau der chinesischen Mauer, 1930), a short story of an unfinished wall, I offer a "sneak preview" of several barbarian operations that will be laid out in this book and present some of its main threads:[1] the relation between civilization and barbarism; the features and functions of what I call "barbarisms"; the relation of the concept of barbarism to questions of knowing; its involvement in comparative acts; and the ways in which we can imagine a creative recasting of this concept. The wall and its construction system in Kafka's story function as a model for mapping out the structuring principles of this book as a whole.

In "The Great Wall of China," barbarism unravels as a force that ruptures the epistemological premises of established discourses and imbues them with foreign and erratic elements. Through such interventions, barbarism overthrows the epistemological priority of civilization and promises other ways of knowing, which spring out of a constant tension with negation, ambivalence, contradictions, and possible impossibilities.

The concept of barbarism has a significant comparative aspect. The "barbarian" can be seen as a figure of comparison by definition because it is the product of a comparative act: someone receives the label "barbarian" after having been compared to, and found the opposite of, the civilized subject. The barbarian is the measure against which civilization acquires its self-validation. The comparative gesture embedded in the barbarian is part of a hierarchical comparative framework that establishes "civilization" as the referent of supremacy and the measure of excellence. It is therefore a fake comparison played out between two constructions devised by the (civilized) subject: the "civilized" and the "barbarian." The outcome of this comparative "act" is always the same: the comparison with the barbarian makes the civilized look good. Self-proclaimed civilized subjects need to measure themselves against barbarians, and they always win this competition, since both parts of the comparison are products of their own representational system.

The figure of the barbarian, however, does not always fall prey to quasi-comparative acts to the benefit of civilizational discourse. Precisely due to its comparative nature, the barbarian can operate between worlds. Acting in the interstices of languages (in the broadest sense of the word), the barbarian can create fissures in the languages and objects involved in comparative encounters. Barbarism can be involved in a mode of comparing that demands a radical change of perspective as well as a shifting of the grounds of the comparison.

Barbarism and Civilization:
An Unfinished Business

The narrator in "The Great Wall of China" is one of the Chinese builders of the wall. He aspires to put together a historical inquiry by combining the fragmented, inconclusive, and contradictory narratives and theories that surround the construction of the Great Wall of China. The project of the wall was meant to reinforce China's ideal of national purity and keep the country isolated and protected from contamination from the barbarous outside world. Nevertheless, Kafka's narrator informs us that the project ended up defeating its purpose because of gaps rumored to exist between several blocks of the wall. The incompleteness of the wall—the fact that pieces are missing along its perimeter—is the result of the so-called system of piecemeal construction, which takes center stage in the narrator's exposition. "Piecemeal construction" denotes the practice of building different blocks of the wall in different places at the same time, which would be joined together at a later stage. According to the narrator, some of these blocks were possibly never joined, leaving openings in the construction. In the story, we read that the piecemeal construction "is one of the crucial problems in the whole building of the wall" (Kafka 1999, 238). Thus, his narrative sets out to shed light on this system.

His first question concerns the incongruity between the wall's purpose and effect. If the purpose of the wall was to offer "a protection against the peoples of the north," the narrator wonders, "How can a wall protect if it is not a continuous structure? Not only can such a wall not protect, but what there is of it is in perpetual danger" (235). The wall is porous, vulnerable to its outside. Yet the construction "probably could not have been carried out in any other way" (236). His first explanation is based on psychological and practical reasons. The piecemeal system ensured variation and change of scenery for the supervisors of the construction. By moving around to build different parts of the wall, the supervisors could see finished sections on their way, renew their belief in their work, and feel they contributed to a great project that unified the nation. "Thus," the narrator concludes, "the system of piecemeal construction becomes comprehensible" (238).

But not quite. In the narrative there are only provisional conclusions, constantly overthrown by new ones. Thus, the psychological explanation gives way to a theological or transcendental one. The narrator brings in the "high command" (die Führerschaft) as the invisible authority behind the decision for the piecemeal construction—an authority whose decrees are not to be questioned. "And for that reason," the narrator remarks, "the incorruptible observer must hold that the command, if it had seriously desired it, could also have overcome those difficulties that prevented a system of continuous construction" (240). Yet the narrator immediately notices a paradox: "But the piecemeal construction was only a makeshift and therefore inexpedient. Remains the conclusion that the command willed something inexpedient [unzweckmäßig]. Strange conclusion!" (240). By suggesting that the decision of the high command was improper and ineffective, the narrator corrupts his own statement of belief in the unlimited power of the command. He thereby imbues his previous statement with a "barbarism," a trace of self-canceling doubt, which leads his reasoning to an impasse ("Strange conclusion!"). The fact that he corrupts his own statement makes his address to an "incorruptible observer" ironic and, indeed, "inexpedient." While the narrator constructs an "incorruptible observer" who *must* accept the infallibility of the high command, his narrative is replete with logical errors and paradoxes, bound to corrupt any "incorruptible observer."

The narrator continues his line of questioning: "Against whom was the Great Wall to serve as a protection? Against the people of the north." His reply is again instantly questioned and negated: "Now, I come from the southeast of China. No northern people can menace us there" (241). Not only have they never seen those barbarian nomads but even if they existed, the land is so vast that the northern people would never reach the southern villages. Once more, the narrator employs a strategy that Bianca Theisen calls "self-referential negation," whereby "a statement invites and seems to entail the following one, only to then be negated and cancelled by it" (2006, 3). If the barbarians posed no threat, then the question that logically follows is, again, *why* the wall needed to be built: "Why, then, since that is so, did we leave our homes . . . our mothers and fathers, our weeping wives, our children . . . Why?" (Kafka 1999, 241).

For an answer he resorts again to the high command, which he now believes "has existed from all eternity, and the decision to build the wall likewise" (242). According to this new explanation, the construction of the wall had neither to do with a barbarian threat nor with the Emperor's decision. It has no origin or cause whatsoever, since it has always existed. For the narrator-historian, this sudden cancellation of all causality behind the wall's building makes the question of *why* utterly impertinent— "inexpedient." The recourse to the high command as an all-explanatory mechanism undermines the purpose of his narrative. If the decision has always existed, then why explore its causes in the first place? However, what seems to make the whole inquiry pointless may also be read as an exposure of the arbitrary structures according to which causes and effects are constructed as such. If the decision for the wall always existed, then the perceived *causes* for the wall's construction—protecting the country from barbarians, safeguarding the purity of the nation, strengthening its unity—come after the decision for the wall and are produced as the wall's effects. The Emperor's decree for the wall's construction, the lifelong devotion of the Chinese people to its building, and the construction of outside others as threatening barbarians, are all effects—not causes—of the wall. By suggesting that national identity and the categories of "civilized" and "barbarian" are effects of discourse, the narrative deessentializes them. This deessentialization also highlights one of this book's main premises: Barbarians do not exist as such but are constructions of a discursive structure that produces others as threatening and inferior.

The decision for the wall's construction has no origin but merely effects, which are expected to be enhanced with the actual construction. However, a glitch appears in this project as soon as the theoretical decision for the wall turns into an actual construct. The actualization of the wall endangers the ideological structures that demanded its construction, because the system of piecemeal construction leaves fissures in the Empire's borders, making them vulnerable to invasions from the outside. If the purpose of a wall is to seal borders, then this wall is strategically useless. The greatest monument to China's civilization is also the greatest proof of its inability to exclude foreignness from its territory. As Wendy Brown argues in her recent study on walled states, while walls may appear as "hyperbolic tokens" of sovereignty, in fact their presence betrays an instability at the core of the message they are trying to convey. Therefore, walls can be signs of the *waning* of a nation's sovereignty (2010, 24). In Kafka, the Chinese wall becomes an ambivalent symbol of power as well as vulnerability.

Although the narrator fails to adequately account for the wall's construction system, it is noteworthy that those who have a better grasp of the project are the barbarian nomads themselves. It is probable, the narrator informs us, that the nomad tribes against which the wall was built "kept changing their encampments with incredible rapidity, like locusts, and so perhaps had a better general view of the progress of the wall than we, the builders" (Kafka 1999, 235–36). As Stanley Corngold observes, the design of the wall is incomprehensible, "except, perhaps, to the nomads whom it exists to ostracize." This, Corngold argues, opens up the great paradox "that the builders are dependent on the beings from whom it is their entire purpose to obtain independence" (2002, 105).

The paradoxical dependence of civilization on its barbarians is thereby underscored. Civilization aspires to establish a proper locus from which to speak, exert power, and identify others as barbarians. In practice, however, this locus is precarious and unstable: the civilized center (in Kafka's story, the Empire of China) is never identical to itself, as it can exist only in relation to a barbarian exteriority. This reflects the paradox of a civilized society priding itself on its self-sufficiency yet needing inferior or subjugated others in order to reaffirm this self-sufficiency. Thus, although civilization appears to be the powerful, superior term in the opposition with the barbarians, its dependence on them also makes it vulnerable.

Presented as inexpedient, the system of piecemeal construction itself can be viewed as a barbarism—a foreign, inexplicable element—at the heart of China's civilization. The barbarism that this system constitutes does not come from the outside but is internally generated: it is the decision of the high command. This fact, as we have seen, puzzles the narrator. Why would civilization (wittingly or not) produce the barbarisms that undermine the completion of its own project? This question gives rise to opposing assumptions. Does the piecemeal construction signal civilization's self-destructive drive, which makes it plant the seeds of its own potential demise in the form of gaps in the wall? Or does this barbarism in fact protect the Empire from turning into an isolated, self-regulating system without connections to its outside? Following the latter assumption, the real threat to civilization does not come from the nomads but from the desire for national purity and the exclusion of foreignness. The piecemeal construction blurs the borders between inside/outside, civilization and barbarism, enabling their interpenetration. By allowing foreign elements to enter, this design may fail to protect civilization from its outside, but it safeguards its potential for change and renewal.

The incomplete wall in the story underscores the unsettled relation between civilization and barbarism. The relation between civilization and barbarism is an unfinished business, with different, unpredictable effects each time it is activated. Through openings in the "wall" of civilizational discourse barbarism enters as a force that foils the completion of this wall and enables alterity to affect its structures.

Possible Impossibilities and Three Incomplete Walls

In the second part of "The Great Wall of China," the narrator focuses on the strange relation between imperial center and periphery *within* the wall of China. Although the opposition between the *intra* and *extra muros* is not very convincing in the story (the barbarian nomads have not even been seen), inside the wall incongruities and improbabilities thrive. Within the Chinese universe, the people and the Empire are barbarian to each other, as they live in different worlds. In the narrator's description of the Empire's modus operandi, especially of the way common people relate to it, a universe replete with barbarisms comes alive. These barbarisms—in the form of paradoxes, hyperboles, irregularities, incompatibilities, and strange mixtures of heterogeneous orders—pertain both to notions of time and space and to the relation between fiction, myth, and reality.

The relation between the Empire in Peking and the "common people" is marked either by miscommunication or by total lack of communication. Regarding temporality, the people in China live in a mythical past, which they perceive as the Empire's present. Information about dead emperors and their dynasties travels so slowly that old stories reach people as "news" thousands of years after occurrence. "Battles that are old history are new to us," writes the narrator. And while nothing is known about the present Emperor, "long-dead emperors are set on the throne in our villages." The living Emperor, on the other hand, "they confuse among the dead" (Kafka 1999, 245). The past is kept alive as present.

At first glance, this unorthodox temporality indicates that people live out of sync with the present, trapped in a mythical past. However, their time-conception also results in a perpetual performance of the past in the present. In this "present," "the wives of the emperors . . . vehement in their greed, incontrollable in their lust, practice their abominations *ever anew*" (245, emphasis added). This repetitive performance of the past *as* present ensures that the past is never solidified but is constantly transformed from a present perspective.

The flow of information in the country is reminiscent of the way we view stars from the earth: most visible stars have been destroyed for millions of years. In Kafka's story, however, not only is history performed as present but the inverse is true as well: for the Chinese people, the present of the Empire is already history. The narrator recalls that when a beggar came to the village to read a revolutionary leaflet by the rebels of the neighboring village, the villagers sent him away without believing a word he said. Although the text of the leaflet gives vivid descriptions of "the gruesomeness of the living present," the dialect in which it is written sounds archaic to them. Hence, the content of the leaflet is perceived as ancient history. "So eager are our people to obliterate the present," writes the narrator. The gruesome present of the neighbors is a barbarism in their own present—a foreign sound dismissed as obsolete, unworthy of attention (246).

China's parallel temporalities usually do not interfere with each other. But whenever they cross each other momentarily—as in the last example—they imbue each other with barbarisms, which unsettle people's time-conception and the truths by which they live. By juxtaposing these temporalities in the story, the narrator unleashes barbarisms that turn the familiar into something foreign and erratic and challenge the secure contexts of people's lives. The elements I call "barbarisms" have a relational meaning: their identification as barbarisms is dependent on the context in which they appear. Thus, when there is no contact between different temporal frameworks in the story, the same elements I here call "barbarisms" may very well reinforce rather than undermine the borders of each temporal framework.

The reality of Peking and the existing Emperor are just as foreign and inaccessible to common people as the northern barbarians they have never seen. "Peking itself is far stranger to the people in our village than the next world," the narrator concedes (246). Yet this does not deter them from keeping the myth of the Empire alive. The sacred dragon—the symbol of Peking—is always honored in their village, because, the narrator says, no people are "more faithful to the Emperor than ours" (246). The Emperor as symbol and the Empire as myth are far more indispensable to them than "reality." Even if they long to clasp the Empire "in all its palpable living reality," in the end they are not willing to exchange the safety of their mythical present for a chunk of the "real" (247). This would subject their age-old beliefs to the risk of falsification from another reality. Therefore, the reality of Peking is to them a barbarism they try to exclude from their discourse.

By juxtaposing reality and fiction, history and myth, past and present, the narrative does not project these categories as irreconcilable hierarchical oppositions. Nor does it collapse them by eradicating their differences. Because they operate on an equal level in the story's universe, they are able to interpenetrate and affect each other: fiction is no less "real" than reality, for history is shown to be replete with mythical constructions, and the past can be just as "present" as the present, if not more. The discursive priority of positive categories over their inferior opposites—the real over the fictional, history over myth, the present over the past—is overthrown in the story, without the tensions between them diminished.

Kafka's story brings together heterogeneous genres, registers, and orders of signs: an objective and "serious" historical treatise accommodates rational inquiry, parables, digressions, (pseudo)scientific theories, myths, and autobiographical elements. All these genres and discursive orders occupy an equally legitimate position in the common symbolic space of literature. The heterogeneous orders and elements in the story are brought together according to a logic of contiguity, placed next to each other in metonymical relations. This contiguity makes it possible to accommodate contradictory, unfitting elements—barbarisms—in the story without having them cancel each other out.[2] The aporias created by the clashing orders in the story appear as such only because of our indoctrination in a logic of irreconcilable oppositions: fiction versus reality, present versus past, inside versus outside, history versus literature, civilized versus barbarian. According to Gilles Deleuze and Félix Guattari, Kafka's work is a writing machine "made of assemblages of nouns and effects, of heterogeneous orders of signs that cannot be reduced to a binary structure."[3] The story invites us to shift our preconceptions so that we can see these binaries not as a deadlock of irreconcilable contradictions but as a space of *possible impossibilities*, where elements can coexist and compete with their opposites.[4]

These possible impossibilities bring us back to the question of the piecemeal construction, but from another perspective. While the narrator is unable to solve the enigma of the piecemeal construction, I argue that the narrative *performs* the design the narrator is unable to explain through reason. The story erects several blocks—mini-narratives comprising parables, digressions, autobiographical incidents, scientific theories—of what promises to be a whole: a historical inquiry. But after erecting each block, it moves on to the next without resolving the relation between these contiguous pieces. An argument or line of thinking is pushed to an impasse, and then another one starts, so the reader almost forgets the previous "block" was left open and incomplete. The result of this "piecework" is a narrative of loose ends and contradictions, which the reader is encouraged to accept as such.

In their study on Kafka, Deleuze and Guattari discuss the role of discontinuous blocks as a design in Kafka's stories, reflected in his "broken form of writing" and his "mode of expression through fragments" (1986, 72). This discontinuity corresponds to the image of the fragmentary wall in "The Great Wall of China." The discontinuity of the blocks, Deleuze and Guattari argue, does not prevent them from being in contact with each other. Indeed, as we see in "The Great Wall of China," the mini-narratives and diverse orders in the story are not entirely disconnected but "touch" each other, exposing each other's inconsistencies.[5]

The openings in the story's "wall" enable disobedient elements to dismantle the normative ground from which positive categories draw their power. In the story, "reality" and "history" are not the normative standards against which "myth" and "fiction" are measured but simply other modes of knowing and understanding the world. The story's incongruous juxtapositions confound our understanding of these categories and turn it into a "creative misunderstanding" as "a means by which to get a different hold on things" (Levine 2008, 1041).[6] The story creates small ruptures in the way we understand reality, history, myth, the present, and the past.

Like the incomplete wall in the story, and Kafka's story itself as an unfinished wall, the question of barbarism, its past and present uses, its violent history, its open future, and its creative operations constitute a long wall from which a few pieces are erected in this book according to a piecework method. Openings are deliberately (and inevitably) left between these pieces. These openings may function as gateways for new perspectives, questions, criticisms, distortions, constructions, and deconstructions, some of which may materialize in future projects. Barbarism itself is here treated as an unfinished concept, with fissures in its discursive performances. Though barbarism is a notoriously saturated concept, if we approach it through Kafka's suggested design, we can focus on the possible openings in the wall erected by the history of the notion of barbarism, through which creative recastings may come about.

Like the coexisting impossibilities in Kafka's story, the concept of barbarism I propose allows contradictory—positive as well as negative—meanings to coexist in the concept. Therefore, making an either/or choice between a negative and a positive or "good" barbarism represents a false dilemma. An affirmative refashioning of barbarism emerges through a constant tension between the conventional, negative aspects of this concept and its critical, productive potential.

Finally, just as the main theme in Kafka's story—the wall's construction system—is performatively inscribed in the story's own construction, the object of this book is also involved in its methodological tenets. The notion of barbarism becomes a methodological tool, which may affect our ways of knowing, comparing, and theorizing.

Barbarism and Knowledge

The motivating force of the narrator's inquiry is his desire for knowledge. He wishes to gain insight into the wall's construction, as well as into the institution of the Empire, which is "unique" in its "obscurity." The knowledge surrounding the Empire is nontransparent, immersed "in a fog of confusion" (Kafka 1999, 242). Although the Empire in Peking is the center of power and thus also the supposed source of knowledge dissemination, the knowledge transmitted by the center is endlessly delayed, forcing the Chinese to live by ancient knowledge and laws. "In part because of the distances," Michael Wood writes, "Kafka's China is a place of misinformation and wild legend, also of claims to arcane knowledge" (1996, 331). Information is scattered in the vastness of the land.

The Emperor and his subjects live in a different here and now. The Chinese "think only about the Emperor," but "not about the present one," because they do not know anything about him (Kafka 1999, 243). The Emperor they know is an almighty, immortal symbol, but the Emperor in Peking is a vulnerable human being with weaknesses. "The Empire is immortal, but the Emperor totters and falls from his throne," his malicious courtiers "perpetually labor to unseat the ruler from his place," and dynasties regularly "sink" and disappear. However, "of these struggles

and sufferings the people will never know" (243). It is, in fact, their ignorance that allows them to construct the Empire as an unchanging, eternal
mechanism, unaware as they are of its precariousness and instability. In
the narrative, this instability is suggested through verbs that show change
of position, and particularly removal from a stable locus, such as "totters," "falls," "unseat," and "sink." The people's ignorance buys them a
stable epistemological framework on which to build their lives. They are
suspicious of new knowledge about Peking coming from imperial officials
who visit them, because the people are unwilling to give up their own
construction of the Empire as a stable and invincible institution. If present
emperors are dethroned and assassinated, the people do not hear about
it—nor do they wish to hear about it.

The same kind of knowledge that determines their relation to Peking
also typifies the people's relation to their purported external enemies, the
northern nomads. Although the narrator and his people think they know
the nomads through old books and artistic representations, this mediated
knowledge has never been verified by empirical facts:

We read of them in the books of the ancients; the cruelties they commit in accordance with their nature make us sigh in our peaceful arbors. The faithful representations of the artist show us these faces of the damned, their gaping mouths,
their jaws furnished with great pointed teeth their half-shut eyes that already
seem to be seeking out the victim which their jaws will rend and devour. When
our children are unruly we show them these pictures, and at once they fly weeping into our arms. (241)

Despite the vividness of these descriptions, they have never seen those barbarians. The word "faithful," with which the narrator refers to the artist's
representations, can be read as another barbarism subverting the subse-
quent description of the barbarians. This adjective not only adds an ironic
undertone to the hyperbolic tone of the description but also underscores
the extent to which the people's mediated, mythical knowledge of the
other is constructed as an unbiased fact.

Even more inaccessible than knowledge about the enemies is the
knowledge the Empire disseminates to its people. To illustrate the inaccessibility of this knowledge, the narrator recounts the parable of the
Emperor and his messenger. From his deathbed, the Emperor "has sent
a message to you alone" and has instructed his messenger to deliver it.

But the messenger can never reach his destination because he has to pass through endless obstacles. He has to go through the "chambers of the innermost palace," the stairs, the courts, the "second outer palace," then more courts, more palaces, and "so on for thousands of years." Even if he were to reach the outermost gate, he would never fight his way through the imperial capital, "the center of the world," "*crammed to bursting with its own sediment*" (244, emphasis added). The choice of words in the latter phrase suggests the kind of sedimented knowledge that resides in the imperial center. No information can travel from the palace to the common people because the Empire is a closed, protected system. The messenger, who tries to channel knowledge to the outside, stands no chance against the imperial labyrinth and its closed epistemological framework.

So far, the kind of epistemology nurtured by the Empire and its people displays the following characteristics. The Empire produces multiply mediated knowledge, which is almost impossible to pervade and threaten. Knowledge *about* the Empire is constructed by the people as certain and stable, although in the narrative it is exposed as unstable and precarious. It has a symbolic center, Peking, although its production is not based on actual communication between center and periphery but on mythical narratives and misinformation. Knowledge from or about the Empire cannot tolerate openings to the outside, and hence both need to be protected against questioning. We could call this a "civilized epistemology."

The parable of the Emperor and the messenger indicates the limits of civilized power and knowledge, presented as a solipsistic system of self-entrapment. However, if the Empire's concentric walls prevent knowledge from moving toward the outside, the openings in the Great Wall may signal the hope of an escape toward another epistemology—a barbarian way of knowing.

Who is "in the know" in the story? The Emperor controls imperial knowledge. In the people's perception, he is omniscient. Nonetheless, on other occasions the builders seem to know more than the ignorant Emperor and the nomads of the north: "Unwitting peoples of the north, who imagined they were the cause of it [the wall]! Honest, unwitting Emperor, who imagined he decreed it! We builders of the wall *know* that it was not so and hold our tongues" (242, emphasis added). The narrator and the builders know more about the wall's construction because they know the decision for it, just as the high command, has always existed. But then again, the builders know less about the wall's construction than the nomads do, who, as mentioned previously, "had a better general view of the progress of the wall" than the builders did (236).

This constant transference of the locus of knowledge leaves no stable position of knowing in the narrative. All agents in the story—including the reader—know and do not know, think they know but do not know ("unwitting people"), and think they do not know but know more than they think. The source of knowledge is constantly displaced. Before knowledge manages to settle in the narrative, it is on its way to another position. This is also evident in the narrator's inquiry: every conclusion is immediately overthrown by a new question or a new contradictory element. The epistemology the narrative performs challenges China's civilized epistemology through a constant falsification and questioning of existing knowledge.

The previous characteristics can be regarded as aspects of a barbarian mode of knowing, or a "barbarian epistemology." In this mode, knowledge is provisional and transitional and does not get the chance to transform to hegemonic power. A barbarian mode of knowing acknowledges the contingent character of discursive categories, and thus the possibility of their disarticulation, through which new categories may be created or existing ones may be redefined.

Oscillating between knowledge and nonknowledge, a barbarian epistemology could be conceptualized as a mode of "(not) knowing." This (not) knowing is the result of a radical self-questioning that ensures the renewal of knowledge. In the story, (not) knowing—as opposed to ignorance—seems to be the result of an active educational process: "The farther one descends among the lower schools the more, naturally enough, does one find teachers' and pupils' doubts of their own knowledge vanishing, and superficial culture mounting sky-high around a few precepts that have been drilled into people's minds for centuries" (242). From the narrator's observation, we can infer that moving higher in the educational ladder does not bring people closer to positive knowledge. On the contrary, it increases doubt and questioning. In yet another counterintuitive observation, the narrative suggests that the ultimate goal of education is the intensification of doubt—learning to "unknow" what one knows.[7]

Despite the manifestations of a barbarian mode of knowing in the narrative, the narrator's inquiry ends in a surprising, if not disappointing, manner for the reader. The narrator decides to put an abrupt end to his inquiry and not push his thinking further. This decision is related to an observation just made that the lack of communication between the people and the Empire lies not only with the governmental organization but also with the people themselves:

There is also involved a certain feebleness of faith and imaginative power on the part of the people, that prevents them from raising the empire out of its stagnation in Peking and clasping it in all its palpable living reality to their own breasts, which yet desire nothing better than but once to feel that touch and then to die. (247)

Although the people long for a touch of "the real," they are not willing to exchange their own reality for another one, because they lack "imaginative power." It takes creative imagination—the ability to step out of one's familiar framework—to taste another kind of knowledge of reality. Myth is for them the safe place to be, while "the real" here is "the other": a barbarian knowledge, which threatens their ground.

Remarkably, the narrator finds that "this very weakness should seem to be one of the greatest unifying influences among our people; indeed . . . the very ground on which we live" (247). Therefore, he eventually backs down before the danger involved in his inquiry, as "to set about establishing a fundamental defect here would mean undermining not only our consciences, but, what is far worse, our feet. And for that reason I shall not proceed any further at this stage with my inquiry into these questions" (247–48). Myth safeguards civilized knowledge from barbarisms and is indispensable for the nation's identity construction. Therefore, he decides that his narrative cannot accommodate any more questioning. Civilized knowledge does not jeopardize itself by opening up to foreign knowledge or self-interrogation. The narrator's desire not to disrupt this established mode of knowing appears to overpower his initial desire to know more, know differently, and push the limits of knowledge. Is this a triumph of civilized knowledge over the narrative's traces of another way of knowing? I do not think so. There is a discrepancy between what the narrator *says* he is doing in the end and what his narrative *does*: falsifying knowledge, displacing its source, inserting barbarisms into familiar frameworks. The performative aspects of his speech contradict the meaning of his final statement.

Although the narrator's historical inquiry hits a wall, the end of his inquiry need not be seen as the end of the story. There is another short piece by Kafka, which could be read as a postscript to "The Great Wall of China," entitled "The News of the Building of the Wall: A Fragment" (Die Nachricht vom Mauerbau: Ein Fragment).[8] This fragment recounts an incident from the narrator's childhood and contains the first news about the building of the wall, brought to the narrator's father by a boatman passing by their village. Although the identity of the narrator is not elucidated, it is probable that the same narrative "I" in "The Great Wall of China" writes this piece too.

As the designation "fragment" suggests, it is an open piece, and its beginning and end are missing—or not (yet) written. A fragment is something broken off from a whole, and as such it can be read as another opening in the "wall" of the main story. It suggests a way out of the impasse with which the narrator's historical inquiry in "The Great Wall of China" ends. In the English edition of Kafka's short stories used here, this fragment is placed after "The Great Wall," thereby inciting the reader to disregard our narrator's final statement (i.e., that he will not "proceed any further") and to seek further, read on.

The account in this fragment is filtered through the imagination of a child, who years later records his memories of the incident. Although he has no recollection of his father's exact words to him, the narrator tries to reproduce his father's reproduction of the boatman's words. This is what he comes up with in the final sentence of the fragment:

An unknown boatman . . . has just told me that a great wall is going to be built to protect the Emperor. For it seems that infidel tribes, among them demons, often assemble before the imperial palace, and shoot their black arrows at the Emperor. (249)

In this narrative, the "truth" about the wall's construction is filtered by no less than four levels of mediation: the boatman, the father, the child, and the adult-narrator. As this fragment suggests, reality does not exist as such, since knowledge of the world is always inevitably mediated. Unlike in the (pseudo)historical account in "The Great Wall of China," in this fragment, perhaps because it belongs to a different genre (an autobiographical, literary account), this mediation is not a problem that needs to be overcome in order to retrieve the "historical truth." Rather, it is a challenge. In the main story's China, the endless reiteration of certain "facts" in the popular imagination reinforces mythical knowledge. However, these repetitions, reproductions, and mediations are inevitably also subject to alterations. The four levels of mediation in this fragment suggest that there is not only an eternal perpetuation of the same (myth) but also the possibility of a repetition with a difference that could challenge mythical structures.

The final sentence of the fragment brings the reader face-to-face with the overblown myth around the wall's construction. This myth involves "infidel tribes," "demons," "black arrows," and so on. But if the Chinese in "The Great Wall of China" are trapped within the wall that their mythical present imposes on them, for the reader a small fissure in this wall is presented through this fragment. Since this is a fragment, the reader is invited to write her own, different ending to this myth. The age-old myths of civilization might be repeated differently within the space of literature.

The fragment may function as an opening to another narrative or an indexical sign that promises another kind of knowledge. As Walter Benjamin writes in his essay "Franz Kafka: On the Tenth Anniversary of his Death," the doctrine Kafka's parables interpret does not exist: "All we can say is that here and there we have an allusion to it. Kafka might have said that these are relics transmitting the doctrine, although we could regard them just as well as precursors preparing the doctrine" (1999b, 119). The doctrine of Kafka's stories is irretrievable, not because the reader does not dig well enough behind the story but because it does not yet exist. It therefore requires the reader's "imaginative power," which can overcome the "feebleness of faith" the narrator ascribes to the Chinese. This is, I contend, a barbarian doctrine: it is unintelligible and foreign to the reader, but it promises a new grammar and way of knowing.

This doctrine could be described in terms of the (not) knowing of barbarism, as previously delineated. The parenthetical "not" foregrounds barbarism as a negative concept pregnant with positivity. As a mode of (not) knowing, barbarism is imbued with positivity as a potential—a promise, rather than a given, self-evident quality. (Not) knowing thus refers to a kind of knowledge that does not yet exist—just like the doctrine of Kafka's stories, according to Benjamin.

Barbarism and Comparison: The Tower and the Wall

In "The Great Wall of China," the narrator's inquiries also lead him to a comparison between the Great Wall and the Tower of Babel. The comparison between the wall and the tower is presented as the theory of an unidentified scholar, who not only compared the two projects but also asserted "the Great Wall alone would provide for the first time in the history of mankind a secure foundation for a new Tower of Babel. First the wall, therefore, and then the tower" (Kafka 1999, 239). According to this scholar's theory, the ancient Tower of Babel failed because its foundations were too weak. The wall of China was thus supposed to provide the solid foundation for the new Tower of Babel. The narrator questions the rational grounds of this theory: "How could the wall, which did not form even a circle, but only a sort of quarter- or half-circle, provide the foundation for a tower?" And if the scholar's comparison was meant only in a spiritual, abstract sense, then, the narrator wonders, "Why build the actual wall, which after all was something concrete" (239)? The narrator finds it curious that the scholar's book even contained architectural plans for the tower that would be built on the basis of the wall.

What I find most remarkable about this comparison is its grounds. There are several reasons—some pointed out by the narrator himself— why this comparison would be inappropriate. Discourses, genres, and even temporal frames are mixed without further justification: an ancient biblical myth belonging to the Judaic and Christian traditions is compared with an actual historical (though mythically invested) project from the Chinese tradition, within a fictional narrative in which the narrator declares to be offering a historical account of the wall. The temporal order is also reversed: "First the wall, therefore, and then the tower," the narrator notes (239). The real wall is supposed to help reconstruct a better version of the mythical tower. The concrete and literal are confused with mythical, spiritual, and metaphorical orders of signs, as the comparison presents us with the possible impossibility of a wall providing the foundations for a (formerly mythical) tower.

Although the reader may be tempted to read the conjoining of the two projects as an allegory, the story makes sure to underscore the materiality of the project by testing its architectural feasibility. As Wood notes, one cannot forget that, most important, "we are talking about a material Wall and a material Tower, whatever their spiritual meanings or grounding might be" (1996, 334). The coexistence of the figurative and the literal in this comparison, as well as throughout Kafka's story, calls for a simultaneously literal and allegorical reading. In this reading, "literal" and "allegorical" are not mutually exclusive categories but part of the same pluralized order.

Despite the narrator's questions about the viability of the comparison, in the scholar's theory, as presented in the story, this interpenetration of orders of signs does not pose a problem. In fact, it forms the very ground on which this unlikely comparative act unfolds. As Natalie Melas proposes, in comparisons there can be "a minimal form of incommensurability, which produces a generative dislocation without silencing discourse or marking the limit of knowledge. This minimal incommensurability," Melas argues, "opens up the possibility of an intelligible relation at the limits of comparison" (2007, 31). By operating at the limits of comparison, the encounter between the two projects in the story creates its own comparative grounds instead of yielding to predetermined frameworks.

Comparisons need both similarity and difference between two objects. Since both parts in this comparison stand on unstable ground, the challenging question is what the two projects have in common. On a first level, both the wall and the tower seem to express a desire for unification and for the exclusion of alterity. The wall embodies a desire for a unified nation of China, purified from the barbarians and barbarisms of the outside world. The Tower of Babel was the project of a united humanity of the generations following the Great Flood, which all spoke a single language. The tower can thus be seen as a celebration of a unified humanity, devoid of foreignness. As Jacques Derrida writes in "Des tours de Babel," just before the tower's deconstruction, the Semitic family "was establishing its empire, which it wanted universal, and its tongue, which it also attempts to impose on the universe" (1985, 167). This ambition for universalization, accompanied by the fear of translation and dispersion, creates the momentum for the tower's construction. The project was to build a tower that would reach heaven. This ambition captures the telos of the desire for absolute unification: unity with God through the crossing of the borders between heaven and earth. The hubris of their ambition—which was not to glorify and praise the name of God but rather to make a name for themselves—brought on God's punishment in the form of linguistic confusion and the scattering of this unified people throughout the earth.

Both projects are incomplete. The wall, built with the method of piecemeal construction, is porous and does not offer protection from outside barbarism. Likewise, the project of Babel is not only left unfinished but has exactly the opposite outcome from its initial aspirations. In building the tower, the Semites wished to *"make a name for themselves"* and to "assure themselves, by themselves, a unique and universal genealogy" (Derrida 1985, 169). Instead, the project ends in linguistic confusion: The builders end up speaking different languages and thus become barbarians to each other. After Babel, language becomes a never-ending process of translation (Rickels 1987, 111). As Derrida argues, the goal of the tower's builders—to found a universal language and a unique genealogy—brings in a colonial violence or linguistic imperialism and "a peaceful transparency of the human community," both of which are interrupted by God's punishment (1985, 174). When God imposes his name, "Babel," he limits the universality of "the universal reason" he imposes by subjecting humans to "the law of translation": transparency and univocity become impossible (174).[9]

Both projects fail to fulfill their purported goals—the desire for linguistic or national homogenization and the eradication of barbarism(s). "The 'tower of Babel,'" Derrida writes, "does not merely figure the irreducible multiplicity of tongues; it exhibits an incompletion, the impossibility of finishing, of totalizing, of saturating, of completing something on the order of edification, architectural construction, system, and architectonics" (1985, 165). The incompletion of these projects suggests the failure of any project striving for total unification, homogeneity, and elimination of difference. It thereby figures the impossibility of excluding barbarism from any (seemingly) self-sufficient construct. Every ideology of national purity in the case of the wall, or linguistic imperialism in the case of the tower, will run up against barbarisms: gaps in the wall through which foreign elements may flow in and out, or confounded tongues subject to translation and thus never self-identical.

The commonality of the two projects could thus be summed up as follows: Instead of universalizing or reinforcing the system of the self and invalidating the domain of barbarism, both constructions end up in a proliferation of barbarism(s). The narrator has doubts about the scholar's "illegitimate" comparison of the wall with the tower.[10] However, the paradoxes, reversals, and "inexpedient" juxtapositions throughout his narrative incite the reader to approach this comparison through a radical change of perspective. I would thus propose the following: What if we assumed that both projects did not fail but succeeded in their objective? What if the builders of the Tower of Babel, condemned to the nightmare of a single tongue, secretly wished for the barbarism of translation and gladly gave up the tower's construction as soon as they got that gift disguised as God's punishment? What if the Great Wall of China was never meant to protect from barbarians but to enable the flow of barbarisms—in other words, what if the goal was not the wall but the building of the gaps between its blocks?

If we view the tower and the wall as *successful* constructions, their motivating force would not be national purity or (linguistic) imperialism but rather *the desire for barbarism*. This desire is not the Orientalist eroticized desire for the other or the colonialist attraction to barbarians and the drive to decipher their mysteries. Nor is this the self-destructive desire of a decaying civilization that awaits the arrival of barbarians. What runs through both unfinished constructions is the desire for a kind of barbarism that deterritorializes and ruptures the unifying, centripetal structures of civilization. This barbarism emerges both through the wall's gaps and through the confounded languages of the tower's builders, which decenter them and introduce them to foreignness and incomprehensibility.[11]

The desire for barbarism that permeates the tower and the wall is what keeps civilization from turning into a solipsistic construct. Paradoxically then, this kind of barbarism protects civilization from entropic decline and self-destruction and sustains the hope for renewal and transformation. This barbarism can come either from outside or from inside civilization's wall. Thus, it is the prerogative neither of civilization's "others" nor of civilization itself. Either way, it takes effect at points of intersection between the inside and the outside, where the borders between them become permeable—as in the gaps in the wall. The failure of the tower and the wall may then be redefined as the promise for another solution to the fear of the outside and the nightmare of a universalized tongue.

The desire for barbarism I see ingrained in these two projects does not have a stable origin in an intentional subject—the builders, the Emperor, or the architects of either the wall or the tower. It can be seen in Deleuzian terms as a process without an origin or destination. For Deleuze and Guattari, desire does not point to a lack but is positive in creating connections and assemblages (Colebrook 2002, 92). This kind of desire invites us to regard the wall's gaps or the unfinished part of the tower in productive terms. Instead of seeing missing or incomplete parts, we could see a desire that connects people by reordering them in different constellations: The people of China are connected to their "barbarians" through the wall's gaps, while the builders of the Tower of Babel develop different ties, based on difference and diasporic relations rather than on uniformity.

Desire is an immanent force that creates contiguous connections—not oppositions.[12] In Kafka's work, Deleuze and Guattari write, "Desire could never be on a stage where it would sometimes appear like a party opposed to another party" (1986, 50). In Kafka's story, viewing the tower and the wall in terms of a desire for barbarism entails setting aside the oppositional parties that govern their respective narratives—human versus divine power or the Chinese nation versus barbarians—and that supposedly motivated these constructions. The desire for barbarism deterritorializes our viewing of these architectural constructions.

In order to conceptualize barbarism as a desire animating the two constructions, we have to momentarily detach ourselves from the traditional biblical narrative of Babel or the narratives around the wall of China. The shift of perspective necessary to see the constructions in terms of desire is a demand Kafka's narrative makes on me. Something in the narrative's unfinished wall and tower invites us to suspend the knowledge we inherit from these stories, in order to view these constructions and the narratives that surround them differently. I seek such a change of perspective in my approach to barbarism, despite, but also through, its preestablished significations and uses. This book initiates a process of unknowing barbarism, provisionally, in order to cast it otherwise.

The shift of perspective in the comparison between the tower and the wall channels the negative evaluation of these projects (unfinished, inexpedient, incomplete) into a more affirmative direction. Instead of their being failed projects of civilization or humanity, we can view them as achievements of another kind of barbarism. This would be in line with Deleuze and Guattari's approach to Kafka's work as "characterized by the total absence of negation" and "a rejection of every problematic of failure." For them, it is not Kafka's work that fails but the attempt to reduce it to something else and make it fit external categories that leads to failure. The work itself is the bearer of "an affirmation without reserve."[13]

This invites an approach to barbarism as a potentially affirmative notion rather than as the failure of civilization's project. This recasting of barbarism is more than a play on words. Claiming that the wall in the story remains incomplete indicates a hidden unity behind the interrupted blocks—the image of a perfect wall without gaps awaiting its completion. This unity poses as a positive ideal to which the incomplete wall is destined to refer and on which it conceptually depends. Reversing this logic by making the interrupted wall—not its lost unity—the primary focus transforms its gaps and fissures into positivities instead of absences signifying something else. Thus, if we assert barbarism as an affirmative notion, we could explore its relation to its antipode (civilization) on a different ground, without having to use civilization as the necessary and primary reference point.

It takes a daring act of comparison—that of the anonymous scholar in Kafka's story—for the reader to see the desire for barbarism as the connecting thread between two otherwise incommensurable projects. In order to grasp their commonality, one has to break out of the regular contexts of these projects and stand on a "barbarian" comparative ground, on which the vertical and the horizontal of a tower and a wall, the mythical and the historical, the literal and the allegorical, illuminate each other in unexpected ways.[14]

Kafka's story, with the improbable encounters it stages, becomes a testing ground for comparison. This is how I imagine the comparative potential of the concept of barbarism. Operating between objects and languages, barbarism uses moments when comparing seems obstructed or when objects seem incommensurable as occasions that may yield surprising insights about the objects involved and may shift our perspectives. By bringing together objects from different media, genres, and languages, this book uses the question of barbarism as a connecting thread to construct its own comparative grounds and fashions a mobile context for these objects, formed by their unique constellation in these pages.

Barbarism as a Paradox-Object

In "The Great Wall of China," the coming together of contradictory narratives, self-canceling syllogisms, clashing temporalities, and improper comparisons results in a world of possible impossibilities. In this world, paradoxes are not only allowed to exist but perform critical operations, which bring about small shifts in the ways we know and envision our past, present, and future, or the ways we read established narratives, such as those of the Tower of Babel and the Great Wall of China.

In sync with Kafka's story, barbarism can be considered a "paradox-object."[15] As such, it simultaneously contains a destructive and creative potential: the potential to subjugate and oppress others but also to debunk authoritative discourses; to do violence and to question violence; to carry a long negative history and to point to new ways of knowing and speaking; to reinforce oppositional thinking and to promise the overcoming of binaries. The negative, Shoshana Felman remarks, "has always been understood as what is reducible, what is to be eliminated, that is, as what by definition is opposed, is referred, is *subordinated* to the 'normal' or to the 'positive'" (2003, 101). In the face of this discursive tendency, I argue that the indisputable negativity in barbarism does not necessarily reduce the concept to the absolute opposite of the "positive"—that is, to a concept definable only by an appeal to a normative system that determines what the "positive" and "negative" consist of. The contradiction shaped by the positive and the negative in barbarism is not something that needs remedy but a constellation that can challenge conventional notions of the positive and the negative through what Felman calls "the scandal of their nonopposition" (104). Barbarism is both positive and negative, and neither positive nor negative.[16]

It is not easy to predetermine whether a certain use of "barbarism" will yield creative effects. The antagonism between the destructive and affirmative tendencies in the concept cannot be resolved. But the alternative of a clear-cut distinction between a "good" and a "bad" barbarism is less appealing. Such a distinction would simply mean exchanging one binary for another.

Because it is never fully independent from categories of the negative, the epistemological and methodological potential of barbarism is never fully present, realized, or complete. It points to something not-yet-realized, a not-yet-existing mode of knowing, comparing, or speaking. This does not mean that the outcome of barbarian operations cannot be envisioned beforehand and thus remains completely unconditioned. A barbarian operation can be initiated through a particular strategy, which prefigures a certain outcome and thereby partly structures the future. This structuring, however, has no guarantees: it can be launched in a certain direction, but the precise coordinates of its destination are unknown—we cannot know where it will land.

The piecework method of Kafka's wall of China makes the critical workings of barbarism possible. But who performs barbarian operations? Are these inscribed in Kafka's text, or do they spring from the reader's act? Are they located in the "noise" of the other's language or in the self that is alert to this noise and allows herself to be changed by it? Barbarian operations may unravel at the moment when both these forces intersect. The noise of barbarism is prompted both by the other's language and by the self that is receptive to it. When two foreign objects, discourses, or subjects listen to each other's barbarian noise, they may allow a different kind of barbarism to take effect—if only for a moment.

As a paradox-object, barbarism challenges us to open ourselves to barbarian encounters, improper comparisons, and different ways of knowing. With such operations in mind, barbarism can be "relaunched" in the cultural field as a force that challenges the logic of opposites and the discourses that capitalize on this logic and nurtures the potential for other modes of understanding our global and local realities.

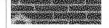

Thinking Barbarism Today

> Opposing arguments are easy to mount. Changing the terms of an argument is
> exceedingly difficult, since the dominant definition of the problem acquires, by
> repetition, and by the weight and credibility of those who propose or subscribe it,
> the warrant of "common sense." Arguments which hold to this definition of the
> problem are accounted as following "logically." Arguments which seek to change
> the terms of reference are read as "straying from the point." So part of the struggle
> is over the way the problem is formulated: the terms of the debate, and the "logic"
> it entails.
> —Stuart Hall, "The Rediscovery of 'Ideology'"

In his reaction to the terrorist attacks on the twin towers on September 11, 2001, British prime minister Tony Blair stated about the perpetrators that "their barbarism will stand as their shame for all eternity"
and described "this mass terrorism" as "the new evil in our world."[1] On
July 7, 2005, the UN Security Council condemned the terrorist attacks
in London, which took place during the G8 summit in Scotland, as "barbaric acts." Blair added: "It is particularly barbaric that this has happened
on a day when people are meeting to try to help the problems of poverty
in Africa and the long-term problems of climate change and the envi-
ronment."[2] In March 2004, President George W. Bush condemned the
beheading of US citizen Nicholas Berg in Iraq by "terrorists" as "barbaric." In a visit to the United States, German foreign minister Joschka
Fischer described the same killing as "a cold-blooded barbaric act."[3]

The striking frequency with which the terms "barbarism" and "barbarian" come up in political rhetoric since the events of September 11, 2001 is indicative of a rekindling of debates around the notions of culture, civilization, and barbarism. I here delve into these debates by scrutinizing examples from recent political discourses, particularly the rhetoric of the US administration after the events on September 11, 2001, but also some milder variants of this rhetoric. I also discuss certain critical responses to this rhetoric, which reflect various theoretical perspectives, including conservative, liberal, humanist, left-wing, relativist, and deconstructionist, paying particular attention to the ways by which they signify and use "barbarism" and "civilization." Despite their divergent arguments and theoretical underpinnings, in most of these approaches the term "barbarism" remains a negative signifier, trapped in an opposition to a positive notion of civilization. Even when the opposition is criticized, reversed, or deconstructed, there remains an unfulfilled call for a new mode of speaking through which "barbarism" could be redeployed in more constructive ways.

The Culturalization of Politics and the New Civilizational Rhetoric

The recent popularization of the rhetoric on barbarians and civilization has coincided with a shift in the criteria according to which global divisions and political conflicts are perceived. As it has often been argued, after the fall of communism global dividing lines are not so much determined by the market or by political ideology—capitalism versus communism or democracy versus totalitarianism—but by culture.[4] In the words of Samuel Huntington, "The velvet curtain of culture" has taken the place of the Cold War's "iron curtain of ideology" (1993, 31). Especially after 9/11, Mahmood Mamdani argues, culture is projected as "the dividing line between those in favor of a peaceful, civic existence and those inclined to terror" (2004, 18).

This "culturalization" of political conflict, which Mamdani calls "culture talk," goes hand in hand with a moralization of global conflicts (17). As political philosopher Chantal Mouffe argues, "Nowadays the political is played out in the *moral register*" (2005, 5). This entails that the we/they opposition is not determined with political categories but defined in moral terms (5). Therefore, instead of "a struggle between 'right and left' we are faced with a struggle between 'right and wrong'"; the "we/they" distinction is "visualized as a moral one between good and evil" (5). Within this discourse, cultural differences are essentialized. In the words of Slavoj Žižek, "Political difference—differences conditioned by political inequality or economic exploitation—are naturalised and neutralised into 'cultural' differences, that is into different 'ways of life' which are something given, something that cannot be overcome" (2009, 119). The moralization and culturalization of global conflicts may account for the increased popularity of the vocabulary of barbarism and barbarians. The figure of the barbarian conveys both the *moral* inferiority and the irreconcilable *cultural* difference of the other. Hence, constructing the other as barbarian enables the perception of the other as an enemy needing destruction rather than as a worthy adversary.

Samuel Huntington's *The Clash of Civilizations and the Remaking of World Order* (1996) is one of the first and most characteristic expressions of this culturalization of conflict. Huntington sketches the image of "an era in which global politics is shaped by cultural and civilizational tides" (309). He argues that conflicts are no longer political or ideological but premised on cultural and, particularly, religious differences. His model reduces conflicts among nations to a "clash of civilizations" and recasts political and economic tensions as cultural differences. Thus, for Huntington "civilization" turns into "the organizing feature of post–Cold War politics" (Tsing and Hershatter 2005, 38).

Huntington's narrative is marked by oppositional thinking in terms of "the West" and "the rest," or civilization and barbarism. In the growing conflict between Western civilization and Islam that he detects, the latter is identified as the main threat to the West.[5] In addition, Huntington holds multiculturalism in the United States responsible for the corrosion of the coherent and unitary US national identity (305). He claims that "multiculturalism at home threatens the United States and the West" and rejects the possibility of a "multicultural America," because "a non-Western America is not American" (318).[6] This outlook reinforces the opposition between civilization and barbarism, since it conceives civilization as a strictly delimited domain, which should keep all foreign, barbarian elements outside its borders. Western civilization, Huntington contends, is "unique" and needs to be preserved and protected from all the internal and external threats it currently faces.

Huntington divides the world into eight civilizations. He thus uses the term "civilization" in the plural and in a seemingly neutral way, in order to denote different ways of life. However, he also talks about "Civilization in the singular" with a capital "C," to denote a "mix of higher levels of morality, religion, learning, art, philosophy, technology, material well-being and probably other things" (320). His use of "civilization" in the plural is not at odds with the term's generic singular use as a moral category and a marker of a highly developed standard of living. Huntington envisions the future prospect of a "universal civilization" based on commonly shared values and practices. To form this civilization, "peoples in all civilizations should search for and attempt to expand the values, institutions, and practices they have in common with peoples of other civilizations" (320). The prospect of a universal civilization is in constant struggle against forces of barbarism in the world. Thus, whereas modernization has improved "the material level of Civilization throughout the world," a series of contemporary phenomena suggest that "Civilization" is currently under assault: "On a worldwide basis Civilization seems in many respects to be yielding to barbarism, generating the image of an unprecedented phenomenon, a global Dark Ages, possibly descending on humanity" (321).[7]

In Huntington's diagnosis, the unprecedented threat to "Civilization" is associated with a current decline of Western power. Thus, the West is implicitly regarded as the source of civilizational norms. As political theorist Wendy Brown argues, even as Huntington calls all civilizations to fight barbarism together, in his view "only the values of the West can lead this fight: what will hold barbarism at bay is precisely what recenters the West as the defining essence of civilization and what legitimates its efforts at controlling the globe" (2006, 181). Therefore, Huntington's use of "civilization" in the plural is not particularly neutral. It cloaks rather than negates the Western superiority with which the term is invested (180).

In Huntington's account, barbarism remains the great opposite both of "Civilization" and of every "civilization." It is the evil force that threatens Civilization and that all civilizations should resist. As Hunting-ton notes in his concluding paragraph, "In the greater clash, the global '*real* clash,' between Civilization and barbarism, the world's great civiliza-tions . . . will . . . hang together or hang separately" (1996, 321).

Although the culturalization of global conflicts, as we see it in Hun-tington, Bernard Lewis, and others, already had an underlying moral dimension at the time of its introduction in the 1990s, this dimension becomes more pronounced after the terrorist attacks on September 11, 2001.[8] The rhetoric of the Bush administration after September 11 played a significant role in the establishment and popularization of a religious and moral framework within which citizens of the West were called to under-stand global conflicts. Culture, religion, and moral values became the key terms of a new "civilizational discourse" that has been popular in the West since the last decade of the twentieth century. This discourse comprises different strands, which range from aggressive approaches (the "war on terror" and "zero tolerance" policy against the world's "new barbarians") to a more nuanced rhetoric, which puts the emphasis on tolerance for other cultures, universal human rights, and the promotion of "civilized" values. Although these strands may seem oppositional, they, in fact, often depart from similar premises.

The rhetoric of the Bush administration exemplifies a rather aggres-sive version of civilizational discourse. In public speeches by President George W. Bush dating from September 11, 2001, until the Iraq phase of the "war on terror," one of the most recurrent words is evil. He speaks of "the forces of evil," "the world of evil," the "evil ones," the "evildoers," and so on. The word evil even comes up repetitively within the same sentence or paragraph, as in the following: "The people who did this act on America . . . are evil people. They don't represent an ideology, they don't represent a legitimate political group of people. They're flat evil. That's all they can think about, is evil. And as a nation of good folks, we're going to hunt them down."[9] The references to forces of Evil (the terrorists and those who harbor and support them) versus forces of Good (America and its allies) are accompanied by religious vocabulary, often enhanced by biblical quotes.[10] Thus, the world is divided into two camps: "the axis of evil" versus the Western "free world." The "good" side is not just Amer-ica but America as representative of (and practically synonymous with) civilization: "This is not, however, just America's fight. . . . This is the world's fight. This is civilization's fight," and thus the "civilized world is rallying to America's side."[11]

This rhetoric, which to an extent was also taken up by leaders in Western European nations after September 11, divides the world through a series of oppositional pairs. On the one side we find notions such as civilization, America, freedom, liberty, compassion, strength, courage, justice, humanity, morality, and honor, while on the other side we find evil, terrorists, criminals, fear, cruelty, barbarism, cowardice, and hatred. The civilized world appears to be at war with the world of evil: a world of terrorist networks and their allies who hate America and the West. Those who do not side with the United States (including "relativists" or "undecideds") automatically join the axis of evil, according to Bush's famous dictum, "Either you're for us or you're against us" (or, in one of its variations, "Stand with the civilized world or stand with the terrorists").[12] This discursive framework, as Jamie Warner (2008) remarks, "became the accepted paradigm for American foreign policy." Bush's "either/or construction," Warner argues, "not only had the effect of demonizing the terrorists, it also worked to demonize anyone who questioned either side of the binary or even the construction of the binary itself." If, according to George W. Bush, "the civilized world is rallying to America's side," the implication is that whoever does not side with the United States is part of the evil spread by the "new barbarians."[13]

In Bush's civilizational rhetoric, violence and military force are legitimized as means either of defending civilization against the barbarism of other regimes and groups or of conferring liberal, "civilized" values (such as individualism, tolerance or freedom) on other cultures. This rhetoric was not new. A comparable rhetoric was employed in the context of European colonialism for the purpose of distinguishing "illegitimate" from "legitimate" forms of warfare: the uncivilized needed to either be punished or saved by the civilized in the name of civilization (Tsing and Hershatter 2005, 39). Brown refers to the rhetoric of the Bush administration as a "liberation theology": a "mission to free the unfree world both in the name of what is good for others and in the name of what makes the world a safer place" (2006, 165).

The assumption that the civilized world is dealing with evil forces leaves no room for understanding the enemy's perspective and motives. No one should negotiate with evil; the barbarian enemy needs to be eliminated. In this discourse, barbarism is the norm of the enemy's behavior. When the civilized "we" commits barbaric acts, these are viewed as isolated incidents. According to Bush, the decapitation of Nicholas Berg, a US civilian working in Saudi Arabia, "shows the evil nature of the enemy we face—these are barbaric people." By contrast, the "abhorrent" torture practices in Abu Ghraib "don't represent our America" and do not reflect "the nature of the men and women who serve our country."[14] This kind of barbarism is seen as unfit for the West.

This discourse is not exclusive to official political rhetoric but is adopted and adapted by many social or political theorists and historians alike.[15] A "milder" strand of civilizational discourse uses a rhetoric that focuses on tolerance, human rights, and universal values. This strand reflects a humanist ideology and the belief in universal values applicable to all cultures. Political philosopher Seyla Benhabib, for example, argues that resolving cultural conflicts should be based on "universal respect and egalitarian reciprocity" (2002, 132). Both conditions require "free" subjects who are "self-interpreting and self-defining beings whose actions and deeds are constituted through culturally informed narratives" (132). While the discourse employed by the Bush administration withheld tolerance (the "zero tolerance" policy on terrorism), this strand of humanist and universalist civilizational discourse confers tolerance on others (Brown 2006, 203).

Critiques

How is the rhetoric of "zero tolerance" compatible with the latter discursive strand that advocates tolerance and human rights? Both strands are part of a discourse that guards the definition of civilization by (implicitly or explicitly) identifying it with Western liberal values. In *Regulating Aversion*, Brown (2006) offers an in-depth critical analysis of these variants of Western and specifically US civilizational discourse. In her analysis, tolerance is identified as the crux of contemporary civilizational discourse.

From the mid-1980s, as she observes, there is "a global renaissance in tolerance talk" that, especially at the turn of the twenty-first century, coincides with multiculturalism taking center stage in discussions of "liberal democratic citizenship" (2006, 2). Brown shows how Western liberalism disguises power and cultural imperialism under a discourse of tolerance. In contemporary civilizational discourse, she argues, the liberal subject poses as having a unique capacity for tolerance—a capacity identified with civilization (166). This is accompanied by the belief that nonliberal societies—especially those designated as fundamentalist—are "inherently intolerant." Western societies, according to Brown, "become the broker of what is tolerable and intolerable" and cast other social and political formations as incapable of tolerance, and thus as barbaric (166). Because the liberal West is deemed capable of tolerance and respect for all other cultures, Western principles and values can pose as "*universalizable*" and culturally neutral without being considered "culturally imperialist" (170).

As Brown convincingly argues, the discourse on tolerance is based on hierarchical oppositions: "When the heterosexual tolerates the homosexual, when Christians tolerate Muslims in the West, not only do the first terms not require tolerance but their standing as that which confers tolerance establishes their superiority over that which is said to require tolerance" (186). The "object" of tolerance is therefore produced as inferior, not partaking in the "universal values" of the Western subject. Thus, Brown contends, the discourse on tolerance in the modern West is a power discourse that produces "the universal and the particular, the tolerant and the tolerated, the West and the East . . . the civilized and the barbaric" (187). In this rhetoric, the West poses as the generous "tolerator" of minorities. Civilizational discourse identifies tolerance with the West and constructs nonliberal societies as loci of a potential "intolerable barbarism" (6). The sovereign tolerant individual of the West is presented as a necessary condition for countering the barbarism that fundamentalism breeds.

In February 2002, Bush stated that the United States has "a historic opportunity to fight a war that will not only liberate people from the clutches of barbaric behavior but a war that can leave the world more peaceful in the years to come."[16] In this statement, Brown argues, it is not hard to see how the "opposition between civilization and barbarism, in which the cherished tolerance of the former meets the limits of the latter . . . provides the mantle of civilization, progress, and peace as cover for imperial militaristic adventures" (2006, 179). Thus, Brown regards contemporary civilizational discourse as a "colonially inflected discourse" that sets the standards of what is tolerable, acceptable, or civilized and consequently provides a legitimation for new forms of imperial state action against intolerant, barbaric, nonliberal subjects (191). This civilizational discourse places the differences between Western and non-Western societies in a binary rhetorical scheme. On the one side of this scheme we usually find liberalism, tolerance, freedom, individualism, civilization, and the West, while on the other side we find fundamentalism, oppression, intolerance, collective identities, barbarism, and the non-West (190).

Brown problematizes the use of terms like "barbarism" and "barbarians" in Western politics and liberal discourse and exposes their ideological underpinnings. However, she does not suggest that the vocabulary of this discourse—with "barbarism," "civilization," and "tolerance" as key terms—can (or should) be discarded. Rather, she invites the reader to be alert to the ways in which this discourse operates and to develop alternative speech and practices in order to "configure conflicts through grammars of power rather than ontologized ethnic or religious feuds" (295).

The kind of deconstructive critique of liberal discourse that Brown performs has its own critics too. Žižek, for example, criticizes a theoretical approach that Brown, at least partly, adopts in her study, although he does not specifically refer to Brown's work. Žižek voices his objections to what he calls "the 'radical' postcolonial critique of liberalism" that "remains at the standard Marxist level of denouncing false universality, of showing how a position that presents itself as neutral-universal effectively privileges a certain (heterosexual, male, Christian) culture" (2009, 126). This "standard postmodern anti-essentialist position," which, according to Žižek, typifies politically correct critics of the left, "is no longer enough" (126, 128). The Marxist point about the gap between what appears to be universal—democracy, human rights, freedom—and the particular interests behind it—economic exploitation, class domination—fails to see that the appearance of these universals is "*not* a 'mere appearance,' but has a power of its own" (128). Thus, following Žižek, the "symbolic fiction" of human rights discourse cannot simply be dismissed as an illusion or a covering of a different reality (namely, particular Western interests and ideology), because it has its own "real" effects (129). All universals receive particular contents. Therefore, there is no point in asking whether a certain universality is "true or a mask of particular interests" (132). The universal form of what we call "human rights" is inevitably tied to the particular interpretation it receives at a certain historical moment. The tension between the professed universality of human rights and their meaning at a particular historical moment, Žižek contends, is not an anomaly but "part of their identity" (130–31).[17]

Another reaction to contemporary civilizational discourse comes from a relativist perspective, which is often—not always justly—conflated with postmodernism. According to this perspective, truth-claims and cultural or moral propositions about what is civilized and barbaric would not be absolute and transcendental but should be evaluated on the basis of the particular perspective and context in which they are issued (Bérubé 2005, 305). From a relativist viewpoint, terms like "barbarism" and "barbarians" tend to lose their meaning and relevance: since we are all barbarians from the perspective of other cultures, we have no right to confer these labels on others as objective moral judgments. Naming other cultures or individuals "barbarian" only reflects our own perspective and moral preferences.

The approach labeled as "postmodern relativism" has received vehement attacks since September 11, 2001. Already by September 22, 2001, Edward Rothstein had written an article in the *New York Times* entitled "Attacks on US Challenge the Perspectives of Postmodern True Believers." On September 24, 2001, Roger Rosenblatt declared in the title of an article in *Time* magazine that "The Age of Irony Comes to an End." Whereas, Rosenblatt wrote, in the postmodern "age of irony, even the most serious things were not to be taken seriously" and "nothing was real," the attacks on the twin towers changed all that for good. According to the same article, academics and intellectuals would now have to acknowledge what is "real" and "serious." "Are you looking for something to take seriously?" Rosenblatt asks; the reply: "Begin with evil" (79). As Peter Beinart remarked in an article in the *New Republic*, after 9/11 "ambiguity became impossible" and "dissent . . . immoral" (quoted in Fish 2002, 27).

These attacks were not left unanswered. Stanley Fish, a well-known proponent of relativism, defended postmodern relativism against what he called a "scapegoating" directed at anyone who after 9/11 still dares to claim things like "there are no universal standards of judgment" (2002, 27).[18] As Fish observes, the gist of the critiques against postmodernism was twofold: first, the events on 9/11 "prove postmodernism to be wrong," and second, "postmodernism is somehow responsible for September 11" (28). For the polemicists of postmodernism, the unwillingness to accept that there are moral truths worth defending, which has weakened the nation's "moral fiber," is a result of the radical cultural relativism injected into American life by the "virus of Postmodernism" (27, 30). Since postmodernism disavows the existence of universal principles or a "transcendent ethical perspective," the same argument continues, it leaves us no grounds on which to condemn the attacks on the twin towers and terrorism in general.[19] The relativism of postmodernism makes it impossible, many argue, to objectively tag the perpetrators as "terrorists" or "barbarians." A relativist would argue that those viewed by the West as barbarians or terrorists could be "freedom fighters" from the perspective of other groups.

Fish, however, fends off the claim that relativism does not leave room for condemning barbaric actions. Nothing prevents us from denouncing certain actions, Fish argues, but we can do that without resorting to an "abstract vocabulary of justice, truth and virtue" or to universal absolutes, which every party defines differently (2002, 28). Condemnation can be issued on the basis of "the historical reality" of "our way of life" (28). Reducing the enemy to the "abstraction of 'Evil,'" a "shape-shifting demon," or a barbaric and irrational being is a dangerous political strategy: it underestimates our enemies and prevents us from understanding their motives and from finding the most effective way to counter their threat (29–30).

The relativist approach, in which the "barbarian" is a matter of perspective and not an absolute moral category, was channeled in new directions and more nuanced versions during the first decade of the twenty-first century. Richard Bernstein's *The Abuse of Evil* (2005), for example, replaces Huntington's "clash of civilizations" with a "clash of mentalities" within (and outside) the West. Scrutinizing the discourse of "good versus evil" in post-9/11 America, Bernstein notices that this discourse of simplistic dichotomies represents a mentality "drawn to absolutes" and moral certainties. To this he contrasts a mentality that questions rigid oppositional thinking and absolutes in politics, which he names "pragmatic fallibilism." This mentality does not fall far from the relativism attacked after 9/11. Contrary to what adversaries of relativism contend, Bernstein argues that renouncing absolutes does not entail lack of commitment "to act decisively in fighting our real enemies" (2005, viii). On this point, he is on the same page as Fish.

Another set of recent reactions to civilizational discourse shares the tendency to reverse the key terms and oppositions of this discourse: "civilization," "culture," and "barbarism." Žižek reverses Huntington's thesis of the "clash of civilizations" by arguing, in a Benjaminian vein, that "every clash of civilizations really is a clash of underlying barbarisms" (2009, 150). Thus, the clash between the Arab and the American civilizations is not between "barbarism" and "respect for human dignity" but "a clash between anonymous brutal torture and torture as a media spectacle" (150). Social and cultural anthropologist Arjun Appadurai adjusts Huntington's model to argue that we are "in a worldwide civilization of clashes rather than in a clash of civilizations" (2006, 18). Through this reversal, he draws attention to conflicts and tensions within each of the cultural formations Huntington calls "civilizations," particularly within the Islamic world and the West.

The Clash of Barbarisms: The Making of the New World Disorder (2006) by Lebanese-French political theorist Gilbert Achcar reverses Huntington's title by using the negative opposites of "civilization" and "order."[20] Achcar argues that violent conflicts and terrorism today, including the attacks on September 11, do not reflect a clash between civilizations with different value systems but rather a clash of the dark sides of these civilizations. In the course of the historical "civilizing process" each civilization generates its own forms of barbarism (84). These are not abnormalities in the civilizing process but "an expression of one of its potentialities, one of its faces, one of its possible offshoots" (Traverso 2003, 153, quoted in Achcar 2006, 84). These forms of barbarism tend to surface in periods of crisis. Both the Bush administration and al-Qaeda, rather than the Western or Islamic civilization as such, embody this barbaric side.

That the West does not embody the essence of civilization but a form of barbarism is another quite popular reversal of the barbarism/civilization dichotomy. Critics, particularly from the Left, scrutinize recent practices of torture and violence by the United States as phenomena that weaken and invalidate the distinction between the West as "civilized" and the "barbarian terrorists." Recent studies draw attention to both Western barbarism in the twenty-first century and the history of twentieth-century Europe as a history of barbarism—or a history wherein barbarism and civilization are inextricably linked. In *Barbarism and Civilization: A History of Europe in Our Time* (2007), for example, historian Bernard Wasserstein presents barbarism and civilization as marching side by side in the history of twentieth-century Europe.

So far, I have laid out the following reversals: Huntington's "clash of civilizations" turns into a "civilization of clashes" (Appadurai), a "clash of barbarisms" (Žižek, Achcar), or a "clash of mentalities" (Bernstein).[21] In some of these reversals, barbarism and civilization (as moral categories) are seen as coexisting sides within all civilizations. Other reversals project the West as a domain of barbarism instead of the beacon of civilization. The critical value of such reversals is undeniable. Despite their critical function, however, they neither debunk the hierarchy between barbarism and civilization nor try to shift the semantic content of barbarism. Rather, they shuffle the referents of the terms involved. The terms themselves retain their conventional meanings and valuation (civilization is good; barbarism is bad), but they switch places or represent different sides of an argument. Although the arguments made through these reversals may, indeed, be different from, and opposed to, popular manifestations of civilizational discourse, they do not change the terms on which the debate is held. Reversals may criticize an argument or viewpoint but do not radically disrupt an established binary or cause a crisis in the terms, which could lead to resignifications and alternative modes of use. Civilization remains the superior part of the opposition, while barbarism continues to be a negative signifier for violent, irrational, and brutal behavior, whether this behavior is attributed to the West, to terrorists, to Muslim fundamentalists, or to every civilization.

French intellectual Bernard-Henri Lévy (2008) unravels another noteworthy reversal of the referent of "barbarism," which also fails to question its meaning. In *Left in Dark Times: A Stand against the New Barbarism*, Lévy detects barbarism not only in the challenges Western societies face today by terrorists and "evil others" but also in the turn the Left has taken in cultural debates. He associates the Left with a "new barbarism."

In what is, in my view, a rather simplistic and caricatured dismissal of Left intellectual thought today, Lévy takes issue with what he sees as a current crisis in the European (and American) Left, which has moved away from what he believes the Left stands for. Although he explicitly positions himself on the Left, Lévy contends that Left intellectuals today are "flirting with evil" and have betrayed the true commitment of the Left, namely, its antitotalitarian and antifascist ideals. Contrary to these ideals, Lévy argues, the Left today endorses anti-Semitism and either allies with Islamism or treats Islamism with "the indulgence that tradition demands for the humble and the ill-fated" (167). Moreover, he criticizes the tendency of the Left to short-circuit and dismiss liberalism (which becomes a "bad word") as well as "the idea of Europe, the politics of human rights, or the dream of an all-embracing concept of humanity" (209). Lévy sketches the turn of the Left and its "new evil" tendencies in religious and at times apocalyptic terms. In doing so, he sometimes comes *rhetorically* close to the discourse of George W. Bush and his administration.

The French context, in which Lévy is situated, has produced several defenses of liberalism. Some of them house more nuanced humanist approaches. French-Bulgarian philosopher Tzvetan Todorov's *The Fear of Barbarians* (2010) represents a kind of liberal humanism growing as a popular counterdiscourse to the allegedly relativist postmodern position.[22] Todorov looks at Western countries today as dominated by fear, specifically the fear of barbarians. Reactions of the United States to the attacks on September 11, including military interventions in Afghanistan, Iraq, and elsewhere under the banner of the "war on terror," exemplify the dangers of giving in to this fear (7). His central thesis is that our fear of barbarians threatens to turn us into barbarians. Guantánamo and Abu Ghraib have become symbols of the kind of barbarism this fear breeds. While "we" (by which Todorov refers to the West) set out to defend democratic and humanist values, we end up sacrificing and betraying them (7, 106).[23]

Todorov defines barbarism and civilization as universal moral categories, applicable to all cultures.[24] He rejects relative and relational definitions, according to which barbarism is a matter of perspective, and adopts an absolute definition: "Barbarity exists in itself and not merely in the gaze of the naive observer" (2010, 20–21). By narrowing the meanings of "barbarian," he formulates the following definition: "Barbarians are those who do not acknowledge that others are human beings like themselves" (16). His definition reverses the traditional signification of the barbarian as less than human by locating barbarism not in the purportedly subhuman other but in the act of *perceiving others as nonhuman.* The terms "barbarism" and "barbarian," according to Todorov, should be applied to the actions and behavior of those who ostracize others from humanity or treat others as inhuman, monsters, or savages (18). He stresses that only actions, attitudes, and behavior can be deemed barbaric—not individuals or civilizations as such (22). This is for Todorov the only rightful and legitimate use of these terms—the rest are abuses. Todorov maintains that despite its abuses, the notion of "barbarism" needs to be sustained.[25] In his definition, barbarism remains the great opposite of civilization, and both terms become exclusively moral categories, conferring absolute value judgments (33). Todorov asserts the unity of humanity despite differences between particular cultures. It is this unity, he argues, that allows us to distinguish, always and everywhere, which acts are barbaric and which are civilized (51).

By listing a set of binary pairs, Todorov categorizes certain conditions or traits as inherently barbaric or civilized. For instance, equality before the law is civilized while discriminatory laws are closer to barbarism; a tyrannical state is more barbarous than a liberal one; magic is more barbarous than science; a dialogue that allows speakers to exchange views on an equal level is much more civilized than a harangue; endorsing an idea "on an act of faith" or because you were told to is barbaric, while to accept a proposition based on reason is civilized; within the same community, a "person who knows its codes and traditions" partakes in civilization more than an ignorant person who has limited understanding of these codes (23–24). The list goes on.

The normative standards Todorov forwards as markers of civilization or barbarism do not project a culturally neutral universal truth. Rather, they reflect the liberal and humanist values of Western democracies, wherein Enlightenment ideals, particularly the belief in reason, play a pivotal role. Thus, even though Todorov opposes the idea that some cultures are by definition civilized while others are barbaric, the "absolute" and "universal" values on which he bases his definition of civilization and barbarism are fostered within a particular cultural space: they are the legacy of European Enlightenment and represent today's liberal democratic West.[26] Of course, when the West deviates from these values—for example, by exercising torture—that is undoubtedly, according to Todorov's definition, also barbaric. But such phenomena in the West are usually seen as exceptions—the "rule" being that Western humanist values condemn torture. For Todorov, the West is not by definition civilized (no culture is) because it does not always follow the lessons of its own values. Nevertheless, for him the West, and Europe in particular, is the source and broker of these values and thus the defining essence of civilization.

Although one can easily agree that torture, tyranny, prejudice, or legal discrimination is reprehensible, I take issue with Todorov's contention that the features and conditions he lists as "civilized," as well as his own definition of "barbarism," represent absolutes: universal values, which always determine whether an action, condition, or mode of thinking is civilized or barbaric. In the final pages of his book Todorov writes: "No merit lies in preferring good to evil when we ourselves define the meaning of these two words" (197). Although his definitions of "barbarism" and "civilization" partly run counter to the traditional meanings of these terms, I cannot help reading Todorov's statement as an unwittingly self-ironic comment on the absolute character of his own definitions.

While Todorov's nuanced humanist argument is in many ways opposed to the civilizational rhetoric of the Bush administration and its supporters, it does not radically break with this rhetoric. Both approaches share the contention that the civilized has to be distinguished from the barbaric in absolute, oppositional, and universally valid terms. For example, Huntington's conviction that "cultures are relative" while "morality is absolute" seems to tie in well with Todorov's vision. In both visions, the West is the implicit source from which civilized values emanate. This entails, as Brown also suggests, that making the world less barbaric would demand "the liberalization of the world" (2006, 154). In a similar spirit, Todorov views the project of the European Union as "an attempt to make the way the world works a little more civilized" (2010, 195). Although he claims not to identify civilization with Europe and points out the barbarous sides of European history, he clearly projects the European value system as an exemplar of civilization.

Contrary to relativist approaches, Todorov's humanist perspective does not invalidate the notion of barbarism but pleads for its judicious application to certain kinds of behavior and actions instead of to particular groups of people. The only way to avoid abuses of "barbarism" and the "barbarian," Todorov contends, is to delimit and specify the precise content of these terms and to narrow down and absolutize their definitions. In his definition, barbarism and civilization remain entangled in an oppositional and hierarchical relation. Their absolute antithesis leaves no room for intertwinement between the meanings and functions of these terms. In his view, reducing their different meanings to a single stable definition in which barbarism remains the negative pole of civilization will enable us to identify barbarism whenever and wherever we experience it.

Shifting the Terms of the Debate

Although I share Todorov's main thesis that the fear of barbarians threatens to turn us into barbarians, his approach to the concepts of barbarism and civilization runs counter to what I propose here. Instead of narrowing the meanings of barbarism, I plead for their pluralization. Instead of keeping barbarism as far as possible from civilization by absolutizing its meaning, I focus on the complex dynamics between the two concepts. Through the *intertwinement* of these notions, barbarism—taken as a relational concept with shifting meanings—can challenge the certainties of civilization and expose its "universal truths" as discursive ruses.

Most approaches to the popular uses of barbarism and barbarian in contemporary Western politics presented here either relativize "barbarism" in ways that invalidate its use and render the term practically redundant or invest both "barbarism" and "civilization" with universal values and plead for using the terms in "the right way," based on a vague consensus on what that way may be. Even critical reversals of these terms do not change their meanings or the dynamics between them but usually shuffle their referents. In all these uses of barbarism, whether they belong to official political rhetoric or to critical oppositional voices, the meaning of barbarism and the barbarian remains generally intact. Even when it shifts a little, as in Todorov's vision, the fixity of the barbarism/civilization opposition and the negativity with which barbarism is invested are treated as a given.

Recycling the same relation between civilization and barbarism perpetuates the logic of their opposition. We may have a better chance countering the discursive violence of barbarism when we try to pluralize and open up the term rather than police its meanings and uses. The violence involved in such "policing" should not be overlooked. This does not mean that problematic uses of barbarism should remain unquestioned—far from it. But the terms by which this questioning takes place may be more crucial for the effectiveness of the questioning than the argument itself.

Instead of banishing barbarism from our vocabulary (radical relativism); instead of solidifying its negative meaning and its opposition with civilization (universalism, humanism); and instead of reversing the opposition by simply shifting its referents, we could imagine a different semantic space for this concept, in which its discursive violence could take critical and constructive directions. This different future for barbarism can be envisioned not only against but also through its long history. Only through an understanding of the historical memories that this term carries and of its shifting relation to civilization throughout history can we begin to think of ways to modify its performativity in present and future contexts.

3

It's All Greek to Me

THE BARBARIAN IN HISTORY

> Caught—both seized and entangled—in a binary opposition, one of the terms
> retains its old name so as to destroy the opposition to which it no longer quite
> belongs, to which in any event it has never quite yielded, the history of this oppo-
> sition being one of incessant struggles generative of hierarchical configurations.
> —Jacques Derrida, *Dissemination*

"It's all Greek to me." We use this idiom when we have no idea
what another person is talking about—when the speech of our interlocutor sounds like "blah blah." What is intriguing about this phrase is that it
succinctly captures the relational nature of the barbarian. At the time of
its inception in ancient Greece, the term "barbarian" was the exact opposite of "Greek": it was applied to foreigners who did not speak Greek and
whose language was therefore incomprehensible, sounding like "bar bar."
To say "it's all Greek to me" today, then, constitutes a firsthand reversal of
Greekness as the standard against which the barbarian becomes defined.
Being or speaking Greek is clearly no longer the criterion for defining
what is civilized. In this idiom, "Greek" becomes a signifier of incomprehensibility and confusion and, as such, occupies the place of the barbarian
language, which, based on its Greek etymology, is a language the "civilized" subject does not understand.

The designation of somebody as barbarian takes place only in relation to a subject that assumes the status of the "civilized." This becomes

evident if we follow the barbarian in history. The historical travels of the barbarian reveal the various perspectives within European space (and probably even more perspectives outside European space) from which barbarism has been defined. From a different viewpoint each time, barbarians are the non-Greeks and the Greeks, the Christians and the non-Christians, heathens or Muslims, the Romans, the Germanic nations, the inhabitants of the Orient, the colonized peoples of the Americas, Africa, and Asia, the European colonizers, the Jews, the Nazis, Romany, members of the working class, terrorists, neo-imperialists, and many others. Practically every group in Western history has been tagged as "barbarian" by another group.

Nevertheless, in each period and context this category tends to fix upon particular features assigned to certain people as inherent qualities. The relational aspect of the term is subject to an essentialist logic that dictates a static hierarchization between civilized and barbarian. Thus, the term's shifting connotations and referents in history highlight the following paradox: Such a protean and relational concept has always sustained one of the most rigid binarisms in Western history. The persistence of the barbarism/civilization dichotomy in the discursive construct we call "Western history" indicates the dependence of civilization on the notion of the barbarian for its self-definition. The barbarian appears as an abjected outside, which, to borrow Judith Butler's words, is always inside the subject "as its own founding repudiation" (1993, 3).

The changing connotations of the barbarian from Greek antiquity to the present are interdependent with the shifting self-perceptions of the civilized. Therefore, when following the notion of the barbarian historically, the discussion is always also about civilization. Standards that delimit the realm of the barbaric and the civilized are in constant flux. Nevertheless, in history both concepts often appear as naturalized entities. As Joan Scott argues, "History is a chronology that makes experience visible, but in which categories appear as nonetheless ahistorical" (1991, 778). History tends to suppress or "under-state" the "historically variable interrelationship" of categories of identity—in this case, between the "barbarian" and the "civilized" (778).[1] Therefore, unpacking the "barbarian" in its historical complexity is a necessary step to question its present or historical moments of objectification.

This chapter follows the connotations of the barbarian in Western history in its relation to the notion of the civilized. In this venture, I have not opted for a chronologically ordered account or a genealogy of the barbarian. Instead, in order to chart the dynamic position that the figure of the barbarian occupies in Western discourses, I relate its changing meanings and uses to the normative standards that established the basis for the antithesis between civilized and barbarian in different eras and social or cultural contexts. To that end, this chapter lays out a tentative typology of what I call "civilizational standards," which have—in different degrees— determined the definition of the "barbarian" from Greek antiquity to the present: (1) language; (2) culture; (3) political system and ideology (including empire); (4) morality, values, and manners; (5) humanity, humanism, and the human; (6) religion; (7) ethnicity and race; (8) class; (9) gender; (10) progress (including technique and modes of production); and (11) psyche.

These standards constantly shift. If language was the main criterion for the definition of the barbarian in archaic Greece, in other periods the criteria become more political (as, for example, in fifth-century BCE Greece), cultural (as in the Hellenistic period), religious (as in the Middle Ages in Europe), and so on. However, to claim that each standard neatly corresponds to a particular period or cultural context would be an over-simplification. In most periods, even when a certain standard is prevalent, it forms a unique constellation with other standards, which are pertinent to a lesser or greater degree. The construction of the barbarian in Western discourses is premised on intricate constellations of the defining features of self and other.

Adopting the structuring principle of civilizational standards instead of a chronological presentation resists the conception of the history of the barbarian as linear and progressive—an uninterrupted succession of significations. This structuring principle underscores the shifting and contested terrain that the barbarian and the civilized simultaneously occupy. Thus, in this typology the barbarian emerges through a web of cultural, social, political, religious, and (pseudo)scientific discourses and its history unravels as a narrative of contradictions, repetitions, tensions, and unexpected intersections.

The standards brought together here indicate the pervasiveness of the barbarian in various spheres of the Western cultural and ideological space. Further, the multiple standards through which the barbarian is cast reveal multiple histories of the barbarian in the West. There are several ways to tell a history of the barbarian, just as there are at least as many ways to tell a history of Western civilization.[2] Thus, this chapter prepares the ground for pluralizing "barbarism" and the "barbarian" and for contesting their dominant uses.

To examine how the barbarian is produced through different standards, I scrutinize a selection of representative case studies—a kaleidoscope of slices of history through which the barbarian is cast in various ways. The focus is particularly on contexts that enabled shifts in the signification of the barbarian: moments when new connotations are attached to this figure; moments of reversal of the hierarchy between civilized and barbarian, when the "civilized" are projected as more corrupt and barbaric than those others on whom they confer the label "barbarian"; and moments of profound critique and renegotiation of the concepts of barbarism and the barbarian. With a focus on such shifts, the discursive mechanisms producing barbarism and civilization emerge as historically contingent and therefore open to critique and negotiation.

Unpacking the Terms

It would be a good idea.
—Gandhi's reported remark about Western civilization

The barbarian is only one of the countless "others" that the civilized imagination has constructed. Slave, woman, guest worker, migrant, nomad, savage, wild man, cannibal, lunatic, Oriental, Jewish, gypsy, animal, and monster are all categories that enabled (Western) subjects to define themselves in distinction from others, situated beyond the borders of their home, class, society, religion, race, gender, nation, empire, or of humanity. The category of the barbarian is coextensive and imbricated with some of these others.

The "savage" or "wild man" is one of the categories that comes closest to the barbarian, although it is a more recent construction.[3] Many ancient and medieval authors often use these categories interchangeably (White 1972, 19). However, in the eighteenth century and during the Enlightenment they develop distinct uses. The savage represents an uncorrupted and pure human state, closer to nature, but because he is a tabula rasa, he is considered capable of being educated and learning European manners.[4] The barbarian, on the other hand, cannot be educated—he represents "the liberal project gone awry" (Salter 2002, 22). Thus, the savage is often considered redeemable, whereas the barbarian is not (22). Another difference concerns the kind of threat these figures were perceived to constitute. In different periods, according to Hayden White, barbarians were generally considered to live "under *some kind* of law" and to be able to organize themselves "into groups large enough to constitute a threat to 'civilization' itself." Wild men, on the other hand, were thought to live alone and thus "represented a threat to the individual" rather than to society in general (White 1972, 20). This difference between barbarians and savages is also reflected in eighteenth-century models of human societal progress. In such models, barbarism and savagery represent two different stages in societal development, with barbarism situated between "savagery" and "civilization" (Salter 2002, 23).

The constant shifts in the content of the barbarian itself make it difficult to pinpoint what distinguishes the "barbarian" from other related categories. The term carries various connotations in history: it has been used to denote simply the foreigner (a person who speaks another language); suggest decadence, moral, cultural, or racial inferiority; cruel, savage, or inhuman behavior; an infantile, natural, or primitive state; lack of education or manners; and the like. However, if we put together a schematic typology of "others" in Western imagination, the barbarian would probably stand out as the opposite of civilization par excellence: the absolute other, which—as a paradox-object—threatens the frontiers of the civilized world and simultaneously sustains the self-definition of the latter.

Although the focus here is on the construction of the barbarian within what we call "Western civilization," the notion of the barbarian is not an exclusively Western construction. Categories akin to the barbarian appear in the conceptual schemes of many cultures. Such are the Japanese notion of the *gaijin* for foreigner and the Jewish notions of the *goy* and *gentile*, used to denote non-Jews, all of which carry pejorative or even offensive connotations.[5]

However, terms comparable to "barbarian" in other cultures are often premised on different standards than those delineating the barbarian in the West. In ancient Greece, for example, from the eighth to the fifth century BCE, the main criterion for defining the barbarian was language. The geographical dispersal of the Greeks over various coasts and islands, the varied ways of life, and the differences in tradition, culture, and political allegiances among the (Ionian, Dorian, Aeolian) Greek communities prevented a definition of the barbarian based on habitat and lifestyle (E. Hall 1989, 4–5). Lifestyle and habitat, however, were the main criteria for the barbarian/civilized distinction in ancient China, where equivalent terms for barbarians meant "nomads," "shepherds," or "jungle people" (Lattimore 1962, 451, 455).[6] The same importance attributed to habitat can be found among the Sumerians, who identified civilized existence with the sedentary urban lifestyle of the plain. They thus used derogatory terms for the "nomads" and "mountain-dwellers" of the steppe and the highlands (Henri Limet, presented in E. Hall 1989, 5). The Hebrews also attached high value to language as a marker of differentiation.[7] Nevertheless, in their distinction between themselves and Gentiles, religion had a more central place than in the definition of Greek versus barbarian (5).[8] However, as Edith Hall argues, despite the existence of comparable terms, in other ancient cultures there is no equivalent that "precisely and exclusively embraced *all* who did not share their ethnicity" (4).

Homer's *Iliad* (eighth century BCE), according to D. N. Maronitis, may be considered the "womb" of the hierarchical pair barbarian/civilized, although this opposition is only fully shaped and articulated two centuries later (1999, 27). Whether we place the beginnings of the barbarian in the eighth or the sixth century BCE, approximately twenty-five centuries separate the first appearance of the term "barbarian" from that of the term "civilization." "Civilization" is first documented in French in 1767 and in English in 1772, and it first appeared in an English dictionary in 1775 (Williams 1985, 57; Salter 2002, 15).

The modern term "civilization" derives from the Latin *civitas.* Although in modernity barbarism is predominantly understood in opposition to the term "civilization," one should bear in mind that historically the first systematic reference point for the construction of the barbarian was the Athenian *polis.* Therefore, insofar as the Roman *civitas* is the notion in which "civilization" is etymologically grounded, this notion needs to be distinguished from the notion of the *polis*. The Greek polis and the Roman civitas are often used interchangeably to refer to self-governing political communities. However, the conception of citizenship implied in these terms, as well as their antithetical poles, are distinct. Unlike citizenship in the Athenian *polis*, which was based on a dualism between *polites* (citizens) and foreigners (barbarians), the Roman *civitas* was premised on a "complex system of group differentiation" that involved "a gradation of citizenship" (Isin 2002, 6). This difference can also be correlated with the fact that in the Athenian *polis* foreigners were ostensibly excluded from political life, whereas the Roman *civitas* included people from different ethnic origins. As a result of the different forms of Roman citizenship, the term "Roman" "became dissociated from a specific ethnic group and came to connote citizens of the civitas irrespective of their ethnic origin" (Samuel E. Finer, quoted in Isin 2002, 95). While members of the Athenian polis shared a common language and culture, against which their "barbarians" were delineated, the Roman *civitas* accommodated a diversity of cultures, languages, and religions (Román 2010, 25). However, unlike the Greeks, Romans "increasingly thought of themselves as the natural rulers of aliens or barbarians" (Geoffrey E. M. de Ste. Croix, presented in Isin 2002, 94). This aspect of *civitas* resonates in the universalizing aspirations of its modern derivative: the imperialist ideology that underlies the term "civilization" as a Western construct.

Despite its relatively brief history, "civilization" also has a complex genealogy. According to Raymond Williams, its main use was to describe "a state of social order and refinement, especially in conscious historical or cultural contrast with *barbarism*" (1985, 57–58). But civilization also denoted a historical process, which carried the spirit of Enlightenment, "with its emphasis on secular and progressive human self-development" (58). In fact, what is specific about the term "civilization," according to Williams, is the way it combines the meanings of "a process and an achieved condition." As an "achieved condition," civilization conveys a celebratory view of modernity as the most advanced state of human society (58). The static and dynamic conceptions of civilization as both a state and a process are, according to Wendy Brown, reconciled within the Western progressivist historiography of modernity:

Civilization simultaneously frames the achievement of European modernity, the promised fruit of modernization as an experience, and crucially, the effects of exporting European modernity to "uncivilized" parts of the globe. European colonial expansion from the mid-nineteenth through the mid-twentieth century was explicitly justified as a project of civilization, conjuring the gifts of social order, legality, reason, and religion, as well as regulating manners and mores. (2006, 179–80)

In the nineteenth century, the term was thus mobilized within the colonial project and used to justify European expansion (Tsing and Hershatter 2005, 36). Within imperialist ideology, the term assisted conceptualizing the European "civilizing mission" of enlightening the "barbaric" worlds beyond Europe.

In modern European history, civilization is often understood specifically as European (or Western) civilization. As such, it expresses a singular European identity, based on the idea of a secular (rather than religious) unity (Gong 1984, 23). However, the word civilization is now also used in the plural as a "relatively neutral form for any achieved social order or way of life" (Williams 1985, 59). As discussed earlier, its use in the plural does not necessarily contradict its singular use for Western or European civilization. As Walter Mignolo argues, "Civilization" is a geopolitically grounded notion that often turns into "a European self-description of its role in history," while it is simultaneously "disguised as the natural course of universal history" (2005, xvii, 8).

Given that the term "civilization" is a modern construction, its application to premodern periods is inevitably somewhat anachronistic. Thus, when talking about *civilizational* standards in Greek antiquity, for example, we must realize that the notion of neither civilization nor Western history as we understand it today was part of Greek consciousness. Even the idea of a unitary Greek consciousness is debatable. Although in Herodotus's account of the Greco-Persian Wars (499–449 BCE) we already have manifestations of the contrast between the West (Greece) and the Asiatic East (the Persian Empire), in ancient Greece identity was generally structured around city-states.

When I refer to "civilizational standards" that determine the identity of Western subjects in history, these standards do not (always) pertain to the term "civilization" as such but to a central self-defining principle on which dominant groups, nations, or empires in Western history built their sense of superiority vis-à-vis barbarian others. This principle determines the perspective from which the rest of the world is viewed and decides which subjects will be excluded from the sanctioned realm of the self by being relegated to the barbaric. *Hellenicity* and *Romanitas*, for example, are linguistic incarnations of the principle that can catachrestically be called "civilization." Thus, throughout history, the hegemonic discourse I call "civilizational" finds its barbarians in "all those who do not belong to the locus of enunciation . . . of those who assign the standards of classification and assign to themselves the right to classify" (Mignolo 2005, 8).

The fact that the term "barbarian" has a longer history than the term "civilization" leads to an intriguing realization: in the age-old dichotomy within which the barbarian is implicated since its inception, the "barbarian" is the stable term, while its positive opposite changes (Greek, Roman, Christian, European, and the like, until the term "civilization" is coined). This suggests that a stable category for the absolute other is even more essential for the discourse of the self than a stable positive category of self-definition. The assumption that a solid denomination of the other is prioritized over a fixed self-defining category finds support in the mechanism White calls "ostensive self-definition by negation" (1972, 4). According to this mechanism, the self defines itself by pointing at what it thinks it is definitely *not*. Remarkably, Samuel Huntington formulates the same claim but also adds a necessary dimension of conflict and violence to this process: "We know who we are only when we know who we are not and often when we know whom we are against" (1996, 21). Although the persistence of the term "barbarian" in Western history serves the self-definition of dominant groups, it could also turn against this purpose: it could enable us to assert the priority of barbarism over civilization and question the former's dependence on its positive opposite. In other words, the continuous presence of the barbarian in history also harbors the insight that civilization may in fact be the weakest link in this opposition.

My choice to use "civilization" as the overarching concept for the various standards probed here is motivated by the particularity of the concept of civilization compared with other categories of self-definition. It could be argued that "civilization" is simply one standard for defining the "barbarian" among many. Instead, I argue that there is no other concept before modernity that captures the totality of standards in the way "civilization" does. What distinguishes civilization from each of the eleven standards listed earlier is that in principle it can contain all of these standards, together or separately. Huntington's definition of "civilization" demonstrates this point. For him, civilization is a "complex mix of higher levels of morality, religion, learning, art, philosophy, technology, material well-being, *and probably other things*" (1996, 320, emphasis added). In this definition, civilization emerges as an all-encompassing container, accommodating a plurality of standards. As the phrase "and probably other things" suggests, the number of standards under the umbrella of civilization is mobile and open to reordering. The concept of "civilization" thereby turns into a machine for producing different versions of the barbarian tailored to the needs and priorities of the civilized "we."

In this machine, the contents of "civilization" are kept as broad and flexible as possible in order to secure the stability of the opposition between civilization and barbarism. With the introduction of the term "civilization" in modernity, "barbarism" finds a constant and stable opposite. While the standards contained within civilization remain flexible, one thing becomes fixed: "civilization" becomes a powerful conceptual wall for keeping the "barbarian" at bay. In this sense, the introduction of the concept of civilization constitutes a unique modern phenomenon: for the first time the superiority of the (Western) subject is established through a single term that contains a multiplicity of standards that delineate the realm of the self and the barbaric. As a result, even as the status of particular standards changes through time—if, for example, religion and culture replace political ideology as the key to defining civilization—the opposite of the barbarian does not have to change: it can still be expressed by the term "civilization" as a container of all active standards in a particular context.

Of course, similar concepts in earlier periods also accommodated multiple criteria. *Romanitas* functioned simultaneously as a marker of culture, education, and virtue. But the concept of *Romanitas* remains bound to a particular context and empire and is thus not easily transferrable to other contexts or groups that succeeded the Roman Empire. In contrast, "civilization" grants this shifting plurality of standards a permanent conceptual space in language, which did not exist before. "Civilization" is thus paradoxically a chameleonic and dynamic concept meant to solidify a hierarchical opposition in the most steadfast way possible. Whenever the opposition is threatened or weakened, the civilizational machine can shift the defining standards of the self in order to slightly redefine the self and the barbarian without changing the terms—and thus the basic violent structure—of the opposition between them.

"Western history," just as "civilization," is a modern construction. The same holds for the globalizing phrase "*the* West," which came into general usage over the past two centuries (Sakai and Morris 2005, 372).[9] Although the term "the West" is supposed to unify a group of people called "Westerners," this unity comprises a constellation of heterogeneous ideologies, traditions, races, and cultural practices. The West is a collective heritage, partly constituted by non-European influences as well.[10]

Despite the diverse forces constituting "the West," as Edward Said says, the West has "a history and a tradition of thought, imagery, and vocabulary that have given it reality and presence" (2003, 5). Thus, even as a mythical construct, "the West" has pervasive material effects. The terms "the West," "Western history," and "Western civilization" are products of a civilizational discourse that has shaped the thought, language, and imagination of Western subjects in common ways and that perpetuates the logic of civilization versus barbarism, and of the West vis-à-vis the non-West.

The idea of Western history as a linear progressive narrative originating in classical Greece is also a product of modernity. My earliest temporal point of reference here is ancient Greece. This choice does not suggest an endorsement of the foundational narrative that views Greece as the origin of Western civilization. Rather, it is premised on the word "barbarian" as it was incepted in ancient Greece. Moreover, given my Greek origin and background, my focus on the Greek context indicates the inevitable implication of the analyst in her object of study.

When I use "barbarism" and "civilization" in this historical exploration, it is not possible to effectively distance myself from discourses that involve these concepts, which are the discourses that have shaped my identity and education as a "citizen of the West." One option would be to use quotation marks each time I use the term "barbarian" or "civilization" in a way unreflective of my own viewpoint or position. However, quotation marks often create an illusion of objectivity or suggest that the speaking subject is able to distance herself and stand outside a discourse in which she is embedded. This would sidestep my complicity with Western discourses on the barbarian. Therefore, by refusing to position myself on the outside or the margins of this discourse, I see myself as what Mireille Rosello has called a "reluctant witness," participating in discursive constructions I would "much rather not condone," while also trying to resist them (1998, 1).[11]

Civilizational Standards

The standards in this typology do not stand in isolation as strict conceptual frameworks but constitute mutually illuminating and intertwined discursive domains. For example, race, class, and gender are involved in "systems of social stratification" that are "superimposed on one another" and either undermine or enhance each other (Shohat and Stam 1994, 22). Certain standards are applicable only to particular periods, as some of them were not (fully) conceptualized earlier. The standard of "progress," for example, applies primarily to modernity.

There are also standards formally left out of this typology, which enter the discussion under the rubric of other standards. For instance, "geography" is not treated separately but is nonetheless important in this discussion, insofar as the conceptual borders separating the civilized world from the barbarians often coincide with geographical divisions. The barbarian is usually "appointed" to areas outside the borders of a civilized society or empire. The "Orient" is such a mythically invested geographical space, where barbarians supposedly dwell. Hence, geography is a parameter underlying many other standards examined here.

Finally, certain standards are more inclusive than others, and (partially) overlap with or encompass other standards. "Culture" is a case in point. A notoriously complex concept, it incorporates standards such as "religion," "political ideology," or "morality, values, and manners." These standards are nevertheless examined separately because of their specific role in the definition of the barbarian.

Language

Language is located at the heart of the definition of the barbarian. In ancient Greece, language is the first criterion for distinguishing the barbarian. However, it should be noted that despite the Greek etymology of the word barbarian, scholars locate similar words in other early languages, such as the Babylonian-Sumerian *barbaru* (foreigner) (E. Hall 1989, 4). There are thus indications that the Greek word *barbaros* might have been formed under oriental influences.

In the earliest Greek sources, foreignness is already identified with linguistic difference. The word *barbarophōnoi*, referring to those who speak a language other than Greek, makes a first appearance in Homer's *Iliad*, although Homer never uses the word *Hellenes*. Here, the Carians are called *barbarophōnoi* because they speak a different language (Munson 2005, 2). Accordingly, the leader of the barbarophone Carians is qualified as a fool, *nēpios*, which literally means "infantile," like a baby who has not entered the system of language (2). Notably, some scholars, like Julius Pokorny, relate the word *barbarian* with Indo-European words that signify the "meaningless" or "inarticulate," such as the Latin *balbutio* and the English *baby* (E. Hall 1989, 4). Thus, even in its early manifestations the term "barbarian" implies inferiority.[12] Although at the time of its inception and up until the Persian Wars it primarily signified linguistic difference, this difference was sometimes accompanied by a depreciation of other peoples, based on the perception of their language as nonhuman speech (Long 1986, 131). Linguistic difference had other connotations. The word's onomatopoetic etymology (the repetition of the "bar bar" sequence) denoted not just the foreign speech of the other but also elocution or pronunciation difficulties, speaking with harsh sounds or inarticulately, stuttering, or lisping (Long 1986, 130–31; Hartog 2001, 80). Although the term is certainly not complimentary, François Hartog argues that its early uses denote "a Barbarian way of speaking" and not "a Barbarian nature" (2001, 80).

Between the eighth and fifth centuries BCE, the linguistic criterion for the definition of the barbarian is more dominant than political or ethnic-based factors, because there is not yet a strong sense of shared ethnicity in the Greek world. Identity in Greece is primarily constructed around city-states, with considerable differences in laws, political systems, lifestyle, and even language. Although language remains the basis of the dichotomy throughout Greek antiquity, the barbarian is enriched with more negative connotations in later texts, especially during and after the Persian Wars, when the Greek/barbarian opposition acquires clear political, ethnic, and cultural connotations. In this context, foreign speech is a sign of primitivism, intellectual or cultural inferiority, and irrationality (Munson 2005, 2; Long 1986, 130–31; E. Hall 1989, 3–5).

Athenian drama reinforced the Greek/barbarian antithesis and helped consolidate the meanings of both terms. In the plays of Aeschylus, Sophocles, and Euripides, the word "barbarian" means "non-Greek," "incomprehensible," and eventually "eccentric" or "inferior" (Kristeva 1991, 51). Nevertheless, the criterion of language also takes center stage in drama. Comedies, for instance, feature barbarians (foreigners) speaking Greek poorly for the production of comic effects. Moreover, the word "barbarian" is used in both comedies and tragedies to characterize sounds of animals, such as horses and, especially, birds (Munson 2005, 3).[13] The understanding of a barbarian (foreign) language as noise, nonsense, or poorly spoken Greek may also account for the association of intelligible (Greek) speech with reason and intelligence. The orator Isocrates, for example, argues that *logos* is what distinguishes Greeks from barbarians (E. Hall 1989, 199).

However, there are also ambivalent and critical responses to the stereotypes involved in the Greek/barbarian antithesis. The historian Herodotus (ca. 484–425 BCE) is an interesting case in this respect. His *Histories*, and particularly his ethnographic descriptions, deal extensively with language difference and translation. Although in his account of the Persian Wars Herodotus fully endorses the distinction between Greek and barbarian, in his ethnographic accounts, as he zooms in on "barbarian peoples," he offers nuanced analyses of barbarian languages and refrains from generalizations (Munson 2005, 23).

Due to his multilingual competency, Herodotus was in a privileged position from which he could challenge Greek linguistic ethnocentrism (67, 69). For instance, he observes that Egyptians, as Greeks do, call "barbarians" all those who speak another language as well as all "noise-makers," including the Greeks. Within the Greek space, the Spartans confuse *barbaros* (non-Greek) with *xenos* (non-Spartan stranger/guest) and thus include other Greeks under the term *barbaros*.[14] His writings therefore invalidate the supposed "linguistic handicap of non-Greeks" and show "that the barbarian/non-barbarian antithesis is relative" (66).

In the Hellenistic period—usually defined as the period between the death of Alexander the Great in 323 BCE and Rome's annexation of the heartlands of classical Greece in 146 BCE—a simplified version of the Attic dialect known as Alexandrian *Koine* (common) became the official written and spoken language in the eastern Mediterranean until the sixth century CE. This common language, meant to serve the communicational needs of linguistically heterogeneous populations, emerged as a result of the intense cultural exchanges that followed the establishment of Alexander's empire. This simplified version of Greek could be seen as a kind of creolization (or even "barbarization") of the Attic dialect of classical Greece. The spreading of this common language among diverse populations, as well as the processes of hybridization in this period, resulted in the weakening of the role of language in the differentiation between barbarian and Greek.

Even though in the Hellenistic and Roman eras language gradually moves to the background as a standard for defining the barbarian, it does not disappear. It returns in late Roman times, for example, in writers such as Porphyry of Tyre, a Neoplatonic philosopher of the late third century CE. In *On Abstinence*, Porphyry argues that animals also have language, even though we cannot speak or understand it (G. Clark 1999, 119). In order to build his argument about the language of animals, Porphyry refers to the experience of hearing an utterly foreign language that you cannot understand or even recognize as language while other people can:

Greeks do not understand Indian, nor do those brought up on Attic understand Scythian or Thracian or Syrian: the sound that each makes strikes the others like the calling of cranes. Yet for each their language can be written in letters and articulated, as ours can for us; but for us the language of Syrians, say, or Persians cannot be articulated or written, just as that of animals cannot be for any people. For we are aware only of noise and sound, because we do not understand (say) Scythian speech, and they seem to us to be making noises and articulating nothing. (quoted in G. Clark 1999, 119–20)

In Porphyry's views, the "problem" of the other's incomprehensibility is not located with the others (the barbarians) but with the self and its limitations. The suggestion is that everyone is a barbarian to other people. A similar relativization is articulated by Saint Paul in 1 Cor. 14:10–11: "There are, it may be, so many kinds of voices in the world, and none of them is without signification. Therefore, if I know not the meaning of the voice, I shall be unto him that speaketh a barbarian, and he that speaketh shall be a barbarian unto me" (*New Testament*, 1865).

In the same period that Porphyry writes, the word "barbarism" already had a linguistic meaning, signifying faults in pronunciation (G. Clark 1999, 120). The linguistic standard at the heart of the "barbarian" survives until modernity through this second meaning of barbarism. According to this meaning, barbarism denotes mistakes in speech or writing, inferior linguistic forms, or foreignisms and linguistic hybridizations. During the fourteenth and fifteenth centuries, there is an intensification of this linguistic usage of the term in western Europe. Classical languages (Latin in particular) were starkly opposed to the barbaric vernaculars, and foreign linguistic importations were perceived as a barbarization of the pure classical languages. Within Renaissance humanism, linguistic barbarism becomes a negative signifier in the context of a cultural and political program—fed by the nationalist aspirations of the Italian intelligentsia—that sought to defend the purity and superiority of Italian culture against foreign influences (Jones 1971, 403).

Culture

"Culture," as Williams claims, is "one of the two or three most complicated words in the English language" (1985, 87).[15] In a general sense, "culture" is used as a synonym of "civilization" to describe the accumulated habits, attitudes, beliefs, values, behavior, and way of life shared by the members of a society. Specifically, as Edward Said puts it, it involves practices "which have relative autonomy from the economic, social, and political realms, and which often exist in aesthetic forms, one of whose principal aims is pleasure" (1993, xii). In an even more specified sense, the term "culture" is, in Matthew Arnold's view, reserved for the refined and elevated elements in a society, a "reservoir of the best that has been known and thought" (1966, xiii). In the latter case, culture is identified with what we often call "high culture."

"Culture" is no less broad and inclusive than "civilization." Although the two terms partly overlap, they have an intricate relationship. In the nineteenth century, for instance, Mignolo writes, culture "created national unity: national languages, national literature, national flag and anthem, etc. were all singular manifestations of a 'national culture'" (2005, xvii). Thus, "European civilization was divided into national cultures." At the same time, the rest of the world's population was—and still often is— "conceived as having 'culture' but not civilization," because the latter required an advanced level of science and history (xvii). This meaning of civilization in relation to culture has been somewhat relativized since the second half of the nineteenth century when "civilization" started to find use in the plural as a (quasi-)neutral term (Williams 1985, 59). Nevertheless, civilization generally tends to carry universalist claims, while culture poses as more particularistic (Salter 2002, 13). Where civilization is used to express Western identity vis-à-vis the West's "outside," culture often denotes a sense of unity, a mode of living, or a level of achievement *within* a certain nation or group. Hence, certainly in the context of colonialism, civilization has an outward direction, whereas culture tends to emphasize the internal practices and values of a group.[16]

The conceptual complexity of culture makes it difficult to untangle its shifting interaction with barbarism. Historically, the interrelation of these notions takes different forms, which range from absolute opposition to intimate intertwinement or even identification. At certain moments in history culture is an exclusive site of the "we," but at other moments, culture becomes almost a bad word and something that belongs to the domain of the barbaric "they." The following six historical "episodes," in which the fate of "culture" and "barbarism" is adjoined, are juxtaposed to highlight the dynamic nature of their interrelation.

1. The opposition of culture to barbarism, whereby culture belongs to the "we" and barbarism is situated outside the domain of the "we," persists throughout Western history.[17] In Greece, cultural criteria for the opposition between Greeks and barbarians came to the fore in the fifth century BCE, during and after the Persian Wars. Although in the fifth century the opposition had primarily political dimensions—contrasting Athenian democracy and freedom of spirit to the despotism of the East— in the fourth and third centuries BCE, the Greek/barbarian antithesis was somewhat depoliticized (Hartog 2001, 96). Hellenicity was recast as

a cultural category and as a matter of education (*paideusis*) (97). As the Athenian orator Isocrates declared in 380 BCE,

So far has our city left other men behind with regard to wisdom and expression that its students have become the teachers of others. The result is that the name of the Hellenes no longer seems to indicate an ethnic affiliation (*genos*) but a disposition (*dianoia*). Indeed, those who are called "Hellenes" are those who share our culture (*paideusis*) rather than a common biological inheritance (*physis*). (quoted in J. Hall 2002, 209)

In the words of Isocrates, Hellenicity—a quintessentially Athenocentric cultural ideal—becomes a matter of enculturation rather than birth. The prominent role of education in the definition of Hellenicity suggests that barbarians could also eventually become "Hellenized" and enjoy the "fruits" of Athenian culture.[18]

In the Hellenistic era, the individual became the subject of geographically vast states and acquired a "cosmopolitan" consciousness. These (and other) new conditions shaped a completely different framework for self-definition: the city-state system was overshadowed by the "Makedonian dynasts," and many Greeks were transferred to "barbarian" territories (J. Hall 2002, 220). Alexander the Great's policy of fusion and integration of populations weakened the dichotomous character of the Greek/barbarian distinction. Culture as an educational ideal was still identified with Hellenicity and barbarism with its outside, but Hellenicity was a "common good" that either Greeks or barbarians could possess.

As Jonathan Hall argues, the cultural definition of Hellenic identity persisted during Roman rule (224). However, the Romans, who still saw Rome as the center of dissemination of political and cultural influence, partly opposed Alexander's policy of cultural syncretism (Hartog 2001, 152). In the early Roman period, the Greek/barbarian opposition was to some extent revised into a Roman/barbarian dichotomy, although Greek culture remained at the basis of Roman education. *Romanitas* could be acquired through education (Heather 1999, 241). Being barbarian was thus not an irreversible state but one that could be "remedied." This idea can be compared with the "civilizing mission" of European colonialism and the attempts by European missionaries to convert colonized peoples. However, unlike the organized character of the latter "mission," in the Roman Empire there was no systematic plan or intention to (collectively) educate the ignorant barbarians (Goffart 1981, 280). The educational process toward *Romanitas* took place more often on an individual than a collective level. It was primarily the responsibility of the barbarian rather than a mission for the Roman.[19]

2. *Culture* defined as "fine art" has been opposed to barbarism of an intra-European kind. In "Letters on the Aesthetic Education of Man" (1794), written at the dawn of German Romanticism, Friedrich Schiller ponders the paradoxical coexistence of rational Enlightenment and (ethical) barbarism.[20] If "our age is enlightened" and "the spirit of free inquiry has . . . undermined the foundations upon which fanaticism and deception had raised their throne," Schiller famously asks, "how is it, then, that we still remain barbarians?" (1995, 106). Subsequently, he wonders, "How under the influence of a barbarous constitution is character ever to become ennobled?" (108). Seeking an "instrument" for the ennoblement of character, Schiller turns to "fine art," which remains unaffected by the corruption of history and by a "degraded humanity" (108–9). Schiller proposes art as the means for an elevation from the barbarous (immoral) habits and qualities of humankind and from the barbarism of (European) Enlightenment and history. He adds, "Humanity has lost its dignity; but art has rescued it and preserved it in significant stone" (109).

While he puts art on a pedestal, Schiller simultaneously degrades (European) history and reason as the causes for an internal barbarism in European society. For Schiller, art has to be protected from "the corruption of the age," and the artist has to "leave the sphere of the actual to the intellect" (109). The "sphere of the actual," which seems to consist of history, rationality, and everyday reality, has led to a degraded human existence. Schiller views art as somewhat detached from its age. Art embodies an ideal of beauty through abstraction and not from human experience (115). Although art and barbarism are here strictly opposed, Schiller sees in art the antidote to barbarism—a kind of barbarism located within the civilized classes of Europe and the "'refined members of society' led by the aristocracy" (Früchtl 2008, 12). Thus, the correlation of culture with barbarism, which we later find in Walter Benjamin and other critical thinkers, finds one of its early expressions in Schiller (12).

3. Culture also crosses paths with barbarism in the relation between the German concepts *Kultur* and *Zivilisation*, as it took form from the

end of the eighteenth century through World War I. The splitting of the meaning of *Kultur* from *Zivilisation* in German can be traced back to Johann Gottfried von Herder in his unfinished *Ideas on the Philosophy of the History of Mankind* (1784–91). As Williams says, Herder argued that we should speak of "cultures" in the plural, to refer to the "specific and variable cultures of different nations and periods," but also, significantly, to the "specific and variable cultures of social and economic groups within a nation" (1985, 89). The latter sense was taken up by the Romantic movement as an alternative to the "orthodox and dominant '*civilization*'" (89). *Kultur* was used as a positive term for national or folk cultures but also, later, as a critique of the mechanical character and inhumanity of industrial development, which was identified with the concept of *Zivilisation*. The terms *Kultur* and *Zivilisation*, Williams notes, distinguished "human" from "material" development (89).

In this hierarchical distinction, *Kultur* is the positive term, whereas *Zivilisation* carries negative connotations. So much so that the latter is often identified with barbarism—a barbarism of an intra-European kind. As Europe found itself in a period of crisis and cultural pessimism at the fin de siècle—the end of the nineteenth and the beginning of the twentieth centuries—Europeans started questioning rationalism, positivism, and the Enlightenment ideal of progress. The negativity of *Zivilisation* reflected this critical attitude to progress and reason, which was thought to have introduced a new kind of barbarism.

The positive connotations of "culture," as opposed to the association of "civilization" with barbarism, are vividly laid out in Oswald Spengler's famous historical two-volume epic *The Decline of the West* (*Der Untergang des Abendlandes*, 1918–22). Spengler defines *Kultur* as the healthy and creative energy of a people and *Zivilisation* as the decadent spirit of decay (Salter 2002, 71). For Spengler, *Zivilisation* represents a culture's decline—the remains of a culture when its energy is depleted. The loss of creative energy in the West is linked with the prevalence of reason. Spengler—like Friedrich Nietzsche—uses barbarism not only as a negative signifier, referring to the declining Western civilization, but also as a positive notion. The barbarian is seen as a dynamic figure who could remedy civilization (71). The idea of a kind of barbarism that would revitalize Europe gained ground among many European thinkers at the fin de siècle. The cultural critic Matthew Arnold and the historian Jacob Burckhardt are two exponents of this line of thinking (Tziovas 1986, 170–71). Thus, the questioning of civilization through a positive notion of culture (*Kultur*) was also accompanied by attempts to positively redefine barbarism. In these recastings, barbarism is not the opposite of culture. Rather, it is invested with a creative force, just as culture is, according to Spengler.

4. The term *Kultur* in relation to barbarism is also famously used by Walter Benjamin in his dictum from "Theses on the Philosophy of History": "There is no document of civilization that is not at the same time a document of barbarism" (1999b, 248). Benjamin uses *Kultur* where the translator uses *civilization*. Thus, we are not dealing with the old distinction between *Kultur* and *Zivilisation*, since in this case *Kultur* becomes a negative signifier affiliated with barbarism. Benjamin's statement underscores the exploitation of anonymous masses and subjugated others in the name of *Kultur* (here, a synonym for *civilization*).

Along similar lines, Theodor W. Adorno and Max Horkheimer's *Dialectic of Enlightenment* (1947) established strong ties between (European) culture and barbarism. The writers explain in the preface that "what we had set out to do was nothing else than to explain why humanity, instead of entering a truly human state, is sinking into a new kind of barbarism" (1988, xiv). Regarding "barbarism," Adorno and Horkheimer had the totalitarian state in mind, in the form it took under German Nazism and the communism of the Soviet Union. The total annihilation of one's political enemy in these regimes signaled the complete collapse of reason and a regression to barbarism. For Adorno and Horkheimer, this barbarism is not an exception but an "immanent constituent" of Western history (Früchtl 2008, 10). Barbarism is the flipside of progress, Enlightenment, and European culture. We come across comparable views in Michel Foucault's *Discipline and Punish* (1975), Zygmunt Bauman's *Modernity and Ambivalence* (1991), and Giorgio Agamben's *Homo Sacer* (1998). In the writings of these thinkers, barbarism poses as a structural and inherent principle of culture, specifically of modern European culture as the legacy of Enlightenment.

5. Another attempt to counter the inherent barbarism of a culture based on reason came from a very different corner: the artistic movements of Dada and surrealism.[21] Both movements emerged as a response to what

was seen as a crisis in modernity. Dada was a revolt against the barbarism of World War I and of new technology. Surrealism was also a reaction to the barbarism to which progress had given birth. Surrealists and Dadaists took issue with nineteenth-century ideals and bourgeois values and became antipolitical and antinationalistic (Kreuter 2006, 41). Surrealism sought to liberate imagination and thereby achieve "a better grasp on the real," "uninhibited by social, ethical, cultural, and aesthetic restrictions" (Matthews 1991, 115–16). The Dadaists created a new kind of art marked by negativity: antiaesthetic, antirational, antibourgeois, provocative, shocking. But in both movements barbarism also received a positive valuation as a force that resists the rational and conventional structures of European culture. As Stephen Foster writes, Dadaists "turned the negative qualities of crudeness and barbarism into a virtue" (Foster and Kuenzli 1979, 143). Surrealists are regularly referred to as "barbarians hammering at the gates of culture" or as "barbarians storming the gates" of European culture (Vaneigem 1999, 20).

6. In the face of their complex opposition in history, as we move to a more contemporary context, we find the concepts of "culture" and "barbarism" engaged in a constellation that paradoxically makes them synonymous. "Culture is the new barbarism," writes Marxist critic Terry Eagleton in "Culture Conundrum" (*The Guardian*, May 21, 2008). This is how Eagleton develops this claim:

> These days the conflict between civilisation and barbarism has taken an ominous turn. We face a conflict between civilisation and culture, which used to be on the same side. Civilisation means rational reflection, material wellbeing, individual autonomy and ironic self-doubt; culture means a form of life that is customary, collective, passionate, spontaneous, unreflective and irrational. It is no surprise, then, to find that we have civilisation whereas they have culture. Culture is the new barbarism. The contrast between West and East is being mapped on a new axis.

For Eagleton, the separation of "civilization" from "culture" is the product of a contemporary Western discourse identifying civilization with Western liberal societies and culture with nonliberal, non-Western societies based on collective identifications. In this Western liberal discourse, the West appears as civilized because it promotes individualism, whereas nonliberal societies, "enslaved" to their respective cultures, are identified with barbarism. Eagleton elaborates this argument in *Reason, Faith, and Revolution*, where he explicitly recasts the clash between civilization and barbarism as a conflict between civilization and culture: today, civilization means "universality, autonomy, prosperity, plurality, individuality, rational speculation, and ironic self-doubt," whereas culture connotes "the collective, passionate, spontaneous, unreflective, unironic and a-rational" (2009, 155).

Slavoj Žižek and Wendy Brown make the same observation, but where Eagleton sees a split between civilization and culture, they detect two different types of relations *to* culture. According to Žižek, the liberal vision relies on an opposition between "those who are ruled by culture" and "those who merely 'enjoy' their culture" and have the freedom to choose it (2009, 120). This leads Žižek to the same conclusion as Eagleton: From a Western liberal perspective, "the ultimate source of barbarism is culture itself." Barbarism is defined as a complete identification with one's culture (120).

If culture is a source of barbarism, Žižek notes, the conclusion would be that the subject has to be extricated from culture. This is the universal liberal "Cartesian subject," able to step outside its cultural and social roots and assert its autonomy and universality (120–21). According to Brown, Western civilizational discourse presents nonliberal peoples as *owned* by culture and liberal people in the West simply as *having* culture(s). Thus, according to this discourse, "'We' have culture while culture has 'them,' or we *have* culture while they *are* a culture" (2006, 150–51). For the nonliberal subject, culture and religion are authoritative, whereas for the rational liberal subject, culture and religion form a kind of "background," something that can be "entered" or "exited" at will, and is thus considered extrinsic to the subject (153).

In contemporary liberal discourse, barbarism is associated with the condition of being governed by culture. Because Western liberal democracy considers itself "cultureless" or "culturally neutral," Brown argues, its principles are considered "*universalizable*," "above" culture, and thus supposedly applicable to all cultures (170). But the logic of Western liberalism, as Žižek argues, does not reflect a lack of culture; it represents modern Western culture—a culture that becomes intolerant when "individuals of other cultures are not given freedom of choice" (2009, 123).

Political System and Ideology

Systems of governance, regimes, and political ideologies have always drawn strict dividing lines between themselves and their political "other(s)." Designating the political other as barbaric, and thus as an evil enemy and not a worthy interlocutor, is often a means of safeguarding the sovereignty of a regime, whose legitimacy could be challenged if a true dialogue with the political other were to be sanctioned. In the twentieth century, for instance, the setting provided by the Cold War (1945–91) enabled the division of the world along political/ideological lines. In the capitalism/communism divide, both capitalism and communism were tagged as "barbaric," depending on the camp to which one belonged.[22]

The construction of one's political enemy as barbarian varies in degree according to the premises of a political system. Thus, one may argue that a democratic society, founded on the principle of dialogue and participation, is more willing to engage with its others without casting them as barbarians. This would not be the case in a totalitarian or fundamentalist regime, where the political other is a barbarian enemy to be eliminated. Chantal Mouffe sees conflict as a necessary dimension of democratic social life and proposes the notion of the "adversary" as a better alternative to the "enemy." By turning enemies into adversaries, we acknowledge the legitimacy of the other and his or her standpoint, despite our differences (Mouffe 2005, 15–16, 20). As a result, the "them" is not a barbarian but someone we can oppose in a "common symbolic space" defined by democratic procedures (20). However, Mouffe's "common symbolic space," in which conflicts between adversaries can be productive, is only imaginable within the structures of a democratic society. Exactly how democratic societies would engage with adversaries from societies that do not play the political game according to the same rules is a question that remains unanswered. Thus, to my initial proposition about democracies I would add that a democratic society is more willing to engage with its others without casting them as barbarians *as long as these others play by the rules of the liberal democratic system.* Therefore, the other of democracy—such as the subject of fundamentalist societies today—is often tagged as barbaric from a democratic viewpoint.

The identification of the nondemocratic other with barbarism can already be found in the distinction between Greek and barbarian. The Greek/barbarian opposition in the fifth century BCE reflected the opposed political ideals of Athenians and non-Greeks: the democratic ideal that produces free citizens versus the despotism of the barbarians (Persians) (E. Hall 1989, 13, 16, 154). In his recounting of the Persian Wars, Herodotus's distinction between Greeks and barbarians is political: it is the opposition between those who live free in the democratic *polis*, ruled by the law, and those who need masters to rule them (Hartog 2001, 84). These conflicting political ideals define the split between (Athenian) Greeks and barbarians, as well as between Europe and Asia (95).[23]

The (political) definition of Greeks and barbarians in classical Greece was Athenocentric (J. Hall 2002, 86). Democracy was considered an Athenian invention. Consequently, since the wars against the Persians were presented as an attempt to protect democracy against Asian despotism, the polarization of Greek and barbarian served the legitimation of the Athenian leadership among the Greek allied states. As Jonathan Hall argues, the image of the barbarian was constructed as the exact antipode not of Greeks in general but of the citizens who proclaimed themselves "to be the most free" of all, enjoying a democratic society par excellence: the Athenians (188–89). After the wars, the Athenians posed as the saviors and protectors of Greece (Hartog 2001, 84). The alliance that Athens formed following the retreat of the Persians (479 BCE)—the so-called Delian League—turned Athens into the major power among Greek city-states. Under Athenian leadership, this league was the basis for the economic prosperity and hegemony of Athens over the Aegean. The demonization of the barbarian (the Persian) legitimated demands from Athens for a regular toll from its allies (J. Hall 2002, 186–87).

By the mid-fifth century, the allied states could be characterized as an "Athenian Empire" (454–404 BCE). Therefore, the Greek/barbarian antinomy in classical Greece could to some extent be understood in an imperial context.[24] If we place classical Athens in a loosely defined imperial context, empire can be seen as a constant factor in the construction of the barbarian in Western history. Empire holds a key position in this typology of standards, as a political, ideological, and cultural apparatus that produces—and depends on—the discourse on barbarians and civilized.[25]

A clear-cut distinction between civilized and barbarians is essential for an empire to sustain its political, cultural, and military hegemony. As a result, Brown writes, the barbarian "has been continually established vis-à-vis empire and imperial definitions of civilization" (2006, 181–82).

The barbarian figured prominently in the context of the Roman, and later of the Spanish, British, French, and the other western European colonial empires. Modern European empires were not focused on warding off the barbarians from the gates of civilization but aimed at territorial expansion, economic exploitation, and the violent subjugation of the colonized peoples, often coated in the logic of the civilizing mission.[26] As Aimé Césaire argued, the colonizers' mission as "the world's civilizers" relies on turning the other into a barbarian (Césaire presented in Kelley 2000, 9). The idea of the "white man's burden" determined the image of the barbarian in the colonies: the colonized subjects were seen as ignorant, infantile, and waiting to receive the merits of civilization but also as a dangerous threat to civilization. As Shohat and Stam argue, colonialist discourse "oscillates between these two master tropes, alternately positing the colonized as blissfully ignorant, pure, and welcoming on the one hand, and on the other as uncontrollably wild, hysterical, and chaotic, requiring the disciplinary tutelage of the law" (1994, 143).

The supposed barbarian nature of the colonized justified deviations from European standards of civilization in the colonies. Interestingly, the same double standards in the treatment of barbarian enemies are found in Roman authors as well. The historian Ammianus Marcellinus, for example, records an incident in which the Romans violated a truce with a group of Saxons and brutally slaughtered them. Because the Saxons were not equal enemies but a "destructive band of brigands," their slaughter is fully justified from the Roman author's perspective (Heather 1999, 234). The construction of the barbarian as evil and dangerous becomes a ruse for imperial violence.

The gradual decolonization in the mid-twentieth century set off a wave of fierce criticism against European colonialism. The anticolonial movement, with thinkers such as Aimé Césaire (in his seminal polemic text *Discours sur le colonialisme*, written in 1950) and Frantz Fanon, turned the barbarian/civilized dichotomy on its head. By exposing the barbarism of imperial rule and of the European colonial project, they transferred the tag of the barbarian to the European colonizer.

Morality, Values, and Manners

Although morality, values, and manners could all be placed under a broad definition of "culture," it is worth probing the specific ways in which they have functioned as markers of civilized behavior—or barbarism.

In ancient Greek drama, barbarians are distinguished from Greek characters not only by language but by specific moral qualities, which deviated from "Hellenic virtue": Greek monogamy is contrasted with barbarian polygamy, promiscuity, and lax morals, and barbarians are often shown as "emotional, stupid, cruel, subservient, or cowardly" (E. Hall 1989, 17). Cruelty or savageness as a connotation of the term "barbarian" appears on few occasions in Euripides but does not become a standardized connotation until the Roman age and the "barbarian invasions" (Kristeva 1991, 51). It is, however, significant that in classical Greece the term is already an ethical category.[27]

However, barbarians are not always negatively portrayed in Greek drama. There is sometimes a reversal of roles, as in Euripides's *Trojan Women*, where Andromache attributes "barbarian deeds" to the Greeks (J. Hall 2002, 181). The moral distinction between Greek and barbarian is not absolute: Greeks are also capable of lapsing into barbaric behavior. In *Trojan Women*, for instance, although many Trojan characters embody typical barbarian features, it is also suggested that the real barbarism lies with the Greeks, who burn down Troy (Hartog 2001, 82).

Moral virtues are key in the definition of "Roman" in relation to "barbarian." One of the main defining qualities of the civilized Roman was rationality, which could be acquired through education (the study of classical literature produces virtue), ethical stance (control of passions), and living according to the rule of law (*civilitas*) (Heather 1999, 236). The image of the barbarian was constructed as the antipode of Roman virtue: barbarians were slaves to their passions and sexual desires, drank excessively, were unable to form consistent policies and obey written laws, and were not capable of true freedom (*libertas*) (237–38).

The Roman image of the barbarian, which stressed irrationality and lack of discipline, influenced the late medieval conception of the barbarian as well, as soon as the religious definition of the term began to wane (Jones 1971, 397). Even when applied to non-Christians, like the Ottomans after the fall of Constantinople, the term had both religious and moral connotations. It conveyed an image of the Ottoman as the "rapacious barbarian whose ferocity in battle and whose fanatic hatred for Christianity seemed to place Christian Europe in dire jeopardy" (393).

As a moral category, the "barbarian" was not always negatively tinted. In the fifteenth and sixteenth centuries, northern European humanist circles sought to reassess their barbarian Germanic origins (404). Since their ancestors—the destroyers of Rome—were indissolubly linked with the term "barbarian," northern European scholars were stuck with the term as descriptive of their own past. Thus, they tried to endow the barbarian status of their ancestors with connotations of moral principles, virtue, manliness, vigor, and simplicity. Teutonic scholars glorified the barbarian conqueror of the Roman Empire as the "upright, brave and hardy fellow, unencumbered by an articulate but possibly debilitating past" (406).

Although the moral connotations of the barbarian persist throughout Western history, in modernity the concept of civilization becomes particularly associated with a refinement of manners and with social etiquette, both in the English and French contexts (Williams 1985, 58). After the Middle Ages, particularly in the eighteenth and nineteenth centuries, civilization comes to signify an entire modern social process. In *The Civilizing Process* (*Über den Prozess der Zivilisation*, 1939), Norbert Elias traces the "civilizing" of manners and personality in western Europe from the late Middle Ages as a process whereby the standard of human behavior gradually changes "in the direction of a gradual 'civilization'" (2000, x). Elias examines how post-medieval European standards regarding violence, sexual behavior, bodily functions, hygiene, table manners, and modes of speaking were subjected to increasingly strict thresholds of inhibition and shame and became part of a system of social demands and prohibitions (x). The new standards that came to signify "civilized behavior" also determined a "threshold of repugnance," which functions as the line between civilized and barbaric behavior.[28]

In modernity, the negative valuation of the barbarian as a moral category, as opposed to the well-mannered, virtuous, and morally superior civilized subject, has also been subjected to critique and reversal. In the writings of Friedrich Nietzsche we encounter a mobilization of the barbarian as a dynamic figure, capable of revitalizing the decaying European civilization. The figure of the "new barbarian" can be situated within Nietzsche's radical questioning of the foundations of reason, logic, and language in European Enlightenment thought. According to Nietzsche, the Enlightenment belief system is not based on any truth or fact but manages to invent the moral or intellectual foundations it needs and cast them as truth. Nietzsche debunks the Enlightenment ideals of progress and reason and sees European civilization as corrupt and declining. In his writings, the barbarian poses as the solution to this decadence (Salter 2002, 68).

Nietzsche's barbarians are individuals with the energy and will to regenerate European culture by disregarding moral inhibitions. In *The Will to Power* (*Der Wille zur Macht*, 1901), Nietzsche envisions the barbarians of the twentieth century as "elements capable of the greatest severity towards themselves, and able to guarantee the most enduring will" (1968, 464). He describes the barbarian as belonging to "a species of conquering and ruling natures," who obeys his natural instincts and gives vital energy back to European society (479). In some of his writings, Nietzsche's barbarian is equated with his *Übermensch*: an individual who overcomes moral inhibitions in order to impose his will to power, "re-investing barbaric characteristics with moral value" (Salter 2002, 69). Nevertheless, as Salter argues, despite the radical change in European civilization Nietzsche saw as necessary, in his thought Europe is still "the center for the dissemination of these (new) values and power" (70).

Although in the course of the twentieth century social decorum and manners became less rigid as civilizational standards in Western societies, the association of civilization and barbarism with moral values and modes of behavior holds strong today. As shown previously, contemporary civilizational discourse tends to project liberal values (such as individualism, compassion, or tolerance) as markers of civilization, while their opposites are ascribed to the (fundamentalist) barbaric other. In the West today, "tolerance" emerges as a cardinal civilizational value. Jay Newman, a philosopher of tolerance, writes on the subject: "Intolerance is the most persistent and the most insidious of all sources of hatred. It is perhaps foremost among the obstacles to civilization, the instruments of barbarism" (1982, 3). According to Newman, intolerance can be remedied through education, which he views in terms of a civilizing process (discussed in Brown 2006, 183). In her critical analysis of the contemporary discourse on tolerance, Brown explains how this discourse constructs the non-Western other as incapable of tolerance and thus as barbaric. The fanatic, the fundamentalist, and the barbarian are often seen as premodern figures whose sensibility must be rectified by modern tolerant societies (183–84).

Humanity, Humanism, and the Human

The concepts of "humanity," "humanism," and the "human" have functioned not only as criteria for defining the barbaric but also as the opposites of the barbarian and barbarism, just as "civilization" has. But unlike civilization, which finds in the barbarian its perfect antithesis, the notion of the human has found its opposites in several categories, such as the "monster," "God" or "the divine," the "mechanical" or the "technological," and the "animal."[29] "Humanity" can be a synonym for the "human race," but it can also refer to human nature and, by extension, to virtues or states of being that typify this nature. As Martin Heidegger observes in his "Letter on Humanism" (1947), the opposite of humanity or the human takes shape based on the different views on what constitutes "humanity" as "the essence of man" (1998, 244). Thus, while Marx finds "man's humanity" in the notion of society, Christianity views humanity in contradistinction to *Deitas* (244).[30]

In the Roman republic, *homo humanus* was opposed to *homo barbarus*. *Homo humanus*, according to Heidegger, "means the Romans, who exalted and honored Roman *virtus* through the 'embodiment' of the *paideia* [education] taken over from the Greeks" (244). Thus, *humanitas* in this context denotes a specific kind of education leading to virtue, while "barbarian" refers to someone excluded from this educational process. *Homo humanus* is here another term for *homo romanus*, and *humanitas* another term for *Romanitas*. This notion of *humanitas* as *Romanitas* in opposition to the *homo barbarus* is found in the fourteenth- and fifteenth-century Italian Renaissance (244). However, the makeup of what is considered barbarian changes in this new context: it represents the "supposed barbarism of gothic Scholasticism in the Middle Ages," which is contrasted to the *humanitas* of the Greek civilization, as interpreted and filtered through Roman (and Renaissance) humanism (244).

In certain contexts, the barbarian is altogether excluded from the realm of humanity, here defined as "the human race." In the context of European colonialism, the distinction between the civilized and barbarian is often reformulated as a distinction between human and animal. The so-called Age of Discovery, when Spain and Portugal began colonizing new lands in the late fifteenth century, occasions unique encounters between European civilization and the civilizations of these lands. These encounters generated systematic classifications as well as debates in Europe about the status of these "others."[31] Not only were the others of the colonies considered lesser, inferior human beings but they were sometimes also denied human status and treated as beasts. Africans and Asians were put on display all around Europe in anthropological-zoological exhibits or "freak shows" (Shohat and Stam 1994, 108). Academic and popular debates were held regarding the humanity of nonwhite races (Mills 1997, 20). European humanism, as Charles W. Mills puts it, "usually meant that only Europeans were human" (27).

Tzvetan Todorov has recently proposed a definition of the barbarian as someone who does not acknowledge the humanity of others (2010, 16). Although by "humanity" Todorov means "human nature," his definition has an ethical undertone: acknowledging the humanity of others, and thus respecting them and refraining from violence against them, is what distinguishes the civilized from the barbarian. In Todorov's definition, humanity is intertwined with civilization by posing as its distinctive feature and the only valid criterion for recognizing barbaric behavior.

Religion

With the advent of Christianity in the Roman Empire, religion becomes a defining factor in the construction of the barbarian. As the first Christian emperor, Constantine, assumes power, Christianity rises as a powerful force and leads to a rethinking of the categories of self-definition (Miles 1999, 10). Late-antiquity definitions of "Roman," "Greek," "barbarian," "Christian," and "pagan" are, as Richard Miles notes, complex, unstable, and "deeply problematic," because each of these terms accommodated several distinct and mutually opposed significations (10).

In late antiquity, the two religious and philosophical codes of Christianity and Hellenism were in tension in their fight for domination. For Christians, Greek or Greek-educated people signified the barbarian other who does not accept the true faith. But for those who identified themselves as culturally Greek (including Romans), it was the Christians, regardless of origin or education, who were seen as barbarian, because they "had rejected Hellenism for barbarian scriptures" (G. Clark 1999, 122). Porphyry of Tyre, for example, a great polemic of Christianity, is reported to have said the following about a Greek-educated man who "went" barbarian: "Origen, a Greek educated in Greek literature, made straight for barbarism, putting himself and his literary training on the market; he lived like a Christian, lawlessly, but thought like a Greek about the divine and about things in general, insinuating Greek ideas into foreign fables."[32] This statement not only demonstrates the identification of Christianity with barbarism by Greek-educated philosophers but also signals the confusion and crisis around identity in late antiquity. The subject of the statement, Origen, seems to be torn between Greek and Christian affiliations, which were both perceived as the domain of either the self or barbarism, depending on perspective.

As a result of the so-called barbarian invasions and the disintegration of the Roman Empire in the West, the distinction between *Romanitas* and barbarism was recast primarily on the basis of religion. By the end of the seventh century, the barbarian in western Europe was usually the pagan or (Arian) heretic rather than the (Catholic) Christian (Heather 1999, 245). During the Middle Ages, the term "barbarian" generally captured the other of Christendom. However, according to W. R. Jones, for a long time in medieval Europe the term "barbarian" had not been applied to Muslim enemies because the primary stereotype of the medieval barbarian was the pagan. Muslim warriors were often depicted as the "chivalric counterparts of Christian knights"—not as barbarian savages. Even during the Crusades, the term was applied to Muslims only on a few occasions, where it served as a generic synonym for the non-Christian (Jones 1971, 392–93). Only after the fifteenth century and the Ottoman conquest of Constantinople did the word start to be used for the Muslim "antagonists of Christian Europe" (393). However, it is worth noting that from the per-spective of the Orthodox Christian writers of Constantinople, the desig-nation "barbarian" was systematically used for the late Roman emperors. Throughout the Middle Ages, these Byzantine writers viewed the West as "barbarian," lost to "barbarian rulers."[33]

From the fifteenth and sixteenth centuries, with the gradual secular-ization of western European life, the "other" of Europe ceased to be pre-dominantly defined on the basis of religion (Salter 2002, 19). Europeans acquired confidence in the ability of human beings to determine "truth" for themselves and consequently stopped thinking about their lives as ruled only by the divine. At the same time, the encounter of Europeans with the native inhabitants of the "New World" brought racial standards for defining the barbarian more to the foreground.

Nevertheless, religion continued to occupy an important place in the ideological apparatus of early European colonialism, especially in the colonization of the Americas. The material exploitation of the con-quered people in the Americas was often legitimized on religious grounds. Converting the natives to Christianity would lead to their salvation. But whether or not the natives of the Americas could, in fact, be converted was an object of heated debate in Europe. Many Spaniards contended that the natives of the "New World" were incapable of receiving faith. This rea-soning enabled the colonizers' lack of constraint in the violent treatment of the natives.[34] While conversion of the infidels to Christianity served as justification for the conquest of their land, the natives' rejection of the Christian message was proof of "bestial irrationality" and barbarism and thus legitimized violent intervention (Mills 1997, 22).

At the time of the conquest of the Americas, Christian Europe also had its internal barbarian others. The Jews were among the most common victims of religious demonization and stereotyping. When the colonization of the "New World" started, the religious othering already taking place on European ground was extrapolated to the indigenous "infidels" of America (Shohat and Stam 1994, 60). Thus, a discourse of intra-European religious discrimination against Jews was transfigured into colonial racism (60).

With the secularization of Europe, especially during the Enlight-enment, religion receded as a civilizational standard, yielding to race in the divide between Europeans and barbarians (Mills 1997, 23). However, today religion has made a comeback in the rhetoric of civilization versus barbarism. Since the 1990s religion has grown to be one of the key components in the way global divisions and conflicts are perceived. In Western political rhetoric, the "new barbarian" is often associated with the religion of Islam, which is seen as feeding violence and barbarism. Moreover, the religious vocabulary of "good versus evil" was amply employed in Western political rhetoric after September 11, 2001, in order to provide legitimation for military action against the "forces of evil" embodied by terrorists and those who support them.

Ethnicity and Race

"Race" is a category into which one is supposed to be born, whereas "ethnicity" is usually seen as an active affiliation resulting from social and cultural identification with a specific group.[35] But the two categories are interrelated. In the nineteenth century, for example, ethnic distinctions became part of a racial discourse, which viewed them in terms of biological difference (Williams 1985, 214). In modern history, ethnic distinctions are often made through the category of the "nation." The two words are in fact synonyms: nation translates the Greek ethnos. But if ethnicity is usually understood as a "quasi-primordial collective sense of shared descent and distinct cultural traditions," nation—at least by the end of the eighteenth century—acquires a definition that is political at its basis: "a union of individuals governed by one law, and represented by the same law-making assembly."[36]

Ethnicity provides a rather constant basis for the distinction between "us" and "them" in Western history, although it is not privileged equally in every context. In ancient Greece, the Persian Wars played a decisive role in shaping the ethnocentric discourse on Greeks and barbarians by identifying the barbarian with the Persian, located in a specific territory—Asia (Hartog 2001, 81, 84). Confronted with the Persian threat, the Greeks emphasized unifying factors that would set aside the differences among Greek city-states. By constructing the barbarian as the non-Greek, the heterogeneity of the Greeks themselves could appear more uniform (J. Hall 1995, 92–93). However, as Jonathan Hall notes, the notion of

"Panhellenism" (the ideal of the Greeks as a unified *ethnos*) and, accordingly, the perception of all foreign peoples as a collective group, was specific to Athenian rhetoric (2002, 205, 208).

In ancient Greece, race (i.e., "common blood") was not a stable criterion in the ethnic determination of "Greekness," because Greeks had varied ethnic composition and, according to some ancient historians, "barbarian" origins (Munson 2005, 15). However, in works by some fifth-century authors the distinction between Greeks and barbarians becomes essentialized and acquires racial (and, from a contemporary perspective, racist) connotations. In Euripides's *Iphigenia at Aulis*, Iphigenia tells her mother that "it is right that Hellenes should rule over barbarians and not barbarians over Hellenes, for they are slaves while we are free" (quoted in J. Hall 2002, 180, ll. 1400–1402). As Benjamin Isaac argues, Iphigenia's assertion here of the natural superiority of Greeks over barbarians serves imperialist ideology, which finds justification in the notion of natural slavery (2006, 278). In *Politics*, Aristotle also propagates the distinction between *natural* slaves (the barbarians) and *naturally* free men (Long 1986, 150).

Nevertheless, the "natural" (racial or ethnic) basis of Hellenic identity was also contested.[37] In *Statesman*, Plato underscores the arbitrariness of the division between Greeks and barbarians:[38]

Just as if some one who wanted to divide the human race, were to divide them after the fashion which prevails in this part of the world; here they cut off the Hellenes as one species, and all the other species of mankind, which are innumerable, and have no ties or common language, they include under the single name of "barbarians," and because they have one name they are supposed to be of one species also. Or suppose that in dividing numbers you were to cut off ten thousand from all the rest, and make of them one species, comprehending the rest under another separate name, you might say that here too was a single class, because you had given it a single name. Whereas you would make a much better and more equal and artistic classification of numbers, if you divided them into odd and even; or of the human species, if you divided them into male and female; and only separated off Lydians or Phrygians, or any other tribe, and arrayed them against the rest of the world, when you could no longer make a division into parts which were also classes. (2009, 262a–263a)

In this passage, the generic categorization "barbarians" does not correspond to a natural division of the world but appears arbitrary and even counterintuitive. In fact, the passage suggests that all ethnic divisions are artificially construed and are thus philosophically unsound.[39]

In late antiquity and particularly in the Hellenistic period, ethnicity plays a very limited role in the definition of the barbarian, overshadowed by the cosmopolitan ideals of the period. In Roman times, as Heather argues, there was no "overriding ethnic content" to *Romanitas*, since in principle every individual could be educated into becoming "Roman" (1999, 241). Nevertheless, the term "barbarian" still applied collectively to non-Roman nations (*barbarae nationes*) and in that sense was also an ethnic category. According to Liddell and Scott's *Lexicon*, at the beginning of the Roman Empire "barbarian" was used for all non-Roman nations who had not received Greco-Roman education. But as the Roman Empire annexed more people and lands, the term was limited to the Teutonic nations. Walter Goffart argues that "barbarian" as a collective term for these people expresses a Greco-Roman point of view, premised on a flawed perception of the Teutonic nations as homogeneous (1981, 277–78). In fact, these people were "diverse and disunited," with no "collective mind or collective aspirations" (285).

The conferral of a unified Germanic identity to the barbarians of Rome by modern historians can be related to the desire of modern Germans to construct a coherent national account of their past (279). Notably, northern European humanist scholars in the fifteenth and sixteenth centuries embraced the term "barbarian" for their Germanic ancestors and thus also for their own national determination (Jones 1971, 404). A surprising contribution to the German national self-determination—performed not against but through the use of the term "barbarian"—comes from the historians of Constantinople. Whereas historians in the Byzantine Empire portrayed past Roman emperors in a negative light, they praised the barbarians (the Germanic nations) and their heroic leaders (Goffart 1981, 303). Authors in Constantinople even tried to construct a coherent ethnic context and history for the Germanic barbarians—a construction that would provide a foundation for the idea of a unified Germanic identity (303–4).

The rise of nation-states in modern history made "nation" an important factor in the self-determination of Europeans. Nevertheless, the barbarian/civilized distinction in modern Europe, especially in the context of colonialism, is particularly marked by the establishment of *race* as a civilizational standard. The belief of Europeans in their racial superiority vis-à-vis Native Americans and Africans provided a legitimation for the enslavement and exploitation of those natives. At the same time such practices would be condemned within Europe, especially if directed toward Europeans. Nevertheless, the term "barbarian," along with other derogatory terms, also came to be applied to Europe's internal others. There were "*intra*-European varieties of racism" directed against marginalized European nations or ethnic groups—"white people with a question-mark"—such as the Irish, Slavs, Mediterranean peoples, Romany, and the Jews (Mills 1997, 78–79).

In the nineteenth century, *biological* racism was established and sanctioned by (pseudo)scientific discourses. It was accompanied by an obsession for classifications, taxonomies, and a general codification of difference. Socioeconomic distinctions among ethnicities, classes, and sexes were recast in biological terms. Nineteenth-century "pure blood" theories foreclosed the possibility of conversion of the other and led to colonial exterminations. Within Europe, these racial theories fed the ideology that led to the Jewish genocide by the German Nazis (Shohat and Stam 1994, 91). Fascism, especially the form it took in Hitler's Germany, was motivated by the utopian dream of a return to a "mythical past of national-racial purity" (Neilson 1999, 89). The other of the superior race was constructed as barbarian and inhuman, but also as a virus or parasite, threatening to contaminate the "pure race."

Class

In modern European history, the distinction between civilization and barbarism was also mobilized in class distinctions within European nations. During the Industrial Revolution of the eighteenth and nineteenth centuries, the term "barbarian" was applied to "an underclass of disenfranchised, newly urbanized European peasants"—an application that expressed the fears of the middle and upper classes (Salter 2002, 26). The increasing gap between classes in Europe led to a conception of civilization as "the achievement of aristocratic races" (Tziovas 1986, 179). In this context, the discourses of class and race become intertwined. In the nineteenth century, the barbarism and moral degradation of "the British urban poor," as Ann Stoler argues, was expressed through the use of racial metaphors, drawn from the "savage tribes" of the colonies (1995, 125). The interpenetration of race and class discourses is eloquently described by British historian Victor Kiernan:

In innumerable ways his [the European gentleman's] attitude to his own "lower orders" was identical with that of Europe to the "lesser breeds." Discontented native in the colonies, labour agitator in the mills, were the same serpent in alternate disguise. Much of the talk about the *barbarism* or darkness of the outer world, which it was Europe's mission to rout, was a transmuted fear of the masses at home. (quoted in Stoler 1995, 125–26, emphasis added)

The poor classes at home and the primitive barbarians of the colonies were drawn together as the "dangerous classes" that threatened British bourgeois mores (126).[40]

The strict class structure of Europe and the inequalities it produced were also mobilized for pinpointing barbarism within European civilization. For many Enlightenment thinkers, the injustice of class distinctions was one of the main reasons why European societies were more barbaric than tribal societies. Michel de Montaigne in his 1580 essay "On Cannibals" (Des cannibales) condemns the barbarism of class in Europe by contrasting it with a Native American perspective:

They [the Tupinamba] said . . . that they had noticed among us some men gorged to the full with things of every sort while their other halves were beggars at their doors, emaciated with hunger and poverty. They found it strange that these poverty-stricken halves should suffer such injustice, and that they did not take the others by the throat or set fire to their houses. (1958, 119)

Montaigne's reconstruction of this Native American outlook on European class inequality illustrates how irrational and arbitrary the European class system appears from an external viewpoint and enhances his critique of European civilization.

Karl Marx confers the tag of barbarism on the capitalist system of production. In "Estranged Labor" (1844), he lays out how capitalism alienates and enslaves workers to their objects of production. He sees a necessary connection between civilization and barbarism in the relation between the worker and the product of labor in capitalism: the more "civilization" society produces, the more barbarous it becomes for the ones who produce, because workers become entirely alienated from the product and process of production, as well as from their own life activity (Marx 1988, 76). Under capitalism, the life activity of the worker—what Marx calls "species-life" and what distinguishes humans from other animals—becomes just a means for the worker's physical existence. "The more the worker produces," Marx writes, "the less he has to consume; . . . the more civilized his object, the more barbarous the worker; the more powerful the work, the more powerless the worker." Although machines often replace human labor, some of the workers are cast "back into barbarous forms of labor" or turned into machines themselves (72). The barbarism of the capitalist system ironically turns the worker into less-than-human—a machine.

Although class is not one of the most prevalent standards defining barbarism and civilization, it is often a silent factor in civilizational discourse. Thus, class is implicitly involved in one of the definitions of the "barbarian." According to the *Oxford English Dictionary* (2nd ed.), the barbarian is "an uncultured person, or one who has no sympathy for literary culture." This definition encompasses two civilizational standards. The explicit standard here is culture, specifically an elevated form of culture and love for the belles lettres. The underlying standard is class, as Brown also notes, because in this definition civilization is associated with high European culture (2006, 252). This high culture is the privilege of a social and cultural elite—an elite that finds its members among the bourgeois and the upper European classes.

Gender

The figure of the barbarian has often been cast in gendered and sexualized terms. In Western imagination, barbarians are usually invested with features of masculinity and virility, which enhance their supposed unrestrained nature and threat to civilization. The blueprint for this image of the barbarian can be traced back to representations of the Germanic warrior-nations that invaded Rome. Edward Gibbon's *The History of the Decline and Fall of the Roman Empire*, written in the late eighteenth century, is a classic source of masculine barbarian imagery, feeding the

European imagination with images of barbarian hordes at the gates of Rome.

Such imagery has sparked a wide range of fictionalizations of the barbarian warrior. "Conan the barbarian" is probably the most famous barbarian in popular fiction. Conan was created by Robert E. Howard in 1932 for a series of fantasy stories. Conan's long-standing popularity has made him a protagonist in movies such as *Conan the Barbarian* (1982) and *Conan the Destroyer* (1984), as well as in television series, comic books, fantasy fiction, video games, and role-playing games. Conan, John J. Miller writes, is "an icon of thick-muscled, sword-wielding manhood." Although his adventures are usually set in a mythical age, he is often depicted as looking Germanic—an allusion to the Germanic "barbarians" of the late Roman period. Conan "is no knight in shining armor who piously obeys a code of chivalry" (Miller 2006). As Howard writes in one of his Conan tales, "The warm intimacies of small, kindly things, the sentiments and delicious trivialities that make up so much of civilized men's lives were meaningless to him."[41] In Conan's words, "I live, I burn with life, I love, I slay, and am content."[42]

Despite the heavy dose of masculinity with which the barbarian figure has been injected, women have also claimed this trope. If male barbarians tend to be depicted as hypermasculine, female barbarians are shown as "hyper-feminine" and "over-sexualized" (Salter 2002, 55). Nevertheless, female barbarians also assume male features or roles. In ancient Greek tragedy, the opposition between Greek and barbarian is often presented as analogous to that between man and woman.[43] In some cases, transgressive female characters in Greek tragedy either are actual barbarians (non-Greek) or their transgression is considered an endorsement of barbarian customs (E. Hall 1989, 202). The figure of Clytaemnestra in Aeschylus's *Oresteia* belongs to the latter category. The woman who murdered her husband, King Agamemnon, as an act of revenge for the sacrifice of their daughter, Iphigenia, is one of the most dominant women in tragedy (204). Clytaemnestra is often referred to as a "manly woman" (205). Her masculinity is also pronounced through the attitude of her weak-willed husband, who, in succumbing to her lavish demands and wishes, is considered to be disavowing Greek values and resorting to barbarian decadence. As Edith Hall argues, this perversion of the natural order regarding man-woman roles, with the woman taking the upper hand, is considered typical only of the barbarian (Persian) world (205). This is also made clear in Agamemnon's words as he tries to resist the decadence to which Clytaemnestra draws him: "Do not pamper me like a woman nor grovel before me like some barbarian with wide-mouthed acclaim" (quoted in E. Hall 1989, 206, ll. 918–22). Femininity, luxury, excess, hubris, and barbarism are all parts of a "semantic complex" signifying "all that Greek manhood should shun" (206).

Associations between barbarians and femininity also pervade Orientalist discourses. European descriptions of Asian women in the colonies contributed to the construction of a female barbarian figure, typified by lax morals, sexual promiscuity, deceptive seductiveness, the threat of racial contamination, and so on.[44] But the ways gender and sexuality are mobilized in the construction of the barbarian in the colonial context are far from stable. For example, whereas African barbarians were often depicted as masculine, Asian barbarians tended to be portrayed in feminine terms (Salter 2002, 55). Moreover, feminine features were attributed both to women in the colonies and to the Orient itself. As Anne McClintock argues, France and Britain posed as masculine nations, while the colonies were effeminized (1995, 54–55). The Orient was constructed as a female space, whereas Europe—the domain of civilization—was cast in masculine terms. In a representational system that, according to Said, finds its beginnings in classical Greece, the Orient appears as defeated, excessive, irrational, dangerous, mysterious, queer, and weak, while Europe is powerful, articulate, mature, rational, and "capable of holding real values" (2003, 40, 45, 49, 57, 103). European civilization is endowed with a stereotypically male sexuality. Its superiority gives civilization the right to penetrate, decipher, and give meaning to the female Asian mystery.[45] Thus, the gendering of the barbarian ran parallel to the gendering of the Orient itself vis-à-vis Europe.

A noteworthy reversal of the correlation between civilization and male dominance takes place in the rhetoric of nineteenth-century American feminists. Their feminist discourse drew from the discourse on barbarism and civilization in an attempt to reshape traditional valuations of Western patriarchal societies. Nineteenth-century activists for women's rights turned to Native American societies, which they viewed as *gynocratic*, because they were marked by equal gender relations and a social system more just to women (Grinde and Johansen 1991, 226–27). In the eyes of these feminists, Native American societies—traditionally viewed as barbarian from a European perspective—were exemplars of civilization. As Elizabeth Cady Stanton said in an address to the National Council of Women in 1891, "Our barbarian ancestors seem to have had a higher degree of justice to women than American men in the 19th century" (quoted in Grinde and Johansen 1991, 227).

In this reversal of the barbarism/civilization opposition, women appear closer to civilization than men, because male-dominated societies are immersed in barbarism and savagery. Feminists like Matilda Joslyn Gage and Elizabeth Cady Stanton turned away from "civilized" European history and found inspiration in "barbarian" (native) societies. In their rhetoric, gender equality and equal participation in politics and decision making are presented as the ticket for the passage from savagery and barbarism to true civilization (233). Although these feminists deployed the barbarism/civilization discourse in order to challenge male dominance, one must also consider that the patriarchal structures they were trying to overthrow were deeply inscribed in the same discourse.

Progress

The concept of "progress" generally refers to the idea that humanity can gradually become better in various domains such as technology, science, standard of living, modernization, and freedom. In particular, the belief in progress as the cornerstone of European civilization can be attributed to Enlightenment philosophy.

Progressive or evolutionary models often placed barbarism or the barbarian on a scale of development: barbarism was an earlier stage in a course that usually ended with European civilization as the apogee of human progress.[46] Thus, under "progress" I lay out various (pseudo)scientific, philosophical, or social models, in which barbarism or the barbarian represents a stage in a process toward a higher civilized state. The criteria on which such models are premised range from technique, modes of production, and economic system, to hygiene, lifestyle, geography, race, and biology.

Although progress is a modern concept, several premodern theories have mobilized the barbarian in accounts of societal development. The Greek historian Thucydides (460–395 BCE), for example, traces the origins of the Greeks of his time through barbarian groups. His view is suggestive of an evolutionary model, according to which barbarians belong to another temporality and thus represent a more primitive stage of human development. Another Greek historian, Hecataeus of Miletus (550–476 BCE), reports that Greece had been inhabited by barbarians in the past. The views of both historians hold a double implication. First, since Greeks emerged from barbarian nations, Hellenicity was not dependent on blood. Second, barbarism and Hellenicity were conceived in terms of a temporal succession: first there were barbarians, who then progressed to Hellenicity. Of course, Thucydides also observes that there is "a current Barbarian world." Thus, there are barbarians who evolved into Greeks, and barbarians who remained barbarians.[47]

Other theories consider the evolvement toward civilization as premised on *manners* and *social behavior*. The twelfth-century Anglo-Welsh author Gerald of Wales, for instance, uses the term "barbarians" for the Irish, because he perceives their society as less advanced. What he deems barbaric are their uncultivated manners and attitude, their ignorance, pastoralism, isolation from advanced nations, and marginalized way of life (Jones 1971, 396).

While earlier thinkers also placed the barbarian in a temporal frame of development, the systematization of the idea that humanity progresses from barbarism to civilization, as articulated in social, political, or (pseudo)scientific theories, is specific to modernity. Developments in *technique* and *means of production* often pose as standards for determining a society's level of civilization. For instance, in a model developed by French and Scottish philosophers in the mid-nineteenth century, societal development advances in four stages: savage societies (consisting of hunter-gatherers), barbarian societies (consisting mainly of shepherds), agricultural societies, and societies based on the institution of a commercial, capitalist market (European society) (Meek 1976, 14–23; Salter 2002, 16). In the eighteenth century, Johann Gottfried von Herder viewed the stages through which societies acquire culture as the domestication of animals, agriculture, commerce, and the development of science or art (Todorov 2010, 34).[48]

Another model comes from Rousseau's "Essay on the Origin of Languages" (1852), in which barbarism is placed between a savage and a civilized society based on *alphabet* and *writing*. Rousseau writes: "These three ways of writing correspond almost exactly to three different stages according to which one can consider men gathered into a nation. The depicting of objects is appropriate to a savage people; signs of words and of propositions, to a barbaric people, and the alphabet to civilized peoples" (1966, 17).

Hegel's *Philosophy of History* (1837), based on a series of lectures that influenced nineteenth-century European perception of the non-European world, suggests a model in which spatial difference is combined with temporal distance. "The History of the World," Hegel writes, "travels from East to West, for Europe is absolutely the End of History, Asia the beginning" (2004, 103). In his scheme of historical progress, a spatial divide (East-West) turns into a model of temporal development: the East is the beginning and childhood of History; the West is its mature age and its end. Africa is missing from this model, since for Hegel Africa has no history. Similarly, in the context of European colonialism, indigenous peoples in the conquered lands were perceived as living "allochronically" in earlier stages of human life (childhood) or history (primitivism), far behind European modernity and progress.[49]

In the face of evolutionary or progressive models, in history we also encounter several reversals of the barbarian/civilized opposition, whereby more primitive or "natural" ways of life are valued more than civilization. After the "discovery" of the "New World" in 1492 and up to the nineteenth century, many European philosophers, travelers, and writers idealized Native American societies. Native Americans were often depicted as dangerous barbarians but also as "noble savages": close to nature, free, maintaining values such as liberty, happiness, government by consensus, and equality of property (Grinde and Johansen 1991, 2–3). Beginning in the sixteenth century, accounts of societies without class structure and poverty, wherein people lived without jails, judges, or kings, led to a boom of utopian literature in Europe, which lasted until the end of the nineteenth century. In these European narratives, utopian primitive societies functioned as a vehicle for social criticism of a supposedly civilized Europe, aimed both at European colonialism and intra-European social problems (40–41).

One of the most famous reversals of the barbarian/civilized hierarchy is performed in the essay "On Cannibals" by sixteenth-century author Michel de Montaigne, who is said to have introduced the notion of the "noble savage" to the European world of letters. Montaigne portrayed American natives as free, natural, uncorrupted, and more civilized than Europeans. For Montaigne, European practices were more barbarous and unnatural than those of Native Americans. He even showed sympathy for the natives' anthropophagy: he finds their habit of eating people after they have killed them less barbarous than the practice of Europeans to "eat a man alive" and to do that "under the cloak of piety and religion" (1958, 113).

Montaigne goes so far as to question the essentialist use of the term "barbarian": "I do not believe, from what I have been told about these people, that there is anything barbarous or savage about them, except that we all call barbarous anything that is contrary to our own habits" (108–9). Thus, barbarism is not an inherent quality of certain peoples but a name for the uncommon or the unfamiliar. In this sense, Montaigne can be considered an early proponent of cultural relativism. Despite his idealization of the natives of America and his critical outlook on European societies, Montaigne still placed these natives in an earlier stage in progress: "These nations, then, seem to me barbarous in the sense that they have received very little moulding from the human intelligence, and are still very close to their original simplicity. They are still governed by natural laws and very little corrupted by our own" (109). Montaigne's view is contrary to many popular models of progress: he considers lagging behind in progress a desirable state instead of a marker of inferiority. Thus, his essay does not reject the temporal model of progress but reverses its valuation.

In the eighteenth century, thinkers such as Montesquieu and Jean-Jacques Rousseau are also skeptical about the merits of civilization and formulate a critique of their own societies by pleading for the supposed simplicity and purity of savage or barbarian societies.[50] Denis Diderot also provided an inversion of the barbarian/civilized hierarchy by depicting Europeans as the real barbarians:

Barbarous Europeans! The brilliance of your enterprises does not impress me. Their success does not hide their injustice. In my imagination I have often embarked in those ships which bring you to distant countries, but once on land, and witness of your misdeeds, I separate myself from you and I join your enemies, taking arms against you, bathing my hands in your blood. (quoted in Shohat and Stam 1994, 89)

But the barbarian as a vehicle for a critique of civilized societies is not exclusive to modernity or Enlightenment thought. Reversals of the barbarian/civilized hierarchy, whereby the progressed civilized appear more barbarous or corrupt than the barbarians, already appear in Homer's *Iliad*, in Plato's *Republic*, or in the writings of the Roman historian Tacitus (Rawson 2001, 6; White 1972, 27–28). The privileging of a certain kind of primitivism also appears in various philosophical, historical, and literary writings. During the Hellenistic period, the Cynics (445–365 BCE) were advocates of primitivizing life and aimed at releasing "the real Barbarian who lurked at the very heart of the city" (Hartog 2001, 98). Ephorus of Cyme (405–330 BCE) saw primitivism as a more just and pure way of life, and thereby closer to the gods (99).[51] The idea of "alien (barbarian) wisdom" was also popular among many Greek intellectuals of that period (99).

Thus, from the ancient Cynics, to Enlightenment thinkers, to primitivism and exoticism in twentieth-century modernist literature and art, the attraction to the barbarian other is almost omnipresent in Western history. Theories of primitivism, the figure of the noble savage, and other attempts to invert the barbarian/civilized hierarchy all challenged discourses of civilization. As Richard Bernheimer writes about the "Wild Man," "Nothing could have been more radical than the attitude of sympathizing or identifying oneself with the Wild Man, whose way of life was the repudiation of all the accumulated values of civilization" (1952, 144–45). Nevertheless, whether such attitudes focus on the commendable traits of the barbarian or on the barbaric behavior of the civilized, they often feed on the Eurocentric elements they seem to question. By valuing barbarism or primitivism more than civilization, they may question the merits of European progress, but they do not (always) invalidate the idea of progress itself: barbarians may still be used as a vehicle for criticizing European societies and simultaneously remain behind civilization in the scale of progress.[52]

Psyche

Hayden White argues that in modern times concepts of otherness, such as the barbarian, which have served the process of "ostensive self-definition by negation," have been relegated to the category of fiction or mere prejudice (1972, 5–6). While the category of the barbarian was generally applicable only to specific groups of people outside the borders of civilization, in modern times, White contends, a partial demythologization and despatialization of the barbarian has taken place, which has led to a "compensatory process of psychic interiorization."[53] According to White, barbarians or wild men have been debunked as essentialist categories and now exist as sociopsychological categories, describing areas of our psychological landscape rather than distinct portions of humanity (35). This interiorization has led to a "remythification" of the barbarian, which finds expression in the trope of "the barbarian within."[54]

The trope of "the barbarian within" in modernity is indissolubly associated with Freud's psychoanalytic theory. Freud's main contribution to the discourse on barbarism lies in his idea that barbarism is internal to every individual. The barbarian is an aspect of our unconscious, which civilization tries to keep under control. Freud's introduction of psychoanalysis at the dawn of the twentieth century led to a radical shift in the self-perception of the civilized and revealed civilization as more unstable than previously thought.

The interiorization of the barbarian—the idea that barbarism is the irrational side of the human psyche—is older than twentieth-century psychoanalytic theory. In the Roman republic, for instance, although the distinction between Romans and (external) barbarians was the basis of Roman identity, some authors acknowledged the irrational and barbaric side of the human psyche. In a speech celebrating a deal between the emperor Valens and a group of Goths in 370 CE, the philosopher and political statesman Themistius says, "There is in each of us a barbarian tribe, extremely overbearing and intractable—I mean temper and those insatiable desires, which stand opposed to rationality as Scythians and Germans do to the Romans" (quoted in Heather 1999, 236). The idea that there is a barbarian in each of us but that (Roman) civilization is able to restrain this internal barbarism and is thus more rational than its barbarian others does not seem too far from Freud's approach to the issue.

Themistius's rendition of the barbarism within, however, is not issued as a criticism of his Roman peers. On the contrary, it is intended as a reaffirmation of the superiority of the Romans. As Peter Heather argues, Themistius here appeals to the conviction of the Roman elite that its members were more rational than the barbarians from beyond the borders (1999, 236). Remarkably, Themistius makes his point about the internal barbarian by drawing an analogy with the external division between civilized and barbarians as distinct groups. Therefore, even though he observes the barbaric drives within all humans (including the Romans), the understanding of the barbarian as an external other remains his stable reference point. Ironically, his belief in the ability of the Romans to control passions through rationality stands in stark contrast with the brutality of the Roman Empire against its barbarians, which did not show many signs of restraint (238). The idea of the "inside barbarian" was thus not strong enough to challenge the Romans' belief in the legitimacy of their own barbaric acts. The Roman Empire would not allow its foundations to be challenged by making the (internal) barbarism of its own "civilized" citizens an issue.

Freud's ideas were certainly more successful in challenging the self-perception of the European subject. *Civilization and Its Discontents* (1930) is the main source for Freud's views on this matter. The central theme of this study is the irresolvable antagonism between instinct and the restraints of civilization. Freud sees a progression of humans from an unrestricted satisfaction of instincts (a primitive state) to a repression of instincts, which is the precondition for a civilized society. Love is found at the foundations of civilization: the goal of a civilized society is to make its participants happy (Freud 1962, 48). But there is also a destructive drive in civilization. The two drives form civilization's struggle between Eros and Death.

For civilization to be sustained, individual instinct needs to be repressed. This condition generates unhappiness, frustration, neurosis, and self-hatred. While civilization uses the law as an external mechanism for regulating aggression, the internal mechanism that prevents the externalization of aggressive impulses in the individual lies in the production of a *sense of guilt*. Freud elaborates:

What means does civilization employ in order to inhibit the aggressiveness which opposes it, to make it harmless, to get rid of it perhaps? . . . What happens to him [the civilized individual] to render his desire for aggression innocuous? . . . His aggressiveness is introjected, internalized; it is, in point of fact, sent back to where it came from—that is, it is directed towards his own ego. . . . The tension between the harsh super-ego and the ego that is subjected to it, is called by us the sense of guilt; it expresses itself as a need for punishment. Civilization therefore, obtains mastery over the individual's dangerous desire for aggression by weakening and disarming it and by setting up an agency within him to watch over it, like a garrison in a conquered city. (1962, 70)

The repression of drives is thus effected through guilt. According to Freud, our "loss of happiness through the heightening of the sense of guilt" is the price we pay for civilization's advances (81). This control mechanism, however, does not always succeed in keeping our aggressive instincts at bay. In Freud's model, the "return of the repressed" becomes the greatest threat to civilization.

The universalism of Freud's views—the fact that they were presented as applicable to all individuals—destabilized the prevalent belief that barbarism was external to Europe. The barbarian is not another race, nation, or religious group but part of our unconscious. The suggestion that there are barbaric drives in every human being, which civilization represses, presented a challenge to the colonial project premised on the assumption of a fundamental difference between Europeans and colonized subjects.

However, the tension between barbarism (aggression) and civilization (restraint) does not exist in equal degree within all subjects. The synchronous relation established between civilization and barbarism in *Civilization and Its Discontents* is elsewhere in Freud associated with a scheme of societal progress from barbarism toward civilization. In Freud's *Group Psychology and the Analysis of the Ego* (1921), barbarism is linked with group identity, while the individuated psyche is a marker of civilization. In Freud, strong group identity is pathologized as dangerous and irrational and is associated with less advanced social formations. Here, Freud builds on views by Gustave Le Bon, whom he also quotes in *Group Psychology*: "By the mere fact that he forms part of an organized group, a man descends several rungs in the ladder of civilization. Isolated, he may be a cultivated individual; in a crowd, he is a barbarian—that is, a creature acting by instinct" (Freud 1959, 12). Groups represent a state of regression of the psyche. For this reason, groups, even when they consist of civilized individuals, can exhibit mob behavior.[55]

In many readings of Freud's progressive narrative, Brown argues, Western liberal values, with their emphasis on individualism and their disavowal of group identity, stand for the "highest state of 'maturity' for man and are equated with civilization" (2006, 155). In *Group Psychology*, Freud normatively draws "maturity, individuation, conscience, repression, and civilization" into the same semantic complex and opposes them to "childishness, primitivism, unchecked impulse, instinct, and barbarism" (157). Civilized individuals are favored vis-à-vis primitive, barbaric groups, who exhibit collective identifications. However, the individuated psyche does not represent a permanent state of civilization because there is always the possibility of regression from the civilized state to barbarism and irrationality. Thus, Freud's views take away civilization's confidence in its own power by suggesting that civilization's restraint of instinct is precarious and fragile. In "Thoughts for the Times of War and Death" (1915), Freud saw World War I as a great example of this fragility (1985, 65). Therefore, Freud's attitude toward the technological advances of civilization is ambiguous. While he is skeptical of the purported progress of European civilization, he does not reject or condemn it (Salter 2002,74). Whether civilization is a blessing or a curse can be judged only by the outcome of the struggle between instincts and rationality in each particular case.

The barbarian is not a self-identical concept. Its history demonstrates that it carries internal contradictions and diverse narratives that disjoin its identity to itself, unsettle its assumed fixity in Western discourse, and point to its connectivity with several categories and contexts. Its disjoined self-identity guarantees its transformability in the present. According to Mieke Bal, a word or image never forgets where it has been and always carries the memory of its previous uses, but "every re-use of pre-existing material changes it" (1999, 100). The history of the barbarian, then, does not decide the future of this concept in a deterministic, linear manner; its past can also be reshaped *from* and *by* the present. Therefore, the history of the barbarian does not only produce its present but also emerges as an effect of the present.

The outcome of the struggle between historical and new potential uses of barbarism or the barbarian is not predetermined. Neither is the outcome of the relation between civilization and barbarism. Barbarism cannot be fully contained by civilized discourse. Not only civilization can define and mold barbarism—the reverse is also conceivable. The following chapters stage the tension between these concepts in an attempt to chart a new space for barbarism, through which—why not?—perhaps a new typology of *barbarian* standards may take shape in the future.

4

A Positive Barbarism?

> Some concepts must be indicated by an extraordinary and sometimes even
> barbarous or shocking word. . . . Some concepts call for archaisms and others for
> neologisms, shot through with almost crazy etymological exercises. . . . In each
> case, there must be a strange necessity for these words and for their choice, like
> an element of style. The concept's baptism calls for a specifically philosophical
> *taste* that proceeds with violence or by insinuation and constitutes a philosophical
> language within language.
> —Deleuze and Guattari, *What Is Philosophy?*

> It is the inconspicuous aspect—or this *and* the offensive aspect (the two together
> are not a contradiction)—which survives in true works and which constitutes the
> point where the content reaches the breaking point for an authentic researcher.
> —Walter Benjamin, "Rigorous Study of Art"

In the second epigraph, Walter Benjamin locates the crux of an artwork not in the meaning or impression of the work as a whole but in
the insignificant, inconspicuous details.[1] His statement has more consequences for the critic (what Benjamin calls an "authentic researcher")
than for the artwork. The critic is called to take on an entirely different
approach to artworks than the traditional methods employed at the time
Benjamin wrote this essay (1933). Indeed, "the hallmark of the new type
of researcher," Benjamin continues, "is not the eye for the 'all-encompassing whole' or the eye for the 'comprehensive context' (which mediocrity
has claimed for itself), but rather the capacity to be at home in marginal
domains" (2005b, 670). Instead of using a holistic approach to the work

as a unified entity, the researcher is called upon to adopt a microscopic method: to pay attention to those elements not fitting the general pattern of the work but standing out because of some, in Benjamin's words, "offensive aspect." The work may thus contain insubordinate elements, and the researcher needs to bring their offensive potential to the fore. In its focus on offensive, deviant, and marginalized elements, this method has something "barbarian" about it.

The importance Benjamin here gives to details and marginal elements in the study of the artwork is telling for the kind of textual criticism he wrote about and performed in his own work.[2] Typical for this criticism, as he writes in "Rigorous Study of Art," is "the willingness to push research forward to the point where even the 'insignificant'—no, *precisely* the insignificant—becomes significant" (2005b, 668). The insignificant is significant because it holds the key to the work's performance and to the actualization of its material contents: "it is precisely in the investigation of the marginal case that the material contents reveal their key position most decisively" (669). Marginal details often hold a revolutionary potential in Benjamin's own writings. Strange elements or erratic interventions take it upon themselves to redefine tradition and change the course of language and culture. Such elements can be thought of as latent barbarisms in Benjamin's texts that can be activated by the reader.

This chapter probes the meanings and operations of barbarism as a philosophical and methodological concept in Benjamin. The focus is more specifically on Benjamin's notion of "positive barbarism" in his essay "Experience and Poverty" (Erfahrung und Armut, 1933). I examine its relation to other appearances of barbarism in his writings, tracing the ways in which "positive barbarism" in this essay breaks with the traditional valuation of barbarism and enables a resignification of this concept.

Following Benjamin's own instruction in "Rigorous Study of Art," this chapter stumbles upon, and zooms into, an inconspicuous linguistic barbarism within Benjamin's concept of positive barbarism. By disentangling the implications of this detail, I propose barbarism as an errant site, in which newness can break through from a creative accident, an unexpected alteration, a marginal element with an estranging effect. The barbarism within Benjamin's concept of barbarism allows an exploration of how Benjamin's "barbarian project" unfolds performatively in his essay;

in other words, how Benjamin's concept of barbarism is put in practice in his own writing as a methodological tool and textual strategy.

The English translation of his essay disregards the linguistic barbarism in Benjamin's "positive barbarism." The translator's (mis)translation of Benjamin's positive barbarism becomes an occasion for laying out the conditions, the institutional and epistemological implications, and the effects of the translation of philosophical concepts.

The exploration of Benjamin's positive barbarism does not amount to a systematic theory of barbarism.[3] Barbarism in Benjamin remains a concept that exceeds—by being in excess of—any attempt to crystallize its meaning and use, as it constantly subjects itself to new appropriations, (mis)translations, and (mis)interpretations. However, as it opens itself to questioning, its methodological relevance breaks through: it inspires a kind of critical barbarian writing, which may be more constructive than any affirmative, logic-based philosophical project. With this in mind, my own reading is grounded in a close literary analysis of Benjamin's text instead of a strictly philosophical approach. This kind of reading is invited by Benjamin's mode of writing, in which the philosophical is intertwined with the literary and in which systematic philosophical thinking cannot account for all kinds of experience (especially those generated by new artistic media and technology). By focusing on details in the text, my reading probes the operations of barbarism not only as a philosophical concept but, primarily, as a textual and, more broadly, medial performance.

Strange Bedfellows: Positive Barbarism and Poverty of Experience

In 1933 the cloud of fascism starts to fall upon Europe, as Adolf Hitler assumes power in Germany and initiates the persecution of the Jews. That year Benjamin flees to Paris, where he would settle permanently and write some of his most influential essays. During his first year in Paris, Benjamin writes his short essay "Experience and Poverty."[4] The essay starts with an apparent paradox. While the development of technology has led to an "oppressive wealth of ideas," it has simultaneously generated a new poverty of experience. Therefore, in what constitutes one of the "dialectical contradictions of capitalist production," technological development drains the reserves of human experience instead of enhancing them (Bracken 2002, 337). This new poverty can be seen in terms of an inability to communicate experience and leave traces. The experiences of previous generations, Benjamin asserts in this essay, fall short of providing means for interpreting and processing new social forms in modernity: "For never has experience been contradicted more thoroughly: strategic experience has been contravened by positional warfare, economic experience, by the inflation; physical experience, by hunger; moral experiences, by the ruling powers" (2005b, 732).

This poverty should not be understood as lack. Rather, it springs out of excess: an excess of ideas and styles and an oppressive overload of culture. People, Benjamin writes, "long to free themselves from experience." They are not "ignorant or inexperienced," but "they have 'devoured' everything, both 'culture and people,' and they have had such a surfeit, that it has exhausted them" (734). Thus, the answer to this new poverty does not lie in reconnecting with the great past traditions but in professing this poverty in order to explore new modes of being. To do that, one has to take up the work of destruction in order to "start from scratch; to make a new start; to make a little go a long way; to begin with a little and build up further" (732). The name Benjamin chooses for this project is "barbarism"—not barbarism as we know it but a new, positive, concept of barbarism. This is how Benjamin introduces this concept:

Indeed (let's admit it), our poverty of experience is not merely poverty on the personal level, but poverty of human experience in general. Hence, a new kind of barbarism. Barbarism? Yes, indeed. We say this in order to introduce a new, positive concept of barbarism. (732)

The word "hence" in the second sentence, which translates the German *damit*, can express both equality and causality, synchronicity and metachronicity. As such, its function in the sentence is ambiguous. The absence of a verb in this elliptic sentence allows for speculation on the implied activity and transfers the weight of the activity to the word "hence." Does "hence" suggest an equation of this poverty with barbarism ("Hence, [the poverty of experience *equals*] a new kind of barbarism")? Or does it imply that this new barbarism can emerge from the poverty of experience as a creative force out of something negative ("Hence, [this poverty of experience can *lead to*] a new kind of barbarism")?

If we follow the first option, that poverty of experience amounts to barbarism, then this poverty seems to entail a disavowal of culture and a regression to a barbaric state. In this case, barbarism denotes the negative opposite of culture or experience. If we pursue the second option, then this new barbarism is not there already but may follow from the poverty of experience. This poverty may not be so bad after all because it holds the potential to unleash the positive force of a new barbarism.

The two interpretive options for the function of "hence" are not mutually exclusive. In fact, they capture the double tension in the concept of barbarism, as simultaneously carrying a negative, violent force and a positive potential *in* and *from* this violence. Benjamin's new barbarism also has to destroy and clear the way for a new start. The barbarian, who, according to the same essay, belongs to the "great, creative spirits," first engages in destruction in order "build up further" (732).

The sentence just analyzed, starting with "hence," highlights the interrelation of a certain notion of experience with barbarism. Therefore, scrutinizing the notion of experience in Benjamin is a necessary step toward illuminating his notion of barbarism. Moreover, Benjamin's positive barbarism needs to be thought in relation to two contextual conditions, both of decisive significance in Benjamin's thinking: the development of technology and new artistic media, and the threat of fascism. *Experience, fascism, technology,* and *new media* all form an intricate nexus in Benjamin, within which the discussion of "positive barbarism" is placed.

The notion of experience in Benjamin is surrounded by ambiguity.[5] In his early essay "Experience" (1913), Benjamin gives a rather negative account of the notion. In this essay (written when Benjamin was only twenty-one years old), he attacks the tendency of adults to devalue the young by resting on a self-assumed notion of experience acquired with age. In Benjamin's eyes, experience signifies "life's commonness" or "meaninglessness" and is associated with "compromise, impoverishment of ideas, and lack of energy" (2004, 3–4). Experience leads to a life devoid of spirit and condemned to mediocrity and preservation of the status quo. As such, it forestalls novelty and radical change. The "experienced" adult or "philistine" in this early essay cannot create anything. This persona of the philistine is the antipode of Benjamin's later "(good) barbarian," as presented in "Experience and Poverty" as well as in another essay,

"The Destructive Character" (1931). The great, new, and forward-looking things cannot even be "experienced," as Benjamin writes in "Experience," because only in the "inexperienceable can courage, hope, and meaning be given foundation" (4). Only toward the end of this essay does Benjamin consider the possibility of "a different experience" that is immediate, full of spirit and creativity, and thus opposed to the philistine's "comfortable" and spiritless kind of experience (5).

The negative connotations of "experience" in this essay support a reading of the poverty of experience as a good thing. Since inexperience can give rise to radical critique and novelty, the affinity between Benjamin's "poverty of experience" and positive "new barbarism" becomes all the more convincing. Of course the argument in such an early essay as "Experience" cannot apodictically demonstrate the content of experience in "Experience and Poverty." Benjamin's writings are replete with contradictions and reversals, which should make one cautious when using the argument in one essay to interpret another one.

However, the positive potential of a deficit of experience is suggested in "Experience and Poverty" as well, albeit less explicitly than in "Experience." "Experience and Poverty" starts with a similar notion of experience, correlated with age. Here, too, experience is handed down "with the authority of age": "everyone knew precisely what experience was: older people had always passed it on to younger ones" (2005b, 731). This kind of experience has disappeared in modernity. The argument that Benjamin unravels in the beginning of this essay is repeated verbatim in a paragraph from "The Storyteller" (1936). The identical part in these two essays concerns the loss of the ability to communicate experience, especially after World War I.[6] Although Benjamin phrases the new condition in negative terms (loss, poverty, decrease of communicable experience), his appraisal of this new condition in both essays is by no means (only) negative. While the loss of the storyteller's aura seems to be lamented, it is also seen as part of a necessary historical development, which allows "a new beauty" to emerge—and with it perhaps a new kind of knowledge:

And nothing would be more fatuous than to want to see in it [i.e., the end of storytelling as a result of the poverty of experience] merely a "symptom of decay," let alone a "modern" symptom. It is, rather, only a concomitant symptom of the regular productive forces of history, a concomitant that has quite gradually removed narrative from the realm of living speech and at the same time is making it possible to see a new beauty in what is vanishing. (Benjamin 1999b, 86)

Benjamin is not merely nostalgic of the past but sees possibilities in the loss of the old. In "The Storyteller," poverty of experience becomes the condition of possibility for the novel. The same poverty indicates new possibilities in "Experience and Poverty" as well. Both poverty of experience and barbarism are projected as conditions for surpassing the old. For Benjamin, the "divorce" of our culture from experience enables "the barbarians" to do away with the "oppressive wealth of ideas" and "the horrific mishmash of styles and ideologies produced during the last century" (2005b, 732). Because of the poverty of experience we lose a piece of the past, but that past, Benjamin seems to suggest, was perhaps not really worth saving. This poverty stimulates the creative, barbarian spirits to look forward, rejecting the "traditional solemn, noble image of man, festooned with all the sacrificial offerings of the past," and turning "to the naked man of the contemporary world who lies screaming like a newborn babe in the dirty diapers of the present" (733).[7] The end of experience as we knew it frees modern man from the burden of tradition and occasions a clean start.

Other thinkers and writers had also noticed the dissolution of experience and the decreasing "graspability" of the world as a concomitant of modernity.[8] For Benjamin, however, the end of experience as we know it does not mean the end of experience as such. Modernity and its technological developments introduce new modes of experiencing and knowing the world. Although "Experience and Poverty" does not explicitly address these new modes, Benjamin's introduction of a new, positive barbarism in this essay suggests a renewed notion of experience as well.

This new experience is elaborated in "The Work of Art in the Age of Mechanical Reproduction," which explores how technologically reproducible forms of art shift perception.[9] With the technological developments of modernity, as Ernst van Alphen remarks, the loss of experience is related to an excess of stimuli: the subject is overwhelmed by sensory impressions and is exposed to novel sensations (2007, 341–43). For Benjamin, new media, especially film, reveal unknown aspects of reality: what was once familiar now becomes estranged, as the camera introduces the viewer to "unconscious optics" (Benjamin 1999b, 230). Moreover, Benjamin observes that in the case of film reception takes place mainly in a state of distraction, as opposed to the deep concentration art traditionally demands (232–33). The viewer now attains insights through discontinuous impressions rather than controlled and rational observation.[10]

In "The Work of Art," by addressing the changes imposed by new media and art forms on traditional art and its reception, Benjamin tries to counter the fascist aestheticization of politics by politicizing aesthetics (1999b, 235).[11] Fascism, as Eduardo Cadava argues, seeks to "stage the non-political essence of the political" by making the autonomy of art into the "truth of the political" (1997, 47). For Benjamin, the fascist "introduction of aesthetics into political life" can only culminate in war and its aesthetic apotheosis (1999b, 234).[12] This alienates humankind from itself to such a degree that "it can experience its own destruction as an aesthetic pleasure of the first order" (235). The destruction of the unity and authenticity of art, and the end of its function as ritual in modernity, deprives art of its aura and can thereby sabotage the fascist attempt to use art for "redirecting the technical apparatus to the production of ritual values" (Werneburg and Phillips 1992, 45). Restoring the artwork's aura is thus a crucial component of the fascist project. In the face of this project, Benjamin suggests a mobilization of aesthetic production toward political ends. This explains why he sees a revolutionary potential in new forms of art and their destruction of the aura (Cadava 1997, 47).

In this sense, new artistic media such as film could be seen as part of the project of "positive barbarism" in "Experience and Poverty," which is also meant to confront the barbarism of fascism in the year 1933. Benjamin's project, however, does not only call upon new art forms. Existing art forms that have redefined themselves as a result of new media and technological advancements can also participate in the same project. The architecture of Adolf Loos, the paintings of Paul Klee, the works of Dadaists, and the literature of Paul Scheerbart are for Benjamin cases in point. These names figure among the great minds that Benjamin deems capable of carrying out this barbarian project.

Benjamin's positive barbarism, either initiated through art or by other means, is called to challenge the destructive movement of the kind of barbarism that is not only manifest in the threat of fascism in 1933 but has always accompanied civilization in history. As Benjamin remarks in

"Theses on the Philosophy of History," "There is no document of civilization that is not at the same time a document of barbarism" (1999b, 248). The wonders of civilization do not owe their existence just to "great minds and talents" but also to "the anonymous toil of their contemporaries" (248). Benjamin's much-quoted statement points to civilization's dependence on its margins—people excluded by history, the colonized, the slaves, the workers, the proletariat, the masses. The paradox that civilization is grounded in perpetual violence against its inferior others locates barbarism in the heart of the civilized construct.

Benjamin's famous dictum exposes civilization as an irrational construct that has to exert violence to safeguard itself. The same apparent contradiction has been noticed by other thinkers. Karl Marx notes the contradiction between the essence of the modern state (reason) and its existence (unreason) and sees a clash between the state's "theoretical definition and its real hypotheses" (quoted in Althusser 1969, 225). The state cannot sustain itself on the basis of reason, even if ideologically founded on it. In practice, the state exercises irrationality, violence, and barbarism, which alienate the state from its foundation (reason) while they ensure its preservation. Ludwig Feuerbach, who laid the foundations for Marxist thought, saw this contradiction not just as irrational but—like Benjamin—as a necessary connection between reason (the idea of the state) and unreason (its irrational, barbaric reality) (Althusser 1969, 225). As Louis Althusser argues in "Marxism and Humanism," for Feuerbach unreason is not simply the opposite of reason but a "necessary moment" in the realization of reason (225). In other words, civilization cannot be thought separately from barbarism. It needs barbarism both for its theoretical self-definition by negation and for its actualization.

Benjamin's belief in the inextricability of barbarism from civilization, in combination with the growing force of fascism at the time, seems to leave no way out of barbarism. The escape from this impasse will have to come from within the notion of barbarism: stealing the concept away from fascism, disappropriating it, and recasting it affirmatively for a new project. In this way, the concept returns with a vengeance to challenge fascism. The instrument of the enemy turns into a strategy of resistance that allows one to destroy, clear the ground, and then begin "with a little and build up further" (W. Benjamin 2005b, 732).

But if this new barbarism that Benjamin proposes engages destruction, how is it *radically* different from the barbarism of the enemy? To come to this question, other questions have to be addressed first: Is *barbarism* really the name Benjamin gives to this strategy? Does he use the same name for his positive barbarism as that of (let us tentatively call it) "negative barbarism"?

Benjamin's Three Barbarisms

To answer these questions, I first seek out other instances in Benjamin's work where he employs the term "barbarism." A striking case is Benjamin's well-known dictum, discussed previously: "There is no document of civilization that is not at the same time a document of barbarism" (1999b, 248). In German the text reads: "Es ist niemals ein Dokument der Kultur, ohne zugleich ein solches der *Barbarei* zu sein" (Benjamin 1991, vol. 1, bk. 2, 696, emphasis added).

Let us now reread, this time in German, the sentence wherein Benjamin introduces his new barbarism in "Experience and Poverty":

Diese Erfahrungsarmut ist Armut nicht nur an privaten sondern an Menschheitserfahrungen überhaupt. Und damit eine Art von neuem *Barbarentum*. Barbarentum? In der Tat. Wir sagen es, um einen neuen, positiven Begriff des *Barbarentums* einzuführen. (1991, vol. 2, bk. 1, 215, emphasis added)

The term used in the first excerpt is *Barbarei*, and in the second, *Barbarentum*. In the English edition of these texts both terms are translated as "barbarism." A literal translation of *Barbarentum* in English would be something like "barbarianness" or "barbarianhood."

Neither *barbarianness* nor *barbarianhood* exists as a word listed in dictionaries. Remarkably, *Barbarentum* is also not commonly listed in German dictionaries. An exception is the revised edition of the *Deutsches Fremdwörterbuch* by Hans Schulz and Otto Basler (1997).[13] In this dictionary, *Barbarei* is a separate entry extending over six pages (131–36), while *Barbarentum* is listed as a derivative of *Barbar* and receives only a short explication of one paragraph. Judging from its somewhat infrequent presence in dictionaries, I deduce that *Barbarentum* is a rather uncommon word that has not been standardized in German.

In this sense, its usage and status in German differ greatly from those of *Barbarei*, which is listed in all dictionaries as the proper opposite of *Kultur*. If we consider its rarity, archaic sound, and marginal lexicographical status, *Barbarentum* could even be seen as a barbarism according to the second meaning of the word: an "expression not accepted as part of the current standard, such as neologisms, hybrid derivatives, obsolete or provincial expressions" (*Webster's New International Dictionary*, 1913). It can be no coincidence that Benjamin chooses a less standardized term to baptize his positive barbarism: a term less historically charged than *Barbarei* is easier to resignify and invest with a new philosophical and political project.

By opting for a term other than *Barbarei*, Benjamin distinguishes between this positive barbarism and the barbarism implied in *Barbarei*. Since, to my knowledge, Benjamin does not use *Barbarentum* anywhere else, we may infer that *in the context of his writings Barbarentum* is a new word, invested with the potential to disrupt the workings of *Barbarei* in language and in the social and political world. Therefore, I will refer to *Barbarei* as the "old" or "negative barbarism" to contrast it to the newness that *Barbarentum* encompasses in Benjamin's essay. Referring to the "old" or "negative" barbarism in contradistinction to Benjamin's positive barbarism constitutes, of course, a reductive and catachrestic generalization. As shown in the previous chapter, this "old barbarism" (in Benjamin encompassed by *Barbarei*) is not a monolithic concept in history but has a complex genealogy with plural connotations and functions. However, in history barbarism remains a principally negative signifier, placed in constant opposition to a positive notion of civilization. Reference to the "old, negative" barbarism here expresses this dominant traditional valuation of the concept. The term *Barbarentum* itself, however unusual, also has its history of negative uses. Nevertheless, I contend that the term *Barbarei*, given its widespread use in German and its use in Benjamin's writings as the proper opposite (and the flipside) of *Kultur*, can be considered as the "old barbarism" par excellence, in the face of which Benjamin throws his reinvented *Barbarentum*. Therefore, *Barbarentum* can be viewed as new in the context of Benjamin's writings.

In "Theses on the Philosophy of History," as well as in *The Arcades Project*, Benjamin uses *Barbarei* to address the inextricability of barbarism from civilization or culture.[14] In "Experience and Poverty," he employs the unusual term *Barbarentum* for a barbarian project that breaks with the genealogy of *Barbarei*. Apart from *Barbarei* and *Barbarentum*, however, there is a third barbarism in Benjamin's writings: *Barbarismus*, the German term for linguistic barbarism, denoting an error or foreign, unconventional locution. This third barbarism appears in the "Work of Art in the Age of Mechanical Reproduction" in relation to Dadaism. The barbarisms (Barbarismen) that, according to Benjamin, are "abundant in Dadaism" denote "the extravagances and crudities of art," which "appear, particularly in the so-called decadent epochs" (1999b, 230). As an art form, Dadaism aspired to certain effects that could not be fully realized at the time, but only later, with new technical developments and in a new art form: film (230). According to Benjamin, Dadaist works were scandalous and obscene. They used mundane materials, were useless for conventional contemplation, caused "vehement distraction," and destroyed their own aura by being displayed as reproductions. In their aspirations, Benjamin argues, and especially in their distracting elements and tactile quality, Dadaist works were (unwittingly) "promoting a demand for the film," although they denounced the market values typical of the film industry (231).

The barbarisms Benjamin finds in Dadaism can thus be delineated as follows: extravagances; crudities; erratic, unexpected, or shocking elements; and artistic effects that deviate from a certain artistic tradition and set of expectations and cannot be fully realized and appreciated at the time of their creation, because the (technical) means for their full realization do not yet exist. These barbarisms anticipate something new—possibly a new art emerging through a distorted and transformed version of the old. As such, they are elements of a new language, which is not yet fully formed.[15] Notably, for Benjamin these barbarisms are also defined by a lack of intentionality (Dadaism "was not conscious of such intentions" [231]). This does not mean that the Dadaists did not intend to achieve certain effects with their works—they certainly did. But the barbarisms Benjamin talks about capture the unintended and unpredictable effects of their works, which were fully materialized only later, in other art forms. These barbarisms herald a future "barbarian" language, the rules and grammar of which do not yet exist.

The way Benjamin uses *Barbarismen* in "The Work of Art" places this third kind of barbarism in the vicinity of the project of *Barbarentum*.

Kevin McLaughlin goes so far as to argue that the positive barbarism in "Experience and Poverty" is in fact indistinguishable from such a literal, linguistic barbarism. Experience, according to McLaughlin, is generally understood in Benjamin as a matter of language, and the poverty of experience should therefore also be addressed in linguistic terms (2006, 11–12). Because experiential poverty in Benjamin has a linguistic basis, McLaughlin argues, Benjamin's concept of positive barbarism in this essay should also be read in terms of literal (linguistic) barbarism. McLaughlin thus equates poverty of experience with barbarism and signifies Benjamin's *Barbarentum* as linguistic barbarism: "Barbarism transposes the concept of a collective experiential poverty onto language" (12).

Although I fully share McLaughlin's insistence on the role of linguistic barbarisms in probing Benjamin's concept of barbarism, McLaughlin's interpretation fails to consider how Benjamin's word for "positive barbarism" is neither *Barbarismus* nor *Barbarei* but a different word: *Barbarentum*. McLaughlin's study, perhaps influenced by Benjamin's English translation, seems to presuppose that all uses of the notion of barbarism in Benjamin refer back to a single term. However, we are in fact dealing with different notions of barbarism in his writings, distinguished from each other not only conceptually but also linguistically. It is remarkable that McLaughlin's study, which takes linguistic (or "literal") barbarism as the basis for the interpretation of Benjaminian barbarism in general, falls short of addressing the linguistic peculiarities (indeed, the linguistic barbarisms) surrounding the different versions of Benjamin's barbarisms.

The meaning and operations of Benjamin's *Barbarentum* extend beyond the linguistic realm. For Benjamin, transformation starts with a radical renovation of language (the redeployment of *Barbarentum* is a case in point), but "language" should be read broadly, as expression through different media. "All expression," Benjamin asserts in his early essay "On Language as Such and on the Language of Man," "insofar as it is a communication of contents of the mind, is to be classed as language. And expression, by its whole innermost nature, is certainly to be understood only as *language*" (2004, 62–63). Even the term *Barbarismus* in Benjamin exceeds its strict meaning as linguistic error or oddity. In the "Work of Art," the term refers to "extravagances and crudities" not only in Dadaist texts but also in visual works and other artistic media.

The three barbarisms in Benjamin are distinct but also intertwined. A mistake, crudity, or foreign element—as Benjamin renders *Barbarismus*—can enter a saturated code, tradition, or form and trigger the destruction and overcoming of *Barbarei* that always lurks in culture, thereby pursuing the project of positive barbarism (*Barbarentum*). A simple way to capture the relation between *Barbarei, Barbarentum,* and *Barbarismus* would be the following: If *Barbarentum* names the project that counters *Barbarei,* then *Barbarismen* can function as catalysts in this project; they can be (accidental) agents of destruction, change, and transformation. *Barbarentum* can thus be realized with the intervention of *Barbarismen,* but the relation between the two concepts is not necessary: *Barbarentum* does not have to be actualized only through *Barbarismen,* and not every *Barbarismus* is related to the project of *Barbarentum.*

Barbarentum and Constructive Destruction

Benjamin's choice for the term *Barbarentum* acquires additional significance in light of the transformative, creative force that he assigns to naming. For Benjamin, names do not just refer to things but participate in their production.[16] In "Experience and Poverty" he calls for a language that could change the world instead of just describe it. Benjamin offers two examples in which language assumes this transformative potential. The first concerns the literary creatures of Paul Scheerbart, German author of fantastic novels and poems. These characters (which are human beings or "people" but lack "humanlikeness") speak a completely new language, which is "arbitrary" and "constructed" rather than "organic." Even their names are nonhuman—an element that brings Benjamin to his second example: the "dehumanized" names some Russians give their children, such as "Aviakhim" (the name of an airline). In both cases, Benjamin writes, we have "no technical renovation of language, but its mobilization in the service of struggle or work—at any rate, of *changing reality instead of describing it*" (2005b, 733, emphasis added).[17]

What these two cases—Scheerbart's creatures and the Russian names—have in common are names that are not humanlike but constructed, technical, or inspired by technology. Why does Benjamin pick these examples to make a point about the transformation of reality through the mobilization of language? If, as Benjamin argues in "Experience and Poverty," modernity and new technological developments contradict experience and incapacitate the language that used to capture this experience, then the new poverty of experience also needs a new language of expression (not necessarily one of words).[18] This new language would not reproduce existing human(ist) forms and names, but it would name the human anew through a constructed language inspired by technique and technological developments. Along these lines, Scheerbart's novels inquire "how our telescopes, our airplanes, our rockets can transform human beings as they have been up to now into *completely new, lovable, and interesting creatures*" (Benjamin 2005b, 733, emphasis added).

Dehumanized and technologized names may thus make humanity more human and humans more "lovable." By implicitly proposing a constructed language with non-humanlike names, Benjamin goes against the grain of humanism. His proposal appears to bring out the technical in the human instead of the human in the technical. However, I argue that it does both. Renaming the human through technology redefines both humanity and technology itself: technology is employed in the service of a better humanity, while it also helps construct this improved humanity. Since both the human and the technological are in need of transformation, what Benjamin's examples propose is a two-way street.[19]

Through these examples, Benjamin's essay envisions a language that embraces the poverty of experience in modernity in order to use technology for reinventing humanity. Dehumanizing language could help rehumanize the human. In this way, the potentially destructive power of technology, especially in the ideology of New German nationalism, could take a constructive direction. Reinventing language based on the new conditions of modernity could lead to a new language able to respond productively to the new kinds of experience that modernity has generated.

In the examples from "Experience and Poverty," the acts of naming call attention to the artificiality in the relation between name and thing. When a child is named "Aviakhim," for instance, no illusion of an organic relation between the child and the name of an airline can be sustained. This relation is constructed *in* the act of naming. "What is crucial about this language," Benjamin writes when discussing the language of

Scheerbart's characters, "is its arbitrary, constructed nature, in contrast to organic language" (2005b, 733). Naming as an act becomes essential for the mobilization of the creative energies of language and the transformation of reality.

The new language "Experience and Poverty" anticipates, reshuffles the relation of names to things in the hope of changing reality. This language is indispensable to the project of *Barbarentum*. Conversely, *Barbarentum* can also be seen as the product of a creative act of (re)naming. Benjamin baptizes his barbarian project with a name different from *Barbarei* in an attempt to stall the deterministic course of the old barbarism.

In Benjamin's *Barbarentum*, the nominalizing suffix *-tum* aspires to counter the exclusionary and violent workings of *Barbarei*, in which the emphasis is on the ostracism of barbarian others or their exploitation within civilization. Instead of exclusion, alienation, or hierarchical power relations, *-tum* conveys the sense of a community or collectivity of new barbarians joined together in a common project. The suffix *-tum* is often used to denote a collectivity, as is the case with *Judentum*. In that respect, the translation "barbarian*hood*" comes closer than "barbarianness" (and certainly closer than "barbarism") to grasping the communal sense in *Barbarentum*. The suffix *-hood* is often used for a group sharing a common characteristic or conveys a sense of bonding.[20] Given the connotations of the suffix *-tum*, Benjamin's *Barbarentum* may function as a critique of the kind of collective identity the National Socialists attempted to foster (based on exclusion and violence) by proposing another kind of barbarian collective with alternative modes of governance and togetherness. The new barbarians constituting this collectivity are human beings in possession of a radical and creative spirit. But the agents of *Barbarentum* need not always be human subjects: these agents can also be the barbarisms of new technologies and artistic media, in which Benjamin sees the hope for new forms of experience in a new language.

Although Benjamin uses *Barbarentum* as a reaction to the destructive and exclusionary operations of *Barbarei*, the violent connotations of *Barbarei*—and perhaps also of the existing meanings of *Barbarentum*, despite its infrequent use—still accompany his new concept. However, in his *Barbarentum*, the destructive sides of barbarism become a prerequisite for the creative aspect of this concept to take effect. Radical newness emerges through destruction. "Among the great creative spirits," Benjamin writes in "Experience and Poverty," "there have always been the inexorable ones who begin by clearing a tabula rasa" (2005b, 732). This "clearing" demands the destruction of the old. Benjamin's recasting of barbarism, John McCole argues, aspires to steal the "energies of barbarism from the fascists, and to reverse the conventional valuations of creativity and destruction" (1993, 157). In his new barbarism, destruction and creation cannot be thought together in a harmonious relation, but they also cannot be thought separately.

Barbarentum sees destruction of the old as necessary, because it *may* lead to a new start. The affirmative quotient of barbarism therefore emerges from a constant negotiation with destruction and violence. Moreover, Benjamin's positive barbarism does not preserve what is but questions everything in its path. This matches the course of action of "The Destructive Character" (1931), an essay in which Benjamin elaborates the features of the new barbarian, which are only briefly sketched in "Experience and Poverty."

In "The Destructive Character," the process of creating possibilities through destruction is laid out in the following terms:

The destructive character sees nothing permanent. But for this very reason he sees ways everywhere. Where others encounter walls or mountains, there, too, he sees a way. But because he sees a way everywhere, he has to clear things from it everywhere. Not always by brute force; sometimes by the most refined. Because he sees ways everywhere, he always stands at a crossroads. No moment can know what the next will bring. What exists he reduces to rubble—not for the sake of rubble, but for that of the way leading through it. (2005b, 542)[21]

The word that catches my attention in the previous passage is "everywhere." Benjamin repeats it three times to emphasize that the destructive character "sees ways everywhere" and once to point out that he "has to clear things from it everywhere." Since the destructive character sees ways everywhere, the future is radically open: "No moment can know what the next will bring" (2005b, 542). This unconditionality creates a wide spectrum of possible futures but also contains the risk of creating monsters instead of angels of change. Accordingly, Benjamin's *Barbarentum*, just like all truly radical gestures, offers no guarantee that it will indeed lead to the desired outcome. There is always risk: the project may take a different and even nightmarish direction, and destruction may be the only thing left.

The destructive character, as Irving Wohlfarth remarks, is a "historical gamble" (1994, 163). He takes a risk that needs to be taken, because at the historical moment wherein Benjamin finds himself there is so much at stake. This brings me back to the questions posed earlier: If positive barbarism endorses destruction, how does Benjamin's concept radically differ from fascist barbarism and destruction? How can Benjamin construe a positive notion of destruction or barbarism that is not simultaneously a sinister foreshadowing of fascist violence? Answering these questions involves scrutinizing the relation between destruction and positive barbarism in Benjamin.

A sentence from "The Destructive Character" is telling in this respect: "What exists he reduces to rubble—not for the sake of rubble, but for that of the way leading through it" (2005b, 542). It is worth juxtaposing this sentence to a statement from "Theories of German Fascism." Benjamin argues that the new theories of war thriving among German nationalists after World War I were nothing but "an uninhibited translation of the principles of *l'art pour l'art* to war itself" (2005a, 314). These two statements imply two kinds of destruction: in fascism, destruction takes place for the sake of destruction (in imitation of *l'art pour l'art*), while Benjamin's destructive character destroys "not for the sake of rubble" but with an eye for the possibilities ("the way") opened through this act; destruction is not an end in itself but a means of creating hope for redemption.

The destructive character is therefore not a Romantic nihilist, wishing to reduce everything to nothing without motive or purpose, but, as Wohlfarth calls him, an "*effective* nihilist," who—in Hegel's words—"enters into his opponent's strength in order to destroy him from within."[22] Benjamin's destructive character destroys in the hope of redeeming humanity rather than letting fascism lead to total destruction.

Destroying is first of all necessary in order to clear the way: "The destructive character knows only one watchword: make room. And only one activity: clearing away." However, the destructive character is not a creator: "The only work he avoids is creative" (2005b, 542). Here we find a difference between the "destructive character" and the "barbarian" in

Benjamin. The barbarian destroys with the intention of constructing something new. In "Experience and Poverty," the figure of the barbarian is surrounded by an architectural vocabulary: the barbarian is a destroyer but also a constructor, who prefers to start from scratch "and *build up* further." The "great *creative* spirits" mentioned as examples of barbarians are those who create a tabula rasa and then "need a drawing table; they were *constructors*" (2005b, 732, emphasis added). The destructive character could thus be seen as the first step in a process that the barbarians take further by engaging in what we may call "constructive destruction." The destructive character destroys to clear the ground; the barbarian destroys but also creates anew.

But in exactly what kind of destruction does the barbarian engage? And even if the barbarian destroys to create anew, how can the idea of the unreserved, cheerful destroyer of all traces be compatible with Benjamin, the tireless collector of past traces? How could Benjamin suggest a complete elimination of tradition—he, the collector who, in Hannah Arendt's words, "gathers his fragments and scraps from the debris of the past," whose ideal work was one consisting only of quotations, and who dedicated himself to collecting excerpts of old and new texts, tearing them out of their context and "arranging them afresh in such a way that they illustrated one another and were able to prove their *raison d'être* in a free-floating state," in the manner of a "surrealistic montage" (1999, 50–51)? Once more, we stumble upon a contradiction in Benjamin's writing. In my view, what Benjamin has in mind is not a complete erasure of the contents of tradition and of the past as such. Instead, destruction can be seen as an uprooting of the authoritative function of tradition in the present and a transformation of the relation of tradition with the here and now.

Benjamin wants the barbarian "to make a little go a long way; to begin with a little and build up further" (2005b, 732). If we put the emphasis on "a little," we detect a small hesitation to annihilate the past altogether—perhaps the dedicated collector's instinct is making a subtle, subconscious manifestation amid the barbarian's destructive drive. But the figures of the barbarian and the collector need not be placed in opposing camps. Even if the collector makes tradition his field of action, in fact he goes against tradition. While tradition is grounded in the authority of the past and values the classifiable qualities of objects in order to make hierarchical distinctions, Benjamin's collector evens out hierarchical orderings and privileges the uniqueness of each object. What matters is that which makes the object part of the present, even if it was created years or centuries ago.[23] "The genuine picture," writes Benjamin, "may be old, but the genuine thought is new. It is of the present. This present might be meager, granted. But no matter what it is like, one must firmly take it by the horns to be able to consult the past" (Benjamin, quoted in Arendt 1999, 48–49). It is from the present that the authority of tradition can be challenged and overthrown. As Benjamin writes in "Theses on the Philosophy of History," "every image of the past that is not recognized by the present as one of its own concerns threatens to disappear irretrievably" (1999b, 247). The present decides, as it were, which fragments of the past are worth saving.

Although with positive *Barbarentum* the emphasis shifts to clearing traces instead of collecting them, this act of clearing is not blind annihilation. It is directed against "the oppressive wealth of ideas," the "horrific mishmash of styles and ideologies produced during the last century," the overloaded bourgeois interior, the overwhelming "culture": all those traces that hinder authentic thought and experience.[24] Destruction, then, could refer to the blasting of a deceptive form of experience in order to construct new relations to objects. Objects are "destroyed" by being wrenched from their established context and placed in novel configurations, which can produce new modes of knowing (A. Benjamin and Osborne, 1994a, xi).

The difference between oppressive tradition and constructive destruction is captured in "The Destructive Character" as follows: "Some people pass things down to posterity, by making them untouchable and thus conserving them; others pass on situations, by making them practicable and thus liquidating them. The latter are called the destructive" (2005b, 542). This is the destructive practice Benjamin favors. Fascist destruction, however, is grounded in, and limited by, the former principle of conservation. Therefore, as Alexander García Düttmann also points out, fascist destruction is not radical *enough* (1994, 35). According to Düttmann, fascism finds its condition of possibility in destruction but does not allow itself to get carried away by total destruction (40). The barbarism of fascism does not seek the destruction of tradition but its preservation— together with the conservation of capitalism. It destroys in order to secure its status quo and its future and prevent any other future from taking place. Fascist destruction seeks delimitation, while the destruction motivated by *Barbarentum* strives for openness. For this reason, the latter is vulnerable and excessive.[25] Benjamin's "positive barbarianhood" destroys tradition by debunking its authoritative function and rethinking the role of the past in the present.[26] For the barbarian, tradition is a toolbox to construct different futures.

Benjamin's ideas on the relation between destruction and tradition echo Friedrich Nietzsche's ideas in "On the Use and Abuse of History for Life" (Vom Nutzen und Nachteil der Historie für das Leben, 1874). In this work, Nietzsche argues that the oppressive weight of history and overload of tradition destroy the healthy energy of a people, and he makes a "barbarian" plea not to suffocate the present with too much reflection on the past. Benjamin's resignification of barbarism can also be correlated with Nietzsche's project of *Umwerthung*—one of the watchwords of his philosophy—which has been translated as "transvaluation" and "revaluation."[27] Nietzsche's project of a "transvaluation of all values" refers to a radical rethinking of the values of the Judeo-Christian tradition and the slave morality it stands for, in favor of more life-affirming values, which endorse instinct, irrationality, and an exaltation of life. Nietzsche not only seeks to negate and invert the values that underlie Western philosophy and tradition but also sets up a new "dialetheic model of valuation," which endorses contradictions within the same value. According to this model, a value can be "both true and false as well as neither true nor false" (Dries 2010, 30, 41). This endorsement of contradictory qualities within the same concept typifies Benjamin's *Barbarentum* as both affirmative and destructive. It also corresponds with the contradictions and tensions Benjamin introduces to several traditional concepts—such as experience, poverty, and destruction.

The term *Barbarentum* in "Experience and Poverty" is paradigmatic in capturing the complex relation between tradition and destruction. The entire essay is structured as a dialectics between different pairs: (richness of) experience and poverty, human and nonhuman/technological, old and new, tradition and destruction, and positive and negative barbarism. At first glance, there seems to be no place for an outside to the structure of doubles—a third element that challenges this structure. However, I argue that the other appears in the text as the remainder of the passage from *Barbarei* to a new *Barbarentum*: the suffix *-ei* of *Barbarei* gives its place to the suffix *-tum* (or, in English, *barbarianhood* replaces the violent *-ism* of *barbarism*). The only trace that remains from *Barbarei* is the "bar bar"—the unintelligible mumblings of a foreign language, which escape the destructive force of the new barbarism to become the starting point for the formation of *Barbar*entum.

The "little" that may survive the destructive force of the new positive barbarism so that one can "build up further" is not a concrete and coherent piece of tradition but a small fragment of that tradition, nonsensical by itself but placed in a new constellation and transformed. This fragment is here the "bar bar"—the promise of a new language that was already ingrained in the old and that can steer, but not determine, the future.[28]

At the same time, Benjamin's use of the suffix *-tum* challenges the deterministic course of *Barbarei*. By replacing the ending (*-ei*) of the old *Barbarei* and its history—a history Benjamin sees as concomitant with civilization—Benjamin's new, positive barbarism points in a different direction. The old barbarism is deprived of its teleology, as the ending of *Barbarei* changes into *-tum*, and from the little that remains ("bar bar") a new start can be envisioned. Could this be another way in which Benjamin's *Barbarentum* tries to change the future and divert the unstoppable course of fascism—the total overcoming of Europe by negative barbarism—by performatively changing the end of this course in the word itself?

Barbarentum does not only try to change the course of fascism but aspires to break the historical continuum of which fascism is only a small part. Based on Benjamin's maxim in "Theses on the Philosophy of History" (1940), barbarism (what Benjamin calls *Barbarei*) is interwoven with civilization. But if barbarism and civilization are two sides of the same coin, then barbarism is unable to disrupt the structures of civilization, because it operates within these structures. By contrast, *Barbarentum* does not only aspire to replace *Barbarei* with an affirmative concept and thereby reverse the hierarchy between barbarism and civilization. It also aspires to disrupt the closed circle of history within which this opposition thrives.

In 1940, when he writes his "Theses on the Philosophy of History," Benjamin does not see a way out of this circle: the intertwinement of civilization and barbarism locks history in a vicious circle. If we remain trapped within this circle, redemption is impossible. Perhaps, then, the exit he did not see in 1940 can be detected in his thinking seven years earlier, in "Experience and Poverty": not *Barbarei*, but another kind of barbarism with the name *Barbarentum* could become the force "to blast open the continuum of history" (1999b, 254). The aim of Benjamin's language, Christopher Bracken writes, "would not be to 'name' the experience of the past but, by uttering a 'word' that interrupts the progress of history, to actualize the present" (2002, 341). That word is here *Barbarentum*.

Barbarentum is not civilization's loyal opposite but a rupture in the edifice sustained by *Kultur* and *Barbarei*. Viewed in this way, "Experience and Poverty" does not suggest a choice between a positive and a negative notion within an oppositional structure, but through *Barbarentum* it shakes the ground on which both the old barbarism and its traditionally positive opposites (civilization, culture, humanism) stand. Benjamin's *barbarianhood* breaks new ground through existing oppositions.

The Translation of Barbarism and the Barbarism of Translation

The conceptual and epistemological implications of *Barbarentum* are inextricable from this term's performance in language, that is, its linguistic deviation from the other two "barbarisms" in Benjamin. The translator of the essay into English, Rodney Livingstone, overlooks the difference of *Barbarentum* by translating it as "barbarism." With this in mind, the question arises: What happens to the complex operations of *Barbarentum* in Benjamin's text the moment it is translated as "barbarism" in English?

If the meaning and philosophical content of *Barbarentum* is inscribed in its form, then "barbarism" is a mistranslation not just because it does not convey the unusual form of the German term but because in failing to do so, it also transforms its illocutionary force.[29] However, Benjamin's own views on translation in "The Task of the Translator," especially his contention that translation should not strive for any likeness to the original, somewhat complicate the assessment of the translation of *Barbarentum* as failed due to its lack of correspondence to the original. "No translation would be possible if in its ultimate essence it strove for likeness to the original," Benjamin writes (1999b, 73). Translation is the original's "afterlife" and marks a process wherein the original undergoes transformation and renewal (72–73). Therefore, following Benjamin, translation should not strive for fidelity to the original.

With Benjamin's views in mind, on what grounds could we evaluate the English translation of *Barbarentum*? Benjamin's suggested independence of translation from the original is not a free pass for any translation that deviates from the original to be automatically considered felicitous. On the contrary: Benjamin's standpoint underscores the significance of translation as a work in its own right. Translation is not a transparency placed over the original but a new text, and as such it can be subjected to critical scrutiny.

The focus here is on the differences translation produces in the materiality of Benjamin's text. In this venture, Lawrence Venuti's views on the translation of philosophical texts are a valuable companion.[30] Although I read "barbarism" as a translation that neutralizes significant aspects of the text's critical performance, my intention is not to dismiss the translation as wrong but to draw attention to translation as an act: not to how (accurately or not) translation reproduces the original but to what it *does*. Thus, I examine its performative effects and the difference of those effects— what Venuti calls the "remainder"—in relation to the source text.[31]

"Reading for the remainder," Venuti argues, "means focusing on the linguistic and cultural differences" that the translation inscribes in the source text (1996b, 28). Venuti calls for a comparison between translation and original that seeks to reflect on "the deviations and excesses of the translation" (29). This kind of reading or comparing is more literary, because it is concerned not only with conceptual analysis but also with the formal properties of language (29). Further, it relates the differences in translation to domestic traditions, institutional practices, hierarchies of styles, and discourses. The remainder in translation, then, is also telling for how concept formation in philosophical discourse is determined by such linguistic or cultural conditions (29).

When translating *Barbarentum*, the translator is confronted with a double foreignness. The German term is not just foreign to English but calls attention to itself because of its difference from the standard term

Barbarei. As the key term in Benjamin's essay, *Barbarentum* demands "a violent translation" that dislocates it rather than domesticates it in Anglo-American discourse.[32] Thus, a translation of *Barbarentum* with a term such as "barbarianhood" would have been more felicitous in preserving the foreignness of Benjamin's term in English and making the reader conscious of its difference from the standard term "barbarism."

The translation as "barbarism," however, assimilates the foreignness of *Barbarentum* into the disciplinary discourse of Anglo-American philosophy. The style that has dominated British philosophy since Bacon and Locke, says Venuti, prefers "current usage," smooth syntax, and "univocal meaning" (1996b, 29). Accordingly, English-language translating prefers "immediate intelligibility" and avoids any "linguistic or stylistic peculiarities that might pre-empt the illusion of transparency" (29). The translator conforms to this tendency by choosing a familiar term. His choice makes recognizable what is foreign; Benjamin's text makes foreign what is recognizable.

Being alert to the remainder makes us more aware, and thus also more critical, of traditions and norms in both Anglo-American and German contexts. It is remarkable that the word "barbarism" in English collapses all three German terms into one: *Barbarismus*, *Barbarei*, and *Barbarentum*. The use of the single signifier "barbarism" in English, as opposed to its partitioning in German into three words, may carry cultural undertones. The use of a single term in English for these related but divergent concepts may be seen as confusing, whereas the German distinction could be read as precise in evading ambiguity. Is this a case of English vagueness versus German precision and clarity? Using one term in English, one could claim, collapses the nuances and distinctiveness of these concepts in German. Furthermore, since they are not linguistically distinguished, these concepts seem to have no *proper* conceptual place in English. Since there is just one "barbarism," challenges or resignifications can come only from within this concept, unless, of course, a term such as "barbarianhood" would be coined.

By using the same term for what (for Benjamin) are different concepts, the translation makes Benjamin's *Barbarentum* part of the same historical circle that ties civilization with barbarism (i.e., *Kultur* and *Barbarei*). As the distinction between the two terms is lost in translation, the conceptual potential of *Barbarentum*—its aspiration to interrupt the historical continuum—is weakened. This potential is intertwined with the word's form. In *Barbarentum* form and content are in tune—they enhance each other.

The way the translation assimilates Benjamin's writing into the Anglo-American academic tradition is also evident in the translation of the phrase in which the term *Barbarentum* is introduced in "Experience and Poverty." Benjamin writes: "Und damit eine Art von neuem Barbarentum" (Hence a new kind of barbarism). There is a small but crucial difference in the way the words are arranged in the translation: a literal translation of "*eine Art von neuem Barbarentum*" is "*a kind of* new barbarism" (or, even better, "barbarianhood"). This formulation indicates that Benjamin's new barbarism is an approximation: "some kind of barbarism," but not quite.[33] This phrasing refuses to absolutize the term and infuses it with an ambiguous quality, which makes it difficult to pin down. This "kind of" new barbarism, as the phrase suggests, is a catachresis for a concept that cannot find precise expression in language. The choice for the uncommon *Barbarentum* enhances this catachresis: *Barbarentum*, as well as the phrasing that surrounds it, indicates that Benjamin's new concept resists linguistic consolidation and univocity.

In the actual English translation—"*a new kind of* barbarism" (emphasis added)—the different position of the word "kind" has semantic consequences. Kind here connotes "species," "sort," or "category." The phrase could thus be paraphrased as "a new *category* of barbarism" instead of "some kind of" new barbarism. This formulation reflects the categorizing impulse in the Anglo-American tradition and the need to ground the term in a recognizable binary structure rather than let it slip away in vague formulations and approximations. In the source text, even if we would read "Art" as "sort" or "category," the implications would still be very different from those of the translation. A translation with "*a kind of new* barbarism" would not suggest just that there are more kinds of barbarism but that there may be other kinds of *new* barbarism as well—so this particular new barbarian project might not be the only possible alternative. In this way, the risk that Benjamin's "new barbarism" may develop into a new singular authoritative system is evaded. In a self-critical mode, Benjamin's formulation acknowledges that other kinds of new barbarisms may come to contest the one proposed by Benjamin and perhaps even replace it more successfully.

The English translation erases the distinctive features of Benjamin's writing. "In criticism and in theater," Betsy Flèche remarks, "Benjamin emphasizes the anxiety of performance: live criticism—'quick,' rather than taxidermic—(or even taxonomic) and dead" (1999, 103). In the phrase "eine Art von neuem Barbarentum," the concept *Barbarentum* is kept purposefully indeterminate, playful, and resistant to "taxonomic" (if not "taxidermic") categorizations. The slight switch of word order in the translation has the opposite effect: it places the phrase on a procrustean bed and adjusts *Barbarentum* to a normative discourse, both by translating it as "barbarism" and by accommodating it within an existing taxonomy and dichotomy.

In domesticating Benjamin's text, the translator commits what Benjamin in "The Task of the Translator" considers the "basic error of the translator"—preserving "the state in which his own language happens to be instead of allowing his language to be powerfully affected by the foreign tongue" (1999b, 81). By minimizing the provocative qualities in Benjamin's phrasing, the translation—whether this was the translator's intention or not—is more concerned with the domestic status quo than with the foreign text. According to Venuti, this translation would subscribe to an "ethics of sameness." This is contrasted with an "ethics of difference," which calls for maintaining the foreignness of the translated concept for domestic readerships, thereby informing and simultaneously provoking the readers (1996b, 30).

Therefore, translating Benjamin's barbarian project is a challenging task. As a philosopher and a critic, Benjamin wants to disrupt the dominant language—not only historical discourse or the language of fascism but also the language of the philosophical canon. His writing challenges the institutional limits of philosophy by mixing philosophical and literary modes in ways that make philosophy's discursive borders visible and more vulnerable to critique. His "barbarian" style involves the use of minor linguistic forms traditionally excluded from major philosophical idioms. In so doing, Benjamin's writing gives saturated concepts a new direction but also marks the limitations in the use of these concepts within the philosophical tradition. His stylistic innovation harbors a political project, which opens philosophical discourse to new kinds of thinking through new kinds of writing. This Benjamin, the innovator of language, is here lost in the English translation.

Looking into the difference the translation inscribes in the source text not only invites a rethinking of Benjamin's text but also makes translation as such visible. Foregrounding the performance of the translation of a philosophical text helps shatter the illusion of the transparency of philosophical language as universal. This, in its turn, can lead to a critical rethinking of academic conventions (Venuti 1996b, 24–25).[34] In this sense, calling attention to the translation also becomes part of Benjamin's barbarian project.

Toward a Barbarian Methodology

Benjamin's essay contains unorthodox conceptual pairings and collocations: constructive destruction, positive barbarism, cultural excess leading to poverty of experience, dehumanized names that rehumanize humans. Moreover, the central notions in the essay hold equivocal and contradictory connotations *within* themselves. Barbarism, experience, poverty, and destruction are all notions with potentially positive as well as negative meanings. Their indeterminacy does not weaken the essay's argumentative force; on the contrary, the essay makes its point *through* these inconsistencies, tensions, and obscurities. Benjamin's text survives its own contradictions because it does not present them as either/or choices or absolute oppositions but as coexisting possibilities. Concepts do not have a clear-cut, consistent meaning throughout the text or throughout Benjamin's writings, because for Benjamin their meanings and functions are not predetermined and their fate has not been sealed.

For Benjamin, there are no good or bad concepts as such. They are invented anew in the act of writing and with every critical reading. Their constant movement—an oscillation between their negative and affirmative functions, between their traditional and novel usages—makes it impossible for the critic to define them conclusively. Benjamin's notion of critique, as it emerges through the performance of concepts in this and the other essays examined here, is not a means of imposing judgment but an act that participates in the creation and transformation of the concepts it addresses.[35] In Benjamin's texts, as Carol Jacobs argues, philosophical concepts present themselves rather than are represented, described, and explicated: "It is an error to search Benjamin's work for stability in the terminology. Nothing works devoid of context, performance. These are texts that must always be read anew, less for the referents they do not seem to preserve than for their *Darstellung*: here lives, works, theories, terms, are saved only like phenomena in ideas, only like stars in a constellation" (1999, 7). Benjamin is not interested in articulating an overall coherent philosophy. What matters is what a concept does (or does not do) in a particular context. His essay "keeps its readers deliberately off-balance" and subscribes to a "methodology of destabilization" (Flèche 1999, 105, 107–8). What the essay seems to say is often contradicted elsewhere. This gives shape to a "barbarian writing" whereby the only consistent principle would be Benjamin's own dictum: "always radical, never consistent" (1994, 300).[36]

The loose ends produced by seeming inconsistencies invite the reader to focus on the particularities of every text, formulation, and word instead of trying to "taxonomize" Benjamin's writings. Perhaps it is part of Benjamin's "barbarian methodology" to insert hidden details in his texts—such as the unexpected term *Barbarentum*—which activate the critical faculties of the reader or translator. "Experience and Poverty" incites us to read it against the grain, not to extract its overall meaning but to search for the oddities and elements that do not quite fit. In this way, as Benjamin writes in "The Fireside Saga," we are transformed from "proud owners" (of texts, words, concepts) into "practical critics" (2005a, 152).[37] The reader or translator of Benjamin's text turns into a potential new barbarian, who starts with minute discrepancies and tries to make "a little go a long way"—perhaps a "way" very different from the one Benjamin himself envisioned.

Benjamin knew that his mode of writing was bound to be "the cause of certain obscurities."[38] But this was part of his method. As he wrote in his opening paragraph in "The Task of the Translator," "No poem is intended for the reader, no picture for the beholder, no symphony for the listener" (1999b, 70). His text is not supposed to serve the reader. Not being "intended for the reader" is not an elitist statement about the work of art (or of translation) but an essential feature of his "barbarian methodology."

His mode of writing produces questions instead of answers, transforms concepts, uses established terms in alienating combinations, and refuses to offer closure. As a result, the "barbarisms" his writing generates haunt the interpretations and translations of his texts and condemn them to incompleteness. In "Experience and Poverty," the open relation between experience and poverty in the title is characteristic in this respect: instead of titling the essay "Poverty *of* Experience," or using some other preposition or subordinating conjunction, Benjamin joins the two terms with a simple "and." The title thus sets up a dialectical relation between the two concepts. "Poverty" and "experience" stand independently in an unsettled relation, which the reader is invited to (re)fashion after reading the essay.

If for Benjamin the original does not dictate the translation's afterlife, this also applies to the fate of his own text. The obscurities, ambivalent passages, and fragmentary sentences make his writing susceptible to creative interpretations as well as misreadings and mistranslations. But this also constitutes the instructive aspect of his writing: the point of his texts lies in both what they say and how they say it. In the words of Eduardo Cadava, "The movement of his language inscribes the lessons he wishes us to learn" (1997, 124).

Benjamin's barbarian methodology involves the partial renunciation of control over his text and its subjection to misunderstandings. This, too, is a quality of Benjamin's "destructive character": "The destructive character has no interest in being understood. Attempts in this direction he regards as superficial. Being misunderstood cannot harm him. On the contrary, he provokes it, just as oracles, those destructive institutions of the state, provoked it" (2005b, 542). The speech of the destructive character instigates misunderstanding, just as the speech of the oracle is replete with enigmatic utterances, polemic statements, and obscure warnings. The oracle, which is here likened to the destructive character, is supposed to predict, and thus also determine, the future by either enabling or preventing certain developments. However, the oracle in Greek antiquity, with its equivocal, confusing, and sometimes almost unintelligible speech, often prefigures the future in the alien, barbarian language of that future. Paradoxically, the oracle's speech, notoriously enigmatic and open to interpretation, signifies the unpredictability of the future as it tries to predict and direct it. The oracle speaks in an elusive, barbarian language, because the future and its language are not yet written.[39] The language of the destructive character, as well as of Benjamin's writings, has comparable qualities: it is inconclusive and open.[40]

By provoking misunderstanding, Benjamin in fact communicates power to the translator or reader of his text, which in their turn can use it, abuse it, redirect it, dismiss it, or hang on to a detail and build something new that makes sense in another era and context. Causing misunderstanding can be a radical form of (self-)critique, because it suggests a willingness to subject your own writing to good or bad translations, readings, and recontextualizations. It entails keeping distance from your own text and ingraining a self-critical attitude in it. Perhaps this self-critical stance is suggested in the enigmatic phrase that concludes the second-to-last paragraph of "Experience and Poverty": "And now we need to step back and keep our distance" (2005b, 735).

Benjamin keeps his distance from his own text as he releases it to the mercy of his readers and translators. This critical distance captures a crucial difference between the barbarism of totalitarian or authoritative regimes and Benjamin's new, positive barbarism: the willingness not only to subvert the enemy's language, the language of others, but also your own, by opening it up to misreadings, reappropriations, and questioning.

The lesson his essay teaches the reader does not lie in the continuing validity of its arguments. To argue that Benjamin's text survives time and continues to be relevant today might or might not be true but is perhaps beside the point. To assume the text's timelessness and continued relevance—as it often happens in studies of Benjamin—could even do violence to the text's instructive power, especially when it leads contemporary criticism to fetishize Benjamin's oeuvre. This fetishization of Benjamin and his work is the kind of objectification his text resists. Benjamin's text is marked by the tireless intention to disrupt the field of the same. But whether this disruption actually takes place depends not on a permanent quality in his text but on its performance. What a certain term, sentence, or essay is able to do in a certain historical moment, it might fail to do in another, future moment. What "Experience and Poverty" could do in 1933 may not be possible now, while in our present a new potential in the text might be activated. This is perhaps the crux of his barbarian methodology and the legacy of his text, as it opens itself to its own self-destruction.

5

Barbarism in Repetition

LITERATURE'S WAITING FOR THE BARBARIANS

> The reign of independent barbarism is now contracted to a narrow span; and the remnant of Calmucks or Uzbecks, whose forces may be almost numbered, cannot seriously excite the apprehensions of the great republic of Europe. Yet this apparent security should not tempt us to forget that new enemies and unknown dangers may possibly arise from some obscure people, scarcely visible in the map of the world.
> —Edward Gibbon, *The History of the Decline and Fall of the Roman Empire*

Reflecting on the second half of the eighteenth century, English historian Edward Gibbon points out that the barbarians, as they were known in Roman times, have disappeared. Nevertheless, he does not believe that the "great republic of Europe"—seen as the domain of civilization—should rest assured. The barbarian threat to civilization is always there in "scarcely visible," "obscure people" (1912, 177). Their invisibility continues to tantalize the civilized imagination and to foster their myth.

Barbarian enemies—so the legends tell us—do not confront the troops of the civilized world on the battlefield. Barbarians are not supposed to have a fixed location, as they hardly ever lead a sedentary lifestyle. They are believed to be somewhere "out there": nomads, roaming vast deserts and steppes; warriors, passing through untrodden mountains; people free from constraints and moral inhibitions, acting on their desires, instincts, and passions—wild, violent, untamable; with monstrous features and strange, inhuman customs; dangerous, dreadful, captivating. Their threat is that of an invasion from the outside into domestic territory, which would violently disrupt a prosperous society and bring about civilization's regression to a primitive, barbaric state. The arrival of barbarians at the gates of civilization is often cast in apocalyptic scenarios engaging civilized humanity as a whole (White 1972, 20). "Waiting for the Barbarians" (Περιμένοντας τους βαρβάρους, 1904), a poem by the Greek poet Constantine P. Cavafy, who lived in Alexandria, Egypt, and the novel *Waiting for the Barbarians* (1980) by South African author J. M. Coetzee, both unravel around the anticipation of such an invasion, which never takes place.

The barbarian operations that take center stage in this chapter are enabled by the demonstrative repetition of foundational categories of civilization. I have probed the implications of Benjamin's use of another name for barbarism (*Barbarentum*), which slightly modifies the common German term (*Barbarei*) in order to redirect its violence toward a new project. Here, I show how Cavafy's poem and Coetzee's novel stick to the conventional categories—"barbarian," "barbarism"—and try to revise them by repeating them into new meanings and effects.

The key concept in this comparative reading of Cavafy's poem and Coetzee's novel is *repetition*. First, repetition takes the form of intertextuality and allegorization. The second concern is how the words barbarism and barbarian can be repeated into new senses in the space of literature and redeployed in ways that create confusion in their established uses.

The concept of repetition here is also linked with two other concepts: "history" and "allegory." Cavafy's and Coetzee's works reiterate history's categories in order to perform another kind of history in literature.[1] Many critics have tried to capture the works' relation to history by allegorizing them. Some critics view either the poem or the novel as a universal allegory of the human condition. Others undertake a historically rooted and contextual interpretation. Although I briefly discuss universalist and historicist allegorizations of both works, I propose another mode of reading, which I call "barbarian allegory." Through the concept of barbarian allegory I envision an alternative approach to history, actualized in the space of literature.

Finally, drawing from Jacques Derrida's and Judith Butler's views on performativity and on the possibility for alteration through repetition,

I probe the workings of the repetitive use of the term "barbarian" in Cavafy's and Coetzee's texts. Through this repetition, the poem and the novel try to shape ground for a new relationality between self and other, beyond the oppositional thinking of "civilized versus barbarian."

The title of this chapter can be read in two ways: it refers to the repetition of the name "barbarian" in literature and to a potential reconceptualization of history and historical categories through literature; and it denotes the constructive barbarism that potentially lies in the operation of repetition itself. In the latter sense, "barbarian operations" can take effect through the repetition of normative and familiar categories in slightly different or subversive ways. Repetition is, after all, inherent in the term "barbarian," which is etymologically grounded in the perception of the other's language as a series of repetitive sounds ("bar bar").

In probing the issue of repetition, I take my cue from the theory of the performative (or speech act theory), which is employed here in its initial conception by J. L. Austin (1962), and particularly in the direction it takes in the poststructuralist thought of Jacques Derrida as a general theory of iterability and in Judith Butler's theory of gender and subject constitution.[2] Austin's theory of the performative focuses on the aspect of language that performs the act it designates instead of just representing, describing, or stating a fact. This describes the performative, as opposed to the constative, aspect of an utterance.[3] Although literary theorists extensively use his theory, Austin's account explicitly excludes literature from consideration. Literature for him is language used "not seriously" and "in ways parasitic upon its normal use." For Austin, performative utterances can be studied only when issued in "ordinary circumstances" and in "serious" uses (1980, 22).

In his version of the performative, laid out in "Signature, Event, Context" (1972) and *Limited Inc* (1988), Derrida takes up Austin's views but underscores the iterability and citationality of any mark as the condition of possibility for any performative utterance.[4] Contrary to Austin, Derrida deconstructs the opposition between "citational utterances" and "singular" or "original" utterances (1982, 326). The citation of an utterance is the condition for the singular to take place. For Derrida, this general iterability is a law of language: for a sign to be a sign, it has to be able to be repeated and cited, even in what Austin calls "non-serious" circumstances, like literature (Culler 2000, 509). As a result, literature, which Austin considers non-serious, parasitic language because it is a form of citation of "normal" language, becomes an exemplary case for Derrida's theory of the general iterability of signs. "Iterability" does not just signify identical repetition—"repeatability of the same"—but "alterability of this same idealized in the singularity of the event, for instance, in this or that speech act" (Derrida 1988, 119). In this sense, iterability makes sure that concepts, utterances, or marks in general are never "safe" from contamination and change (119). The repetition of a concept makes its alteration possible.

Butler extends this view beyond language to address the constitution of subjects through the citation and repetition of norms. According to Butler, we become subjects through repeated acts, which reflect social conventions, norms, and habits. The citation of norms is thus constitutive of subjects. As she argues in *Bodies That Matter* (1993) and in *Excitable Speech* (1997a), the repetition of certain utterances in the social world enhances dominant discourses and their central categories. However, this also means that dominant discourses depend on the repetition of utterances and are thus not self-sufficient. If norms are fortified only insofar as they are reiterated, then the repetition of normative categories could lead to the destabilization of authoritative discourses by producing a citation that challenges the force of the norm (1993, 14–15). The possibility of resistance and change lies in the limited space between the norm and the way it is carried out, which is not always according to expectation. As I argue, in Cavafy's and Coetzee's works, the destabilization of the category of the barbarian comes about through its stubborn citation, which aspires to produce difference in repetition.

Because the force of normative categories is grounded in their repetitive use in different places and moments in time, they have a strong historical dimension. However, their historical force remains tied to their repetitive uses in each present. As Jonathan Culler notes in his discussion of Butler's views, "You can't control the terms that you choose to name yourselves. But the historical character of the performative process creates the possibility of a political struggle" (2000, 515). Here, I show how such a struggle can take place within literature.

Repeating the Title

Cavafy's "Waiting for the Barbarians" is staged in a decadent city, not historically defined, but with allusions to Rome.[5] Diana Haas and George Savidis suggest that Cavafy's main historiographical source for this poem was Edward Gibbon's *The Decline and Fall of the Roman Empire*, which Cavafy was reading at the time.[6] The poem is structured as a dialogue—a person (designated here as "the first speaker") poses a series of questions and another person ("the second speaker") answers them. The questions concern the commotion and preparations the city is making, the reason for which the first speaker wishes to know. The answer to all his questions is the same, repeated again and again, with slight variations and additions: "Because the barbarians are coming today." The reader and the first speaker are therefore informed that everyone is preparing to receive the barbarians, who are coming to take over the city:

What are we waiting for, assembled in the forum?

    The barbarians are due here today.

Why isn't anything happening in the senate?
Why do the senators sit there without legislating?

    Because the barbarians are coming today.
    What laws can the senators make now?
    Once the barbarians are here, they'll do the legislating.

Why did our emperor get up so early,
and why is he sitting at the city's main gate,
on his throne, in state, wearing the crown?

    Because the barbarians are coming today
    and the emperor is waiting to receive their leader.
    He has even prepared a scroll to give him,
    replete with titles, with imposing names.

Why have our two consuls and praetors come out today
wearing their embroidered, their scarlet togas?
Why have they put on bracelets with so many amethysts,
and rings sparkling with magnificent emeralds?

Why are they carrying elegant canes
beautifully worked in silver and gold?

> Because the barbarians are coming today
> and things like that dazzle the barbarians.

Why don't our distinguished orators come forward as usual
to make their speeches, say what they have to say?

> Because the barbarians are coming today
> and they're bored by rhetoric and public speaking.

Why this sudden restlessness, this confusion?
(How serious people's faces have become.)
Why are the streets and squares emptying so rapidly,
everyone going home lost in thought?

> Because night has fallen and the barbarians have not come.
> And some who have just returned from the border say
> there are no barbarians any longer.

And now, what's going to happen to us without barbarians?
They were, those people, a kind of solution.
(1904; translated by Edmund Keeley and Philip Sherrard [1992,
18–19])

Due to its dialogic form the poem is easily imagined as a stage performance. In fact, there are two levels of staging in the poem embedded within each other. While the speakers stage a dialogue in front of the readers' audience, an elaborate stage is being set within the poem by the citizens, the emperor, the senators, consuls, praetors, and orators, anticipating the real actors (the barbarians) to rush onto the city's stage.

Like the poem, Coetzee's *Waiting for the Barbarians* is situated in an undefined town and period. The Magistrate, who narrates the story, is peacefully doing his job in a small town at the edge of the "Empire." The advent of Colonel Joll, a functionary of the "Third Bureau," disrupts the tranquility of his life and brings him face-to-face with the brutal reality of the Empire. Colonel Joll arrives to collect information about "barbarians" supposedly planning attacks against the Empire and causing border troubles. The absurdity of Joll's enterprise becomes obvious when he captures, interrogates, tortures, and imprisons a large group of native fishing people who have nothing to do with any barbarian attacks. From then on, the Magistrate refuses to cooperate with the Empire and its practitioners. He eventually ends up in prison and is tortured after being wrongly accused of treason. He is released again when the people of the Third Bureau leave the town. The barbarian invasion the Empire so much feared does not take place, and the Empire's expeditionary force sent to confront the barbarians is dispersed in the desert and disappears without ever reaching the enemy.

Coetzee borrows the title of Cavafy's poem and thereby acknowledges it as the novel's pre-text. Both works can be placed within a broader intertextual network that engages the theme of waiting for the arrival of the other. This topos has been staged in a series of literary works, from Dino Buzzati's *The Tartar Steppe* (*Il deserto dei Tartari*, 1938) to Samuel Beckett's *Waiting for Godot* (*En attendant Godot*, 1952) and Julien Gracq's *The Opposing Shore* (*Le rivage des Syrtes*, 1951).[7]

To these works one can add several poems that converse with Cavafy's barbarians. Extending over more than ten countries, these poems either respond directly to Cavafy's poem and the questions it poses or borrow its dialogic structure and appropriate it for contemporary situations.[8] Examples in the latter category are American poet James Merrill's "After Cavafy," where the role of the barbarians is filled by the Japanese; Richard O'Connell's "Waiting for the Terrorists," which takes over the dialogic structure of Cavafy's poem to address the events following the attacks on September 11, 2001;[9] Serbian poet Jovan Christić's "Varvari"; and Alistair Te Ariki Campbell's "Waiting for the Pakeha," a poem from New Zealand, in which the natives are waiting for the European settlers.[10]

Coetzee's novel is perhaps the best-known restaging of Cavafy's poem in literature. What is the function of the demonstrative announcement of the poem as the novel's main intertext by the adoption of the same title? In the poem's title, the progressive form of the verb points out the lack of closure in the process of waiting. It is a process without end, as the advent of the object of waiting does not take place in the poem and is eternally deferred. In the novel, the barbarians also fail to arrive. In both cases, the title fails to fulfill its implicit promise: to produce the barbarians as presences. In breaking this promise, the title becomes an *anaphora*, which, according to Shoshana Felman's definition, is an "act of beginning ceaselessly renewed through the repetition of promises not carried out, not kept" (2003, 24). It is because the title does not keep its promise that this promise can be renewed.[11] The anaphora of Cavafy's title keeps reproducing its promise in an array of texts and cultural objects that bear the same title, some of which will also be discussed further.

Iterability, Derrida argues, suggests that the full presence of a text—as an absolute correspondence between the text and its meaning—is never attained (1988, 129). The intention of a text never reaches its *telos*, because the text keeps referring to something else that slips away. An intention, like a promise, ceases to exist as soon as it is realized. The topos of "waiting for the barbarians" exemplifies this law of iterability as the promise of full presence deferred by means of repeating itself. The barbarians' arrival is never actualized, and its promise can therefore be renewed through its repetition in other forms and contexts.

The iteration of the title of Cavafy's poem in Coetzee's novel results in a new event. This event stands as a challenge to the poem, testing the Cavafian theme in different spatial and temporal coordinates. Therefore, Coetzee's repetition of Cavafy's title invites us both to explore the echoes of the poem in the novel and to reread the poem through the experience of the novel.

The Ambivalence of the Speaking Voice

Although Cavafy and Coetzee are situated in very different contexts, their position is marked by a certain ambivalence, which infiltrates the speaking voice in both the poem and the novel. Coetzee's writing is caught up in the ambivalence that characterizes oppositional white South African writing. While trying to interrogate the binary divisions of apartheid society, white writing is inevitably caught up in them. As a result, it is simultaneously implicated in, and opposed to, the hegemonic oppression of colonialism (Kossew 1996, 2, 7). This ambivalence haunts the position of most protagonists in Coetzee's novels, as well as Coetzee's own position as an author.

In a different but somewhat parallel way, Cavafy also occupied an ambivalent position. Originally Greek but living in Egypt, being part of the Greek community in Alexandria and having to work in the service of the British Empire in order to earn a living, Cavafy was caught amid conflicting worlds. Due to his complex position, he remained a marginal figure all his life—a marginality enhanced by his homosexuality. A Greek, a European, and a Levantine at the same time, he was, as Martin McKinsey has called him, "a civilized barbarian" (2000, 42).

Ambivalence and oscillation between belonging and not-belonging mark the speaking voices in the poem and the novel. The position of the first speaker in the poem is quite obscure. The use of the first-person plural in his questions about the city situates him as a member of the community—a citizen of the city. However, his complete ignorance about what is happening places him outside the spectrum of knowledge to which an insider would normally have access.[12]

The first speaker's storm of questions can be attributed to sincere ignorance with regard to the reasons for the commotion. Nevertheless, one can also read in these questions an inquisitive spirit that refuses to passively wait for the barbarians and uncritically assist in the preparations, but interrogates the official course of action, seeks the underlying reasons for the city's frenzy, and questions the rationale of the enterprise of waiting to receive the barbarians. The speaker's questions can be read as a critique of the city's strange resignation and inertia. In this case, with a question such as "Why isn't anything happening in the senate?," the speaker implies that the senate should be more active in times like these.

If the role of the first speaker is to question, the role of the second is to validate the Empire's voice by repeating its official statements in a mechanical way and spreading its propaganda. He is the Empire's parrot. Both the arrival of the barbarians and the city's attitude to their arrival are taken for granted in his replies, which do not betray any signs of doubt.

The repetitive structure of the dialogue, built up as a succession of "why-because" questions and answers, accelerates the rhythmical dynamics of the poem by creating staccato. The iambic meter in the Greek text enhances this rhythmical structure.[13] However, while the structure of the dialogue conveys a sense of anxiety (the heat of the preparations), it simultaneously has a reassuring function, since it turns the poem into a perfectly rational composition: to every question, the voice of civilization (the second speaker) has a clear answer, repeated no less than four times:

"Because the barbarians are coming today." The almost hypnotic effect of this repetition leaves no room for doubting the logic of the answer: the barbarians are coming, and they are the remedy to the predicament of a decaying civilization. The repetition of the reply illustrates the mechanism by which the discourse of civilization sustains itself: it cultivates the illusion of rationality and normalizes its truths by overstating them through repetition.

Nevertheless, the poem's perfectly rational and symmetrical structure collapses in the end. The nonarrival of the barbarians deprives civilization of the only answer it seemed to have and disempowers the second speaker. In light of this nonarrival, suddenly the mechanical repetition of his answer sounds like the stuttering utterances of a barbarian, whose language is perceived as a continuous repetition of the same meaningless sound: "bar bar." His speech loses its ground and status.

Like the first speaker in the poem, the Magistrate in Coetzee's novel is an insider of the Empire, but not quite. Living as he does in a convenient state of ignorance and tranquility, he gradually enters a state of uncertainty and doubt. He ceases to believe in the truths of colonialist discourse and takes an oppositional stance. He realizes, however, that switching sides is not merely a matter of free will, because he cannot avoid his complicity with the discourse of the Empire. As Butler argues, subjects are constituted through social norms and discursive practices (1993, 7). For Butler, there is no voluntarist, intentional subject who "exists quite apart from the regulatory norms which he/she opposes" (15). "The paradox of subjectivation," Butler's argument continues, is "precisely that the subject who would resist such norms is itself enabled, if not produced, by such norms" (15). This captures the Magistrate's predicament. The authoritative discourse of the Empire, within which the Magistrate has been shaped as a subject, is not something he can discard at will, as it is not external to his subjectivity. Caught up in a position where he can neither belong to the oppressors nor to the oppressed, his narrative becomes a battlefield of conflicting discourses.

When Colonel Joll's native prisoners are brought in, the Magistrate sympathizes with them but at the same time watches them from a condescending distance. He does not want them to stay long or return: "I do not want a race of beggars on my hands" (Coetzee 2000, 20). His

sympathy soon gives way to impatience and indignation at "their animal shamelessness," "the filth, the smell, the noise" (20–21). His voice is
replete with contradictions and immersed in the discursive violence of the
Empire, even when he wishes to counter it. Later in the novel he views
the same features he himself had attributed to these natives as a result of
"the settlers' litany of *prejudice*: that barbarians are lazy, immoral, filthy,
stupid" (41, emphasis added). What he had previously taken as a fact he
now regards as a biased and unfair opinion, based on the colonizers' partial judgment.

Once doubt creeps into the Magistrate's life, however, the certainties
of his former life as a blissfully ignorant colonizer are irrevocably shaken.
Nevertheless, even when he questions the Empire's practices, he often contradicts his own critical statements and doubts his actions. After delivering a sermon against the Empire's injustice toward "the barbarians" (the
natives), he cannot help asking himself: "And do I really after all believe
what I have been saying? Do I really look forward to the triumph of the
barbarian way: intellectual torpor, slovenliness, tolerance of disease and
death?" (56).

The Magistrate is not freed from the colonizer's instincts. He takes
obsessive care of a barbarian girl tortured and made lame and blind by
Colonel Joll, and then left behind by her own people. His care, however,
does not fundamentally differ from the practices of her torturer: "I behave
in some ways like a lover—I undress her, I bathe her, I stroke her, I sleep
beside her—but I might equally well tie her to a chair and beat her" (46).
In fondling and kissing her wounds, he recognizes the drive to engrave
himself on her as deeply as her torturers did. Soon enough he realizes that
he and Joll are different sides of the same coin: "For I was not, as I liked
to think, the indulgent, pleasure-loving opposite of the cold rigid Colonel.
I was the lie that Empire tells itself when times are easy, he the truth that
Empire tells when harsh winds blow. Two sides of Imperial rule, no more,
no less" (148–49). It is no coincidence that the novel begins with a description of Colonel Joll's sunglasses, in which the narrator sees a reflection of
himself.

In the barbarian girl the Magistrate sees the possibility of making
contact with the other. Nevertheless, his approach is not free of the logic
of understanding as penetrating and deciphering, typical of the colonial

attitude toward the colonized: "Until the marks on this girl's body are deciphered and understood I cannot let go of her" (33). Her body, however, is impenetrable, "without aperture, without entry" (45). Despite the Magistrate's attempts, the girl remains an unsolved mystery, a stranger.

The girl's blindness makes it impossible for him to exist in her gaze. His gaze cannot be reciprocated, because in her eyes he sees only his own image cast back at him (47). According to Émile Benveniste, subjectivity is produced in the here and now of an utterance. As a result, the "I" cannot just dictate its truths but needs the "you" to sustain its authority and allow it to speak (1966, 225–36). Therefore, the girl's refusal to validate the Magistrate's speech with a response leads the Magistrate to a self-crisis. As Gayatri Spivak argues in her commentary on the novel, "The meaning of his [the Magistrate's] own acts is not clear when he tries to imagine her perspective" (2003, 22). As he continues "to swoop and circle around the irreducible figure of the girl," the meaning he is after, according to Spivak, is "the meaning of the Magistrate as subject, as perceived by the barbarian as other."[14] The girl refuses to yield any determinable meaning through which the Magistrate could articulate his own subjectivity through the other's perspective. Struck by the inability of his language to translate the girl, he starts doubting the signifying capacity of his own language and considers that "perhaps whatever can be articulated is falsely put" (Coetzee 2000, 70). Nevertheless, her untranslatability holds the promise of another language, different from the Empire's fixed set of meanings.

Although the girl is generally cooperative, she speaks only in order to give brief answers on practical matters or to communicate factual information. In response to the Magistrate's inquiries about her torture, she gives him only a strictly factual account of what happened (44). She never gives away emotions; she offers no indication of her desires, wishes, or feelings toward the Magistrate and her torturers; she asks no questions; and she never embellishes her utterances with anything other than facts. The Magistrate perceives her attitude and speech as uncommunicative. There is something ironic in the way the rational speech of a barbarian—devoid of emotions, interpretations, and biased opinions—clashes with the confused, stuttering, self-canceling speech of the Magistrate—the speech of the civilized. Their communicational gap is experienced as such by both sides. She has as little understanding of him as he does of her. "You want to talk all the time," she complains when the Magistrate tells her about his hunting experience; "you should not go hunting if you do not enjoy it" (43–44). Disillusioned by their miscommunication, the Magistrate shakes his head: "That is not the meaning of the story, but what's the use of arguing?" (44). In their interaction, the distinction between civilized and barbarian is transfigured into a difference between two foreign subjectivities, two barbarians, neither of whom makes sense to the other.

The girl causes the Magistrate's narrative to stutter and stumble. He fails to make any confident statement about her, as her subjectivity remains inaccessible—"what I call submission may be nothing but indifference" (60). The girl interrupts the flow of his speech and leads it to dead ends and unresolved question marks. His language turns into the stuttering speech of the barbarian.

However, despite his failure to unfold the mystery of the girl, the Magistrate does not end up imposing his own voice on her in the same way that the Empire constructs its others on its own terms. As Spivak argues, the Magistrate "tries to grasp the barbarian in an embrace that is both singular and responsible" (2003, 21–22). He waits for the girl to talk about her experience in the torture chamber and doesn't make up his own story about her. Despite his willingness to make contact with her, he does not force her into it. He thereby shows his willingness to live with the other, without having access to her subjectivity.

The "waiting" of the novel's title could also refer to the process of waiting for the other to speak without using words that others have chosen for her. Therefore, the girl's silence grants her a form of agency. By refusing to let her tortured body be translated into language, she prevents the violence that the Empire's categorizations would impose on her story (Wenzel 1996, 66). Only in the desert, where the Magistrate takes her to return her to her people, she willingly sleeps with him for the first and last time.[15] The desert—a neutral, formless space outside the Empire's borders—erases with dust and wind the violence of imperial categories. Away from the borders of imperial discourse, the girl comes to him on her own terms.

Perhaps the closest the Magistrate comes to her, even though she is no longer physically with him, is when he becomes a victim of torture himself. When his status suddenly changes from that of a respected official to that of an enemy of the state, the Magistrate is imprisoned, tortured, and humiliated. As soon as he enters this new state of being—from a colonizer to a tortured victim—the Empire cannot understand his voice anymore. For the Empire and its practitioners, everyone who produces meaning alien to their language is reduced to a barbarian. Listening to his howls of pain, the Magistrate's torturers scornfully remark: "He is calling his barbarian friends." One of them adds: "This is barbarian language you hear" (Coetzee 2000, 133). The scene evokes the etymology of the "barbarian," based on the perception of the other's language as nonsensical sounds.

The Magistrate does not embody the position of the barbarian in the same way the natives or the barbarian girl do—the Empire's designated others. His barbarization partly answers to his own desire to redeem himself and achieve what he was not able to achieve in his relationship with the girl. Unable to domesticate her otherness from his position as "civilized," he may be trying to achieve that by becoming the Empire's other. The status of the barbarian is usually violently imposed on others, but at times it can be willingly assumed or claimed.[16] The tagging of the natives as "barbarians" takes place independently of the natives' wills. They become silent objects on which the discursive violence of civilization is exerted. They are the real site of otherness in the novel—an otherness exemplified in the barbarian girl. The Magistrate's barbarian status is partly imposed externally and partly self-assumed. It is the result of a dislocation that, according to Rebecca Saunders, "allows him to conceive of himself as other and to become foreign to the identity mapped out for him by historical circumstances" (2001, 223). His attempt to make himself the Empire's enemy, I contend, may reflect his wish to put himself on equal footing with the girl but also to cleanse himself, as it were, from the guilt of her torturers, which is also his own. His (self-)barbarization is both a brave act of opposition and a selfish act of personal redemption.

His barbarian status should thus be distinguished from the barbarian labeling of those others, upon which a discourse foreign to them is inflicted. The Magistrate is an exponent of the self-proclaimed civilized world and wishes to become barbarian in order to oppose the Empire's practices and fend off his complicity with these practices. The girl and her people—proclaimed barbarians by the Empire—are fishing people and nomads who (possibly) just wish to be fishing people and nomads.

Both the novel and the poem end with a sense of disillusionment and uncertainty, without any revelation that restores meaning and presence. The Magistrate tries to make sense of several signs throughout his narrative. However, all the signs that seem pregnant with meaning remain undeciphered—just as the girl does. No apocalyptic vision endows his actions with meaning. In the final scene of the novel he sees a child playing with snow, who appears to be the child he has often been dreaming of—one of the signs he so eagerly wanted to decode. For a moment, the expectation is raised in him (and in the reader) that at least the meaning of this sign will be disclosed. The last lines of the novel, however, seal the failure of this expectation: "This is not the scene I dreamed of. Like much else nowadays I leave it feeling stupid, like a man who lost his way long ago but presses on along a road that may lead nowhere" (Coetzee 2000, 170).

Cavafy's poem does not offer closure either. The only answer is encompassed in the ambiguous statement that views the barbarians as "*a kind of* solution" (emphasis added). The lack of certainty in these words corresponds to the final words in Coetzee's novel: "a road that *may* lead nowhere" (emphasis added). The final lines in Cavafy are an attempt to cling to the previous order—an attempt, however, severely weakened by the doubt contained in the words "kind of." "A kind of solution" translates in fact to "no solution." "A kind of" reaffirms the shaky ground on which this statement is made, and it is hardly convincing. In Coetzee, the "road that *may* lead nowhere" signals the terrifying openness of the future, when the "truths" that sustain the Empire are debunked. This road may lead to an impasse. However, the word "may" leaves open the possibility of envisaging a different path, a "solution" beyond binary oppositions and enemies constructed for the sake of self-definition.

What Figures between Literature and History

The uncertainty and resistance to closure that the poem and the novel share contrast them with what we could call "history," which is the discursive field wherein the opposition between barbarism and civilization takes center stage. The distinction between fiction and history has been adequately contested by postmodern literary theorists and by historians such as Hayden White, as well as by Michel Foucault's influential work, which has projected history as one discourse among others.[17] Nevertheless, many historians are still, as Derrida remarks, "naïvely concerned to 'objectify' the content of a science" (1992, 55). I see "history" here as a strictly regulated discourse, which, according to Felman, prefers clear-cut choices and binary distinctions (2003, 100). While history prefers sharp distinctions and clear-cut categories, literature, in Spivak's view, "relativizes the categories history assigns, and exposes the processes that construct and position subjects" (Spivak, presented in Scott 1991, 791).

Coetzee addresses the relation of the novel to history in his essay "The Novel Today": "In times of intense ideological pressure like the present . . . the novel, it seems to me, has only two options: supplementarity or rivalry" (1988, 3). The novel that chooses rivalry "evolves its own paradigms and myths, in the process . . . perhaps going so far as to show up the mythic status of history . . . a novel that is prepared to work itself out outside the terms of class conflict, race conflict, gender conflict or any of the other oppositions out of which history and the historical disciplines erect themselves" (3). The kind of novel Coetzee describes here is not ahistorical. As David Atwell remarks, "To decline the politics of historical discourses does not necessarily involve ahistoricism" (1990, 588). Coetzee reacts against the "colonization of the novel by the discourse of history" rather than pleads for a disengagement of literature from history (1988, 3).

The real challenge, in my view, is not to show that history is just fiction or to collapse the distinction between history and literature altogether but to articulate the difference of these discourses without posing an absolute dichotomy between them. This would encourage new readings (or even modes of writing) of history within literature. This is a challenge that Cavafy's poem and, especially, Coetzee's novel undertake.

The Magistrate in Coetzee's novel aspires to be a historian. After his experience of torture, he has a burning desire to write the history of the events he witnessed in a way that will expose the Empire's crimes and unveil the truth. However, he acknowledges his inability to write a history that would account both for his aversion to and complicity with the Empire (Wenzel 1996, 9). This history would inevitably be written in the discourse that the Empire developed to spread its own truth. Trying to find a way out of this predicament, the Magistrate starts his "historical account" in the mode of a fairy tale: "No one who paid a visit to this oasis . . . failed to be struck by the charm of life here" (Coetzee 2000, 168–69). His account is imbued with romantic nostalgia for a past way of life and the desire to escape from historical time. He wishes to return to a world before history, because he realizes that "Empire has created the time of history" (146). This colonization of history by the Empire makes it impossible for him to write a history that would do justice to the Empire's victims. He says, "I think: I wanted to live outside history. I wanted to live outside the history that the Empire imposes on its subjects, even its lost subjects. I never wished it for the barbarians that they should have the history of Empire laid upon them. How can I believe that that is cause for shame?" (169).

For a moment, his flight to a prehistorical world seems the easy way out of his entrapment in the imperial matrix. However, his overall position in the novel contradicts his momentary desire for a flight from history. From the beginning he states his intention to stay within history and put up his fight: "I struggle on with the old story, hoping that before it is finished it will reveal to me why it was that I thought it worth the trouble" (26).

Cavafy's poetry is immersed in history. Remarkably, Cavafy had expressed his historiographical impulse: "I am a historical poet; I could never write a novel or a play, but I feel 125 voices in me telling me that I could write history" (Lechonitis 1977, 19–20).[18] This history writing takes place within his poems. His poetry flirts with historiographical conventions and employs techniques intended to enhance the historicity of what is enacted in the poems.[19] At the same time, the kind of history his poetry performs decenters hegemonic historical accounts in order to illuminate alternative perspectives, marginalized and forgotten characters or events, and obscure or peripheral eras and places.[20]

"Waiting for the Barbarians" is usually counted among Cavafy's "historical poems," even though it lacks explicit spatial and temporal markers. Many interpretations use it as a key alluding to specific historical events. Some critics have tried to establish connections between the poem and contemporary events in Greece or Egypt, where Cavafy lived. Stratis Tsirkas, for example, has argued that the events in the poem reflect recent events in Egypt at the time the poem was written.[21] These events—if we assume they formed a source of inspiration for the poem—reveal another connection between the poem and the novel, as they place the poem in the context of colonialism. According to this interpretation, the people waiting for the barbarians are the people of Egypt, including the foreign communities in the country. These people wanted to be saved from "civilization"—the British Empire, which had ruled Egypt since 1878. The disappearance of the barbarians in the poem alludes to the British army's brutal crushing of the Mahdist uprising in 1898—an Islamic revolt that threatened British power.[22] Thus, the barbarians in the poem refer to the Mahdists, who no longer existed after their defeat.

Cavafy's poem has thus attracted historicist approaches, which read it in the context of colonized Egypt, connect it to political and military events in Greece, or place it in the fin de siècle climate in Europe at the time of its writing.[23] However, even more common is the poem's treatment as a universalist allegory. Edmund Keeley argues that in "Waiting for the Barbarians" the poet does not have "a specific historical event in mind" and leaves the historical context purposefully vague, because he intends to "offer an insight into the larger pattern of history that raises particular places and events to the level of metaphor or myth" (1976, 30). Viewed as symbols within a historical pattern, Cavafy's barbarians are easily applicable to historical situations before or after the poem's publication.

The poem's citation in various genres, ranging from newspapers, exhibition catalogues, and philosophical or theoretical texts to Internet blogs, illustrates its multiple allegorical functions and applications.[24] In newspaper articles and opinion pieces, Cavafy's poem is employed as an allegorical vessel for illuminating global problems and contemporary issues in politics and international relations. It is worth looking at some of these allegorical applications and their thematic diversity.

In "West Needs to Rethink Attitudes to Islamic Civilizations" (*Irish Times*, May 11, 2002), Patrick Comerford reflects on the suspicion and prejudice with which Muslim populations within or outside Europe and the United States are treated after September 11. He ends his piece with a brief discussion of Cavafy's poem, which helps him reach his conclusion: "An imagined external enemy provides excuses for not wrestling with real social and political problems. On the other hand, real dialogue with the Islamic world is the only way of removing prejudice and fears of an imaginary threat."

In "After America; Is the West Being Overtaken by the Rest?" (New Yorker, April 21, 2008), Ian Buruma uses Cavafy's poem to probe the thesis that "America's time of global dominance is finished, and that new powers, such as China, India, and Russia, are poised to take over." In this context, he writes: "All great empires set too much store by predictions of their imminent demise. Perhaps, as the Greek poet Constantine Cavafy suggested in his poem 'Waiting for the Barbarians,' empires need the sense of peril to give them a reason to go on. Why spend so much money and effort if not to keep the barbarians at bay?"

An opinion piece by H. D. S. Greenway, "No More Waiting for 'Barbarians'" (Boston Globe, June 2, 2009), applies the poem's message to the people of Iran after Barack Obama's election as president:

And so it is with Iranians today. For generations America, the "Great Satan," has been at the gates, overthrowing Mohammed Mossadegh in the '50s, serving the Shah through the '70s, shooting down a civilian airliner and backing Saddam Hussein in his war against Iran, President Bush's "Axis of Evil," and on and on go the grievances, convincing Iranians that their ancient civilization risks destruction at the hands of the United States. But now President Obama is saying there need not be barbarians any longer. And Iranians are asking what's going to happen to them without barbarians? . . . For Iranians, the constant of American hostility has been "a kind of solution."

Such uses testify to the poem's appeal in the present. Nevertheless, understanding the work as part of the present does not just mean turning it into an allegorical formula that helps us build an external argument about real-life situations. It involves reading it through contemporary concerns, while being attentive to its singularity and its resistance to reductive allegorical uses.

Just like Cavafy's poem, Coetzee's *Waiting for the Barbarians* has been read both as a universal narrative of human suffering and moral choice, and as an indictment of the violence and barbarity of the apartheid regime (Attridge 2004, 42). Historicist readings have been particularly prioritized in South African writing, especially during the apartheid years, when every "responsible and principled South African writer" was expected to make the country's historical situation his or her "primary concern" (33).

Although these two kinds of readings—universalizing and historicist—may seem incompatible, Derek Attridge argues that they both treat the texts as allegories. Attridge defines allegorization as "a process whereby characters and the events that befall them are taken to represent either wider (in some cases . . . universal) or more specific meanings" (39). The first kind of allegorical reading (universalizing) seeks to extract general statements or truths about the human condition, while the second historicist allegorical reading approaches texts as keys to an external historical situation (33). The main fault Attridge finds with allegorical readings is that they often bypass the details and particularities of the text, as they turn it into a vehicle that should lead to a more significant meaning (60).[25] The formal elements of the text seem to be in the service of an external meaning or message. Once this meaning is extracted, formal elements, narrative techniques, and other details lose their relevance, as a gift's wrapping becomes useless after the gift has been opened.

In a discussion of Attridge's views, Ernst van Alphen locates the problem with allegorical readings in the fact that they often use only limited and selective aspects of the text—those that are useful for its transformation into an allegory. Contingent or seemingly superfluous textual elements or details that do not fit the economy of the allegorical reading are bypassed (2008, 27). Another problem I would add is that an allegorical reading that views a literary work as either ahistorical or as a key to a historical situation outside the text presupposes a clear-cut opposition between literature and history. If literature and history are viewed as completely distinct domains, the only way for a literary work to be historically relevant is by becoming a marker of a historical reality external to it. This overlooks the possibility that literature can offer another mode of history writing, different from that of academic history, without explicitly referring to an external historical context.

In reaction to reductive allegorical readings, Attridge proposes a *literal* mode of reading that focuses on the singularity of the text and on the reading experience. A literal reading draws attention to what the text does rather than what it means, and thus does not rush into saying what a text is "about" (2004, 36–37, 39). It is sensitive to the reading experience and to the impact of textual elements and narrative techniques on the reader.[26] It can be described as a performing of the text that "responds simultaneously to what is said, the way in which it is said, and the inventiveness and singularity (if there is any) of the saying" (60).

Following Attridge's notion of literal reading, Cavafy's and Coetzee's texts constitute unique events anchored in the present of their literary universe. The lack of time/place indications does not prevent these works from evoking moments in history and in the present, thereby improving our understanding of the present and of external situations. However, they refuse to be reduced to a spot in a chronology. In so doing, the poem and the novel become even more historically active. Their iterability is what immerses them in history. A text's iterability, Derrida claims, is "the condition of historicity," because it roots a text to a context and simultaneously "opens this non-saturable context onto a recontextualization" (1992, 63).

But can the singularity and iterability of the literary event be captured only by a "literal reading," as Attridge suggests? Attridge, van Alphen argues, is perhaps a bit too quick to dismiss allegorical readings altogether. According to van Alphen, reading for the meaning of a text, which allegorical readings do in Attridge's definition, is something we always end up doing in one way or another when we interpret a text (2008, 29). Thus, the crucial question is *how* we read for meaning: Do we read to confirm what we already know or to open ourselves to unknown meanings and sensations that works may trigger? Attridge's proposed "literal reading" and "reading for meaning (allegorical reading)," van Alphen concludes, can be seen as complementary: they substantiate each other in "an interplay" between the "affective, experiential dimension of reading" and "the allegorical dimension of meaning." In this interplay, the production of meaning is the result—not the "cause, end, or goal of reading" (30). As long as allegorical readings do not rush into the production of familiar or predetermined meanings, they can be a productive part of a careful interpretive process that makes space for the "not yet known," triggered by the affective operations of the text (30).

In Coetzee's *Waiting for the Barbarians*, the untranslatable symbols and signs, as well as the irreducible otherness of the girl, are elements that exceed the allegorizations we are tempted to produce. In such ways, Attridge argues, the novel simultaneously invites and sabotages its allegorization, thereby delivering a critique on the allegorizing impulse itself (2004, 45). But there might be more at stake here than an implicit commentary on allegory. Instead of dismissing allegorical readings as reductive per definition, I argue that the works invite a new kind of allegorical reading, which suggests another approach to history in literature.

Barbarian Allegory

Words and signs in the Magistrate's narrative often seem to refer to something else. Their promise of meaning invites us to view them as parts of an allegory that promises to translate signs into something different than what they are. Neither the novel nor the poem gratifies the expectations its allegorical structure cultivates.

In a definition that stays close to its etymology, allegory means to "speak other than one seems to speak" (Saunders 2001, 223). Allegorical readings usually assume that the "other" to which the allegory refers is knowable and can be discovered through interpretation. The allegory the novel sets up is different: its allegorical structures point to something unknowable and, in that sense, barbarian. This "barbarian allegory" does not promise a decodable meaning but induces an experience that can still affect our language with its foreignness and produce multiple interpretive possibilities, none of which are final or verifiable. This allegory invites us to read for meaning without presupposing that the meaning of a text is ever determinable. It thus perpetuates interpretation, while alerting the reader to the "barbarian" aspects of a literary text: those elements that escape our understanding without being meaning*less*. A barbarian allegory does not abolish reference; referring to something *other* is part of the definition of allegory. Thus, it does not freeze the signifying transaction, but it problematizes the correspondence of a sign with its referent.

Barbarian allegory describes both a mode of reading and aspects or elements in literary texts that invite and enable such a reading. It is thus a potential in some texts (not all literary texts can function as barbarian allegories) that the reader can activate. The performance of barbarian allegory requires both certain aspects of a literary text and a particular mode of reading. Coetzee's novel can be read as a barbarian allegory because its untranslatable signs bear the promise of a language, the meaning of which cannot be fully determined.

The girl in the novel, for instance, functions as a site of barbarian allegory. Because the Magistrate is unable to "read" her, she maintains her irreducible singularity against the generalizable features of the Empire. Despite her unintelligibility, she has an impact on the Magistrate's language and subjectivity. He may not be able to determine the meaning of her language and acts, but through her barbarian allegory the meaning of his own acts changes as he tries to imagine it through her perspective. As Spivak notes, in speculating about the possible meanings that his subjectivity assumes in the eyes of the barbarian girl, there is "an indefinite structure of possibilities" (2003, 23).

The concept of barbarian allegory is particularly developed in the following scene in the novel, wherein a barbarian language assumes an allegorical function. The scene describes the interrogation of the Magistrate by Colonel Joll. The latter is conducting an investigation concerning supposed barbarian threats to the Empire. Colonel Joll is convinced that the Magistrate has been communicating with the barbarian enemy. He therefore asks him questions in order to clarify the exact meaning of certain wooden slips with barbarian characters, which were found at the Magistrate's house. The Magistrate had excavated those slips at the site of an ancient barbarian civilization. Colonel Joll is not aware of that and assumes that the slips are recent and contain secret messages between the Magistrate and the barbarian enemies: "A reasonable inference is that the wooden slips contain messages passed between yourself and other parties, we do not know when. It remains for you to explain what the messages say and the other parties were" (Coetzee 2000, 121).

At first, the Magistrate is at a loss when he is assigned the task of translation: "I look at the lines of characters written by a stranger long since dead. I do not even know whether to read from right to left or from left to right. . . . Does each stand for a single thing, a circle for the sun, a triangle for a woman, a wave for a lake; or does a circle merely stand for 'circle,' a triangle for 'triangle,' a wave for 'wave'?" (121). The Magistrate has no idea what the characters mean. Nevertheless, he offers Colonel Joll a speculative reading. He first pretends to read the texts on three of the slips as parts of an epistolary exchange: a letter from a father to his daughter, written at times of peace, and two letters informing someone about the brutal death of his brother in the hands of officers. The last two letters allude to the practices of torture exercised by the Empire's practitioners against the barbarian natives. After "reading" those letters, he moves on to another slip:

"Now let us see what the next one says. See, there is only a single character. It is the barbarian character *war*, but it has other senses too. It can stand for *vengeance*, and, if you turn it upside down like this, it can be made to read *justice*. There is no knowing which sense is intended. This is part of *barbarian cunning*."

"It is the same with the rest of these slips." I plunge my good hand into the chest and stir. "They form an *allegory*. They can be read in many orders. Further, each single slip can be read in many ways. Together they can be read as a domestic journal, or they can be read as a plan of war, or they can be turned on their sides and read as a history of the last years of the Empire—the old Empire I mean. There is no agreement among scholars on how to interpret these relics of the ancient barbarians. . . ."

"Thank you. *I have finished translating.*" (122–23)[27]

In this scene, two views on translation are implied, each with different objectives and epistemological consequences. Colonel Joll wishes to have the barbarian signs translated to confirm his suspicion that the signs are secret messages from the enemy. This will legitimize his presence in town and his violent practices. Although he does not speak the barbarian language and therefore needs a translator—the Magistrate—Joll has in fact already decided on the meaning of this translation and will accept the Magistrate's translation only if it confirms his own prefabricated version of it: the messages as threatening for the Empire. Joll's intended translation follows the Empire's tendency to impose its own code on others, turning it into a universal, all-explanatory machine. Following this logic, the Empire translates based on the law of sameness: its translations appropriate every barbarian sign to the imperial code and regulate meaning by delimiting the context in which it can take place (Saunders 2001, 228).[28] In fact, Colonel Joll's intended translation is a pseudo-translation because there is no transference of meaning from one code to another. There is only one code at play, that of the Empire.

In a different way, the Magistrate's translation is also a failure. It is a misreading—and, to be sure, an intentional one. In fact, one could argue that it does not qualify as a translation at all, since the source language remains unintelligible. However, instead of facing the unintelligibility of the barbarian language as an insurmountable impediment, the Magistrate plunges into an impossible translation, which takes nonknowledge as its starting point. His "translation" does not just reproduce a version of the self (the Empire's language) but imbues the Empire's discourse with traces of alterity, which I identify as "barbarisms."

Contrary to the way Colonel Joll imagines translation—as an act that should yield a univocal reading—the Magistrate's translation constitutes an allegorical reading that converts the Empire's naturalized categories (war, vengeance, justice) into barbarian allegories, by "reading" them *through* the foreignness of the barbarian slips. In this way, the language of the Empire and the barbarian language of the slips, to borrow Felman's words, "meet even as they fail to meet" (2003, 63). The Magistrate's reading, Saunders argues, subjects the Empire's terms to multiple interpretive possibilities, while making their determination impossible (2001, 226). The Empire's most popular terms become barbarian allegories, as they are disembedded from their familiar context and read through the signs of a barbarian language.

In their "Treatise on Nomadology," Deleuze and Guattari distinguish between "royal" and "nomad" science. While the former domesticates foreign knowledge, the latter cuts the contents of royal science loose (1987, 405). Bringing this distinction to bear on the novel, we could say that the Empire (as "royal science") appropriates barbarian knowledge, while the Magistrate's "barbarian cunning" (representing "nomad science") unsettles the Empire's epistemological certainties. His translation refuses to gratify the Empire's need for stable contexts and definitions and imbues terms like "justice," on which civilization depends for justifying its practices, with an ambiguous, controversial meaning. Whereas Joll needs a stable signification for the barbarian signs, the Magistrate does not extract constants from variables but sets variables "in a state of continuous variation" (Deleuze and Guattari 1987, 407).

"Justice," one of civilization's favorite categories, is made to coexist with "vengeance" and "war" under the umbrella of the same sign. As a result, its meaning shifts through its proximity to these two concepts. The force of these three terms in imperial discourse is premised on their difference, which allows them to be clearly distinguished from one another. The Magistrate purposefully bypasses that difference in order to underscore their similarity and intertwinement. The virtuous connotations of "justice" are contaminated by the violent connotations of "war" and "vengeance." The Magistrate's translation suggests that "justice" and "vengeance" are indistinguishable from each other in the Empire's practices: justice is often an excuse for vengeance, or vengeance is masked as justice to justify violence. The hierarchical interrelation of these three terms is unsettled, the values they carry become suspect, and their absolute difference fades out, as they all become readings of the same allegorical sign.

The Magistrate counters the Empire's hegemonic knowledge with his epistemological barbarism—his "barbarian cunning": a practice of inserting ambiguous elements that the Empire tries to obliterate from its discourse. Notably, these elements are no other than the Empire's key categories. However, their unorthodox use reveals the contradictions within the Empire's own discourse. The terms and ideological tools of imperial language turn into instruments of subversion. The Empire cannot domesticate the Magistrate's translation, which is the reason that Colonel Joll dismisses it.

Although his translation does not really decipher the barbarian slips, it manages to convey something of the other's language, albeit only the realization that the Empire's linguistic code is just as unstable and stuttering as the mumblings we hear in a barbarian language. His encounter with the barbarian language of the slips generates a temporary suspension of understanding that reveals the limits of the Empire's discourse. The Magistrate ends his part in this scene with the words "I have finished translating." However, his translation does not really "finish," since it does not offer semiotic closure. His allegorical reading seeks to perpetuate interpretation by bringing in ambiguity and polysemy in the fixed relation between the Empire's signs and their meanings.

The Magistrate's reading in this scene could also serve as a model for a different approach to history. The past could be seen as a barbarian allegory: an untranslatable language—just like the barbarian script on the slips—referring to something gone and impossible to grasp as a presence. It is reminiscent of Cavafy's barbarians, who, in the poet's words, are not there "any longer." History, then, can be seen as an attempt to read the barbarian allegory of the past and assign meanings to it by casting it into coherent stories and familiar narratives. Discourses of history generally treat the past as something (at least partly) known and legible. But, as the novel suggests, we could also write history differently by reading the past in the way the Magistrate reads the barbarian slips: as something unknown and irretrievable, which nonetheless, through its foreignness, can affect our language in the present.

By acknowledging the untranslatability of the past, we invite it to haunt our present, because we can never appropriate it and leave it behind as a "finished translation." The barbarianness of the past does not prevent it from being meaningful to us. Due to its allegorical character, it is not a hermetic structure but refers to things and situations other than itself even though its referents are not fully determinable. It therefore has a continuous bearing on our present, as its signifying capacity is inexhaustible.

The conception of history that I draw from the Magistrate's allegorical reading yields different meanings in every present without ever being present. This conception is also suggested in the poem. There, the barbarians' absence challenges their status in the discourse of history. If literature is performative in that it creates the reality to which it refers, then history supposedly refers to an existing reality in the past. However, the poem questions this opposition between literature and history by showing that a fundamental category of history—the barbarian—has no actual referent in "reality."

By turning history's founding terms ("barbarians," "war," "vengeance," "justice") into ambiguous signs, the works read history as "speaking other than it seems to speak"—an "other" that never crystallizes. Thus, both the poem and the novel open up a space within literature for performing history otherwise. The capacity of literature to interrogate other discourses (including itself) can be correlated with its freedom to say everything—a freedom that the strictly regulated discourse of history lacks. Derrida describes literature as an "institution of fiction which gives *in principle* the power to say everything, to break free of the rules, to displace them, and thereby to institute, to invent and even to suspect the traditional difference between nature and institution, nature and conventional law, nature and history" (1992, 37).[29]

For Derrida, this freedom can work both ways: it can be "a very powerful political weapon, but one which might immediately let itself be neutralized as fiction. This revolutionary power can become very conservative" (1992, 38). The fact that literature is explicitly fictional and citational language use—which is the reason that Austin, John Searle, and other philosophers degrade it as "non-serious" language—may suggest that literary discourse can have no impact on "real" situations or "serious" discourses.[30] However, precisely due to its common perception as non-serious, fictional, and citational—in contrast with the supposed seriousness and truth effect of historical discourse—literature is allowed to say everything and can use this freedom to challenge "serious" discourses. Therefore, literature's assumed non-seriousness, to which it partly owes its institutional freedom, is paradoxically what makes it a powerful political tool, able to intervene in "serious" discourses.

As we see in the novel, literature interrogates historical categories by "citing" them otherwise. Whereas reductive allegorical readings either superimpose a specific version of the historical upon the literary or strip a text of its historical relevance altogether, Coetzee's novel and Cavafy's poem perform history through literature's institutional freedom. In so doing, they undercut the hierarchy between the two discourses—history as "serious" language with a bearing on "reality" versus literature as "non-serious" language that only "cites" real situations—without canceling the differences between the two discursive realms. As a result, they enable a critical performance of history through its "discursive other."

Who Are Those Barbarians after All? Barbarians in Repetition

One of the most prominent ways in which the poem and the novel challenge the discourse of history is by using history's key terms in ways that erode their stability and enable their resignification. I explore this operation by specifically following the term "barbarian" in the novel and the poem.

The first question that arises concerns the term's referent. In the poem, since we never see any barbarians, we can only reconstruct the image that the people of the city have created about them. The consuls and praetors are dressed in embroidered togas and are overloaded with dazzling jewelry, because "things like that dazzle the barbarians." The orators are silent, because the barbarians are "bored by rhetoric and public speaking." The image of the city-in-preparation fits the Orientalist stereotype of decadent people immersed in luxury and excess. The citizens believe either that this is what the barbarians are like or that these are the kinds of things the barbarians like. In other words, either the barbarians are constructed according to an Orientalist representational regime or they are imagined to be crude primitive warriors—reminiscent of the Teutonic nations that invaded Rome—who are likely to be impressed by the Empire's luxury and grandeur. The reader cannot test this mental image on real subjects. We receive only a mediated mirror image of the barbarians through the civilized.

In the novel, the identity of the people the Empire names "barbarians" remains unclear. The barbarians against whom the expeditionary forces are sent are supposed to be violent nomadic people who are planning attacks against the Empire. However, the expeditionary forces never reach these barbarians, although they think they sense the barbarians' constant presence. One of the leaders of these forces is convinced that barbarians trailed him at a distance. "Are you sure they were barbarians? I [the Magistrate] ask. Who else could they have been? He replies. His colleagues concur" (Coetzee 2000, 53). The barbarians seem to leave traces without their presence ever being witnessed. Thus, when "clothing disappears from washing-lines" and "food from larders," the people in town are convinced that the barbarians did it, even though nobody catches them in the act. Various theories are devised to account for the fact that the perpetrators are never seen, for example, that "the barbarians have dug a tunnel under the walls" or that they only "come out at night" (134). The barbarians become the Empire's scapegoats. The people end up accusing them for every calamity and crime, such as the flooding of the fields (during which, again, "no one saw them," 108) or the rape of a girl (during which her friends recognize the rapist as a barbarian "by his ugliness," 134).

The accumulation of rumors around them leads to their demonization. They become the personification of evil, ready to "fry your balls and eat them" (164). "Once in every generation, without fail," the narrator observes, "there is an episode of hysteria about the barbarians" (9). But the myth of the barbarians as the ultimate enemy of the Empire needs to find real bodies on which the Empire can exercise its power. These are the prisoners Colonel Joll brings with him, who, according to the narrator, are peaceful fishing people, in no way related to any attacks. The last group of prisoners the Colonel captures is put on public display. As the Magistrate ironically remarks, "Everyone has a chance to see the twelve miserable captives, to prove to his children that the barbarians are real" (113). The Empire's need to legitimize its discourse and prove that the barbarians "are real" by finding—that is, naming—the enemy in material bodies, transforms the miserable prisoners into a dangerous enemy. On their naked backs Colonel Joll writes "ENEMY" with charcoal and orders the soldiers to beat them until the word is erased by blood. The word has to be written on them to make those damaged bodies plausible as enemies, to transform a "literal body into a figurative enemy" (Saunders 2001, 230). "The constative claim," Butler tells us, "is always to some degree performative" (1993, 11). Here, naming creates the enemy. The category "enemy" is literally inscribed by the Empire on the bodies of its subjects. This scene literalizes the symbolic violence of language, thereby underscoring its inextricability from physical violence.

Colonel Joll's act reflects the Empire's need to sustain what Paul de Man calls "the myth of semantic correspondence between sign and referent" by literally attaching the sign to the referent (1979, 6). The actual intentions and deeds of the natives are irrelevant in this process. Only after imposing its clear-cut distinctions does the Empire read its others— that is, read itself in its others. In the same way, the Empire's officials elicit "the truth" from their victims of torture: they project their own truth onto their bodies.[31]

The barbarian other does not exist as an external enemy. Through the Empire's atrocities toward its prisoners a new referent is attached to the barbarian in the novel. The overwhelming reality (in the novel) leads the narrator to adopt the term for the Empire's practitioners. Although, as the narrator remarks, in the Empire's euphemistic vocabulary the torturers of the Third Bureau are probably designated as "security officers" (Coetzee 2000, 129), the Magistrate views them as the "new barbarians" (85) who have come to install terror in town. He realizes that the people of the Empire are enemies to themselves and that Colonel Joll is the product of an irrational society that becomes barbaric in its attempt to protect civilization: "Those pitiable prisoners you brought in—are *they* the enemy I must fear? . . . *You* are the enemy, Colonel! . . . *You* are the enemy, *you* have made the war, and you have given them all the martyrs they need" (125).

In the Magistrate's words, a new kind of inside barbarian is designated, exposing the impulse of the Empire to generate its own excess in a suicidal fashion. The Empire's soldiers, who have settled in town, end up terrorizing the citizens, looting shops, violating laws, getting drunk, and causing trouble. Their behavior is constantly contrasted either with the pitiful state of the barbarian prisoners or with the stories about barbarian crimes that are never witnessed. Consequently, it becomes impossible for the reader to overlook the paradox in the Empire's use of the name "barbarian."

The image the Empire has created for the barbarians is a distorted reflection of itself. During the Magistrate's journey in the desert to return the girl to her people, he and his companions keep seeing specters of the barbarians in the distance, which they never reach. If they move or stop, the specters move and stop with them. "Are they reflections of us, is this a trick of the light?" the Magistrate wonders (74). Like a mirage, the barbarians dissolve before anyone can reach them, pointing back to the ubiquitous presence of the people of the Empire as the real barbarians. This specter hunting in the desert is later also carried out by the Empire's troops, leading to their total dissemination: they freeze, starve, and get lost in the desert, still convinced that they are chasing barbarians. The disintegration of the Empire comes from within.

From the beginning of his narrative, the Magistrate repeats the term "barbarian" in exactly the same way it is used within the Empire's language: to refer to the natives (the colonized subjects) and to the Empire's (invisible) dangerous enemies. The native fishermen, the nomads, the prisoners, the invisible enemies are all called "barbarians" in the Magistrate's narrative. Even the native girl that lives with him is referred to as "the barbarian girl," not simply as "the girl." The Magistrate has no choice but to employ the categories within which he has been constituted as a subject. These categories have been naturalized through their repetitive use in history. I contend that the narrator's obsessive repetition of the word "barbarian" draws attention to this practice of naturalization through repetition. As Butler argues, the repetition of the norm—here, the citation of the name "barbarian"—is the main mechanism through which its power is secured (1993, 15).

However, that same mechanism used by a discursive regime for the indoctrination of its truths can also lead to the regime's delegitimization. There is a deconstituting possibility in the process of repetition, Butler claims, because through it "gaps and fissures are opened up as the constitutive instabilities in such constructions, as that which escapes or exceeds the norm, as that which cannot be wholly defined or fixed by the repetitive labor of that norm" (10). Although the word "barbarian" is repeated in the novel, the material referent of the term either never appears or does not live up to its supposed barbaric nature: the barbarian enemies are not found in the desert, and the native prisoners never display any barbaric behavior. This puts the term under suspicion. At the same time, when the narrator starts using it for the "new barbarians" (the colonizers), confusion is produced. This new use is concomitant with the Magistrate's indignation at the Empire's practices, which leads to his imprisonment.

The Magistrate's turn against the Empire, however, does not put an end to his use of the term "barbarian" for the colonized subjects. Until the end of his narrative, the conventional use of the word for the natives runs parallel to its critical use for the colonizers. Thus, the word becomes a performative operating in a twofold way: while the reader perceives its use for the natives as an infelicitous speech act (the reader fails to see these people as barbarians), its use for the colonizers is more likely to convince the reader and secure uptake.[32] The parallel uses of the term indicate that more than a simple reversal of the barbarian/civilized opposition is at stake. The narrative destabilizes the hierarchy by rendering it unnatural and arbitrary.

One could argue that we are dealing with two different definitions of the term "barbarian." In the first case, the narrator uses it as a (supposedly) neutral, descriptive term to refer to the native others and distinguish them from the civilization of which he is part. In the second case, he uses it to impose moral judgment on the Empire's practitioners. However, through the narrator's simultaneous use of both senses, the novel problematizes precisely the intertwinement of these two senses of the word, which is so commonplace in Western discourses. This intertwinement results in the automatic attribution of barbarian behavior (the second sense) to subjects that simply happen not to be part of the "civilization" of the self. Therefore, the term's operations in the Magistrate's discourse point to the inconsistencies in the language by which Western history signifies the barbarian.

The narrator's voice is limited by the hegemonies against which it utters itself but manages to challenge these hegemonies through a repetition with a difference. The repetitive and somewhat confusing use of "barbarian" in the novel reveals the contested terrain the term occupies. All in all, the uses of "barbarian" in the novel have three different functions. They perform (1) the history of the term's use for naming civilization's inferior others, (2) the history of the reversals of the term's referent, to describe the barbaric behavior of the civilized, and (3) the open temporality of the term, since its subversive iteration in the novel creates a space for resignification.

The operations of the barbarian in the novel invite us to revisit its function in Cavafy's poem. In the poem, the repetition of the word "barbarians" by the second speaker conveys certainty about their coming. The phrase "because the barbarians are coming" is repeated in all his answers (albeit in a slight variation in his first answer) and thus almost sounds like a promise to his interlocutor, the people of the city, and the readers themselves, who are also anticipating the spectacle. The more emphatically the promise is repeated, the greater the disappointment becomes when the promise is not realized. The failure of this speech act stages the failure of the discourse of civilization to bring to life what it has constructed as its outside. The barbarians remain a signifier without a material referent because they have always existed only as part of the discourse of civilization. The poem stages the infelicitous speech act of a discourse trying to play God. Its "let there be barbarians" does not work. The omnipotence of the discourse of civilization is contested, and the transparency of its correspondence to the world becomes opaque.

The people of the city live in a decadent world that is falling apart. To these people, the anticipation of an encounter with the other, even in the form of an invasion, becomes the driving force behind their actions.

In the Western imagination, the barbarian has sparked anxiety and fear, as well as fascination and longing.[33] A mixture of both emotional states overtakes the people in the poem, although desire is the prevailing emotion. The poem inflates the Western topos of the desire for the other to such an extent that it takes the form of a self-destructive wish.

The eagerness of the citizens to welcome the barbarians is comparable to the Magistrate's attraction to the barbarian girl and his desire to make contact with her. Both the Magistrate and the people in Cavafy's city fail to make real contact with the barbarians. But the way they imagine this encounter and the reasons for their failure are different. While the Magistrate refuses to construct the girl on his own terms and tell her story in his own language, the people in Cavafy's poem are unable to imagine an encounter with the other in terms other than their own.

The people in the poem assume to know what the barbarians are like, what their habits are, how they will behave, and how they will rule the city once they arrive. The emperor has even prepared a scroll to give to their leader, "replete with titles, with imposing names." Hidden in these titles and names is the hierarchical structure of the old Empire, which the people intend to pass on to their prospective barbarian rulers. They are convinced that changing rulers is enough to bring their world to a new beginning. However, the script of the Empire in the hands of the emperor contains the "titles" and "names" that safeguard the categories and oppositions that brought their society to an impasse in the first place. As such, they resemble Colonel Joll's act of creating his barbarians by writing "ENEMY" on the backs of his prisoners. Therefore, the citizens leave no room for the arrival of something truly new, because they presuppose an already known other that can be articulated in their language before it has even made its appearance. In this way, the poem sketches a solipsistic society that does not open itself to newness and alterity. Without knowing it, the citizens themselves are responsible for sabotaging their encounter with the barbarians they so eagerly anticipate.

The mythology of the other, Dimitris Tziovas argues in his essay on the poem, is essential for self-affirmation, whereas its absence gives birth to utter bewilderment (1986, 177). The pessimistic mood that overcomes the city when the barbarians do not come is a sign of resignation. The Empire has to come to terms with its own demise, but not in the way it has staged it: not as an honorable defeat from external enemies but as a result of internal contradictions. The society in the poem, to borrow T.S. Eliot's famous line from "The Hollow Men," ends "not with a bang but a whimper." As a result, the citizens redirect their gaze from the outside to the inside. The introspection that follows—and the depressive mood it generates—can be read in everybody's faces ("How serious people's faces have become"), as everyone is "going home lost in thought."

Eventually, the compelling final lines are heard:

> And now, what's going to happen to us without barbarians?
> They were, those people, a kind of solution.

Who speaks these verses and from which position? The identity and status of the voice in these lines has been an object of debate among critics. The lines could be uttered either by the first or second speaker in the dialogue or by a third unidentified voice, which could be that of the poet-observer, reflecting on the situation in the poem with a deeply ironic statement.[34] Based on the structure of the dialogue, we can infer that these lines are uttered by the first speaker, as a reaction to the previous statement by the second speaker, wherein he announces that the barbarians will not come. However, a metrical analysis of the Greek text suggests that these two verses follow the metrical pattern of the second speaker's speech: they comprise thirteen syllables each, as opposed to the decapentasyllabic verse (fifteen syllables) that the first speaker uses in his questions. This brings the final lines closer to the second speaker's sound in the poem.[35]

I contend that these lines are spoken by the first speaker, whose voice is no longer the same. His voice appears altered after the "dreadful realization of the depletion of images of Otherness" (Constantinou 1998, 193). The final voice does not belong to a third-person-observer who witnesses the dialogue from a distance. The agony and struggle for self-preservation implicit in the phrase "a kind of" suggests that this voice belongs to the same discourse that invented the barbarians. But this voice is also changed by self-reflection, which requires a distancing from oneself, a viewing of oneself as other. To this latter dimension it owes its ironic undertone.

The final voice addresses the poem's audience: the readers. Through this implicit apostrophe, the speaker transfers and perpetuates the search for another "solution" in the present of every reading, implicating the reader in this search. Searching for an answer to the question "And now, what's going to happen to us without barbarians?" may lead to a rethinking of the self and a reflection on the conditions that made the encounter with the barbarians impossible. The non-realization of this encounter does not necessarily support a pessimistic view upon civilization. Cavafy himself read his poem with optimism: "Besides, the poem does not work against my optimistic view [about the future]. It can be taken as an episode in the course towards the Good. Society reaches a level of luxury, civilization, and consternation, where, desperate from being in a position wherein it cannot rectify things through a compromise with its usual mode of living, it decides to bring radical change—to sacrifice, to change, to go back, to simplify."[36] Cavafy reads his poem as a warning that society needs "radical change." Whether the "solution" lies in going back to a simpler mode of life, as Cavafy seems to suggest in his comment, or in another mode of being, one thing is certain: the failure of the poem's promise indicates the bankruptcy of existing modes of thought, and as such it can be seen as an act of criticism, initiating a search for another solution.

Cavafy's poem and Coetzee's novel, by disrupting the discourse of "barbarism versus civilization" through a subversive reiteration of its categories, both stand before an even greater challenge: that of constructing a new discursive space after having deconstructed the old. In Cavafy's poem, this challenge is implied in the question, "And now, what's going to happen to us without barbarians?" In the poem, the possibility of another "kind of solution," of a new space wherein the relation between self and other is refashioned, is posed as a challenge, which is left unresolved. Despite the difference in the speaker's voice in the final verses, I still hear it as a voice standing *before* a void, not yet plunging into it. In Coetzee, however, I contend that the narrator descends into that void and lets a negotiation take place between the old and a new kind of discourse. The narrator's language, misreading the foundational concepts of the Empire, carries signs of a transition between the old and the new, sameness and otherness. Nevertheless, this transition is not fully accomplished in the novel, which in the end leaves us on a road "that may lead nowhere."

The narrator cannot escape the limitations of his discourse. However, his barbarism consists in misusing the terms of the Empire's discourse and experimenting with the inconsistencies that come about when these terms are reiterated. In the space of literature, barbarism emerges as an operation that causes shifts in a familiar code by repeating the signs of this code in slightly altered signifying constellations.

A Promise on Shaky Ground

The Empire in Coetzee's novel is falling apart for the same reasons as the city in the poem: not by an external enemy but under the pressure of internal conflicts. Both the poem and the novel expose the barbarian as part of the civilized subject, but nonetheless constructed as an external other that supports the identity of civilization. These works do not just reverse the opposition between civilization and barbarism in order to demonstrate that the civilized are the real barbarians, whereas those tagged as "barbarians" are the innocent victims of Western barbarism disguised as civilization. As Coetzee's novel particularly suggests, it is not enough to recognize the barbarism within civilization and point the finger to the perpetrators of barbaric acts from a supposedly safe distance. Recognizing barbaric behavior is commendable, but it does not resolve the predicament of our implication in these discursive categories that have co-shaped our subjectivity. As the Magistrate's position indicates, our entanglement in the discourses of civilization, Empire, or history marks our complicity with the perpetrators, even if we are not the ones using the instruments of torture. This predicament is too complex to be resolved by siding with the "good guys" or against the "bad guys." Thus, instead of just shuffling the referents of these categories, Coetzee's novel reiterates the term "barbarian" in ways that confound its conventional field of operation.

Faced with the impossibility of discarding the category of the "barbarian," the poem and the novel nevertheless succeed in mobilizing it. Searching for the barbarians, we do not know where to look; our gaze is unfixed. Should we try to discern them beyond the borders of the city or in the vastness of the desert, or should we look around us, in our homes, our cities, within ourselves? And is what we think we see the barbarians or a distorted reflection of ourselves? The barbarian is omnipresent yet elusive.

In both the poem and the novel, the barbarian oscillates between history and literature, challenging the institutional boundaries of these

discourses. The barbarians of history are shown to be mythical constructions with no real referents, while new barbarians—the people of the
Empire in the novel or the people of the city in the poem—are designated
in literature. One of history's favorite dichotomies, barbarians versus civilized, faces a "barbarian invasion" from literature, which imbues the solid
terms of this dichotomy with ambiguity.

Cavafy's poem and Coetzee's novel present the reader with unresolved questions, linguistic bewilderment, obsessive reiterations, infelicitous performatives, and the prospect of an alternative way of speaking and
relating to others—a prospect perhaps explored in Coetzee more than
in Cavafy. The promise they make—the arrival of the barbarians—is a
promise they cannot keep. However, in failing their promise, they succeed
in envisioning another kind of history within literature. This history is
able to survive the repeated broken promise of the presence of meaning
by refashioning its binary structures and "truths" as barbarian allegories:
configurations of inherited signs, which may be meaningful for, and relate
to, our present, but whose meaning is never fully settled. In this performative approach to history, the past is a living part of the present.

These works do not have any clear-cut solution to the predicament
of civilization. They do, however, project the hope—the promise even—
of another "kind of solution" that could guide us to "a road that may
lead" *somewhere*. Some may find the terms in which this promise is made
too weak or vague to be convincing. But attempts to repeat dominant
categories into new senses cannot have a secure outcome. On this shaky
ground of unpredictability, between the "may" and the "kind of" new
solution that could put us on a road to somewhere or "nowhere," a limited but cogent notion of agency is enabled. Cavafy's poem and Coetzee's
novel explore the effects of oppositional thinking, as well as a prospect
that constitutes one of the desiderata of our globalized world: that societies would not need to wait in vain for barbarians but would be more
open to encounters with others on terms other than the ones they have
internalized.

6

Another "Kind of Solution"

ART'S WAITING FOR THE BARBARIANS

C. P. Cavafy's and J. M. Coetzee's explorations of the theme of waiting for the barbarians set the stage for a performance that never takes place but leaves us "on a road that may lead nowhere" and in search of another "kind of solution." Despite (and because of) the barbarians' non-arrival, the structure of the promise in Cavafy's title contains the hope of exiting this stagnant state. Therefore, the promise in "Waiting for the Barbarians" reproduces itself in new contexts. This chapter probes barbarism through a different medium. If so far the question of barbarism has been located in—and limited by—language (either that of history, literature, philosophy, or cultural critique), this chapter hives off barbarism from its purported "natural habitat" to an extralinguistic, and in that sense "barbaric," realm: the visual.

The topos of *waiting for the barbarians* does not captivate only literary works. Perhaps less known than its literary adaptations are its stagings in visual art. Several paintings, sculptures, and art installations visually stage Cavafy's theme and relocate it in new cultural and national contexts. Some of these works bear the same title as Cavafy's poem. Artworks with the title *Waiting for the Barbarians*—albeit in different languages—include paintings by Rotterdam-based artist Arie van Geest (2002); British painter David Barnett (2004), who explores the creative energy of chaos as a barbaric force; London-based artist Linda Sutton; and German artist

Neo Rauch (*Warten auf die Barbaren*, 2007).[1] Cavafy's theme also resonates in Juan Muñoz's comic sound installation *Waiting for Jerry* (1991), exhibited at the Museum of Modern Art (MoMA) in New York, as well as in the sculpture exhibition "The Barbarians" (2002) by British modernist artist Anthony Caro. In Caro's exhibition, Cavafy's poem is quoted in its entirety in the catalogue as Caro's main source of inspiration. The theme of *waiting for the barbarians* appears in other media as well. In music, American composer Ned Rorem's song "Waiting for the Barbarians" was composed to the lyrics of Cavafy's poem and was first performed in 2002.[2] Finally, Philip Glass's opera *Waiting for the Barbarians*, which premiered in Erfurt, Germany, in 2005, is based on J. M. Coetzee's novel.

The focus in this chapter is on two visual stagings of the topos of *waiting for the barbarians*: South African artist Kendell Geers's labyrinthine installation *Waiting for the Barbarians* (2001) and Argentinian artist Graciela Sacco's billboard-type installation *Esperando a los bárbaros* (1996). These artworks take up the question of a possible alternative to the state of waiting for barbarians and ponder different answers to the aporia of civilization. In so doing, they transfer the topos of *waiting for the barbarians* to other mediums, to sites of enunciation beyond the West, and to a contemporary context. They explore what *waiting for the barbarians* might mean today and how art can address the predicament this topos signals.

Neither of these works is a straightforward visual illustration of the theme of *waiting for the barbarians*. Sacco's and Geers's works complicate, revise, and even criticize their literary counterparts. Their allusions to Cavafy's poem and Coetzee's novel create a productive tension between the visual and the textual. While the poem and the novel add different layers to the reception of Sacco's and Geers's installations, respectively, the artworks enrich or challenge existing readings of the poem and the novel.

Through their recasting of *waiting for the barbarians*, these installations intervene in contemporary discussions about barbarism and historical memory (Geers), as well as comparison and cultural translation (Sacco), and become producing agents of a critical mode of thinking by visual means. In my approach to artworks here, I take up Ernst van Alphen's view on art as a form of thinking and on artworks as agents of theory and cultural critique, participating or intervening in the issues they raise (2005, xiii–xiv, 2).[3]

The kind of thinking that Geers's and Sacco's artworks yield is produced "in a singular relationship" to each viewer or visitor: it is the product of a dialogue (Bal 2011, 7). For this reason, the artworks' performance can never be experienced and signified in the same way by all viewers. But this, I contend, does not make writing about these works purely "subjective": a matter of individual interpretation, too particular, and thus irrelevant for others. My analysis is co-shaped by my subjectivity and the specific questions I pose to these works. But it is simultaneously grounded in certain affective operations that each work sets in motion, which bind the experience of all its viewers, making them share an affective space despite individual differences in their perception and interpretation of the work. In this sense, my analysis of these works can be considered intersubjective.

Certain theoretical concepts help me articulate an approach to each work's aesthetic vision and critical operations. The central concept in the analysis of Geers's installation is that of *haunting*. I take my cue from Jacques Derrida's view on history as a practice of *hauntology*, which he elaborates in *Specters of Marx* (1994). Through the concept of haunting, I explore how the installation performs the past in the present, thereby transforming both the visitor's perception of the surroundings and her sense of self. The main concept brought to bear on Sacco's work is that of *staring*. This concept enables me to capture the specific encounter of the viewer with this artwork and to probe the relation between self and other that the work negotiates. Finally, by following the theoretical interventions and barbarian operations these works mobilize separately and in relation to each other, I pose the question of their relation to the political and explore how the political weaves itself in their aesthetic vision.

Inside Kendell Geers's *Waiting for the Barbarians*

The narrative of *waiting for the barbarians* is injected with a teleological vision. The expected arrival of the other signals the utopian future to which modernity's grand narratives aspire. In this narrative, the present is defined by an absence, which becomes its structuring principle. The present is occupied by a utopian future, but this occupation empties out the present from all productive forces: the people in Cavafy's city are not acting—they are waiting. They have turned away from their present and have invested their hopes for salvation in a future that will be actualized when the barbarians arrive. Cavafy's poem already carries the seeds of the deconstruction of this conception of the present: since the barbarians do not arrive, the civilized are forced to deal with their present reality on their own. The question, however, remains: "And now, what's going to happen to us without barbarians?" Geers's installation takes up the challenge of this question in a different "now," in the twenty-first century, the "now" of what is often referred to as a (post)postmodern, postpolitical, postideological era. Revisiting the theme of waiting for the other, this artwork confronts a future-oriented mode of being with another alternative.

Kendell Geers's installation is a labyrinth. With a side length of thirty meters, the entire piece is nine hundred meters square. Its walls are constructed to resemble border fences, whose top edge is crowned with a spiral of razor wire—the type used at military bases and national borders. The installation was conceived for a site outside the Gravenhorst Monastery (currently an art museum) in Hörstel, a small town in western Germany. It was part of the "Skulptur Biennale 2001 Münsterland" in Steinfurt, a project that aimed to bring together the landscapes in Münsterland and the visions of contemporary artists in a series of art installations situated in the German countryside. Geers's installation was set up in 2001, at the beginning of the new millennium and approximately one century after Cavafy's poem was written. The installation's title alludes primarily to his compatriot J. M. Coetzee's novel *Waiting for the Barbarians*, but Cavafy's poem also resonates in the work.

The title's allusion to Coetzee's novel enhances the installation's connection to the South African context, which is a constant reference point in Geers's work. Born in Johannesburg in 1968, Geers started his career in South Africa. In the 1990s, his provocative stance and "artistic bad manners" earned him the title "enfant terrible of the South African art world" (Enwezor 1997, 205; Krost 1998).[4] In 1997, he left South Africa and currently lives in Brussels, participating in group shows, holding solo exhibitions, and setting up art installations in Europe and around the world. As "White, Afrikaner, African and above all South African," Geers occupies multiple ambiguous positions (Enwezor 1997, 203). These complex positions are also reflected in his reception by the art world. Internationally, his work is sometimes viewed as "too African," while for the art world in South Africa he is often someone who has betrayed his "Africanicity" by flirting with the Western art world (Kerkham 2000, 37). Geers resists his labeling as a South African artist, as he objects to the tendency of the art world to view non-European artists as representatives of their cultures and local geographies (Enwezor 1997, 202).

Geers's works create tensions between the local and the global. While the context of apartheid South Africa, in which he was brought up, is inscribed in his art, Geers insists that the atrocities associated with this context have worked themselves into his artworks in a way that makes them "not as much about South Africa" as "about the human condition" (Sans and Geers 2000, 268). Geers's artworks do not only address the specific context in which they appear but also operate within complex networks of signs, drawing from history, literature, religion, the media, pop culture, and highbrow culture (Perryer 2002).

With this in mind, the choice of title for *Waiting for the Barbarians* reflects Geers's strategy of responding to specific situations and simultaneously projecting their connectedness with other contexts. The title alludes to Coetzee's novel and, through it, to the South African situation, but it also engages an extended network of objects that address the same theme. Therefore, it announces the work's dialectic movement between the local and the global, the specific and the general.

Geers's labyrinth sets up a nexus of references, which the viewer is called to activate. Thus, I approach Geers's installation, as well as the other artworks discussed here, as events that take place with the viewer's participation. Their meaning takes shape in a concrete situation of viewer-work interaction (Bal 1991, 8, 13, 15). In Geers's *Waiting for the Barbarians*, the visitor is not simply a viewer: she cannot watch the work from a safe distance but actively participates in it. In my reading of the work, I will be using the persona of "the visitor" as well as the pronoun "we."

The conflation of "the viewer" or "visitor" (a textual construction for my analysis) with the pronoun "we" in my reading of all artworks here is not meant to create the illusion of a homogeneous community of viewers or construct an ideal universal viewer. It is first of all, as Bal argues, an acknowledgment of the fact that the ways we view images are premised on socially based fantasies, which determine our modes of looking on

FIGURE 6.1 *Waiting for the Barbarians,* by Kendell Geers (2001). Permanent installation, Gravenhorst monastery, Munsterland, Germany. Photograph courtesy of the artist.

a collective level (1991, 18). As Geers also notes, despite the differences between viewers, we can still assume a commonality in the way artworks are experienced: "Of course, there is no ideal viewer. I don't pretend that every viewer is the same. But there are things that everybody has in common like the fact that we are all bodies in space, looking at a work of art, reacting to it from within those bodies" (Geers, quoted in Neumaier 2001, 94). In addition, the "we" in my analysis acknowledges my own participation (conscious or not) in the social fantasies that determine the ways we look.

Standing out as a strange object in the countryside and in the peaceful ambience of the monastery, the installation has an alienating effect on the visitor yet invites her to come closer. Contrary to the title's indication, the visitor entering the labyrinth embarks on a quest: an active process of searching rather than waiting for the barbarians. The labyrinth is reminiscent of the ancient Greek myth of the Minotaur, the monster who lived in the labyrinth of Knossos on Crete and was eventually slain by the hero

FIGURE 6.2 *Waiting for the Barbarians,* by Kendell Geers, showing ivy growing around the fences of the labyrinth (original photo in color, reproduced here in black and white). Photograph courtesy of the artist.

Theseus.[5] Like another Theseus, the visitor is enticed to discover the foreign presence in the labyrinth and fantasize about being a hero, fighting the beast, and saving the day. The labyrinth also arouses the inquisitive spirit of the Western explorer, who enters a foreign territory in order to master it, decipher its mysteries, and obliterate or "civilize" any barbaric elements. Thus, in the first place, the visitor is tricked into performing the stereotype of the Western explorer/colonizer. Of course, just as in Cavafy's poem, there is no barbarian presence waiting in the labyrinth. The structure is an empty iron cage: a trap into which the visitor has willingly led herself.

At this point, the quest for barbarians takes a different turn: from hunters we turn into prey entrapped in a cage, which echoes perhaps Max Weber's famous "iron cage."[6] The labyrinth stages the self-entrapment of the civilized subject in a solipsistic, suffocating system. Just as in Cavafy's poem, no barbarians are coming to save us, either because explorers or colonialists before us have exterminated them or because the others of civilization are barred from the labyrinth.

FIGURE 6.3 Detail of *Waiting for the Barbarians*, by Kendell Geers. Photograph courtesy of the artist.

Trapped in the labyrinth, we come face-to-face with ourselves as barbarians. Could we, as civilized subjects, be the barbarians, for which the installation is waiting fearfully, trying to guard itself by means of barbed wire and warning signs? The title suddenly takes an unexpected meaning. In our heads we hear the echo of the Magistrate's words to Colonel Joll in Coetzee's novel: "You are the enemy, you have made the war" (2000, 125).

The visitor's temporary entrapment in the labyrinth invests her with a sense of guilt. The labyrinth interpellates the visitor, as it were, and the visitor responds by accepting guilt. In Louis Althusser's theory of interpellation, the formation of the subject and the conferral of identity take place through an acceptance and even self-ascription of guilt. In Althusser's well-known example, the policeman hails a passerby ("Hey, you there!"), who automatically turns around, acknowledging this hailing as an attribution of guilt (1984, 48). For Althusser, this operation of interpellation or hailing describes the function of ideology, through which individuals are transformed into subjects (48–49).The installation can be viewed as a visual metaphor for the ideological system (or "the law") within which we attain our subjectivity and identity. As products of ideology, in Althusser's theory subjects have limited free will or control. As Judith Butler remarks in her analysis of Althusser's theory, the subject "accepts the terms by which he or she is hailed" and submits to the law (the police) because this readiness to accept guilt "promises identity" (1997b, 106, 108). There is no "I" without this self-attribution of guilt (107).

The installation performs an interpellative address that confers guilt on the visitor. However, unlike in Althusser's theory, in *Waiting for the Barbarians* this guilt does not operate on an abstract ahistorical level. It is historically grounded, because it is the product of accumulated historical processes or events. The artist's own identity helps elucidate this point. The guilt with which Geers's installation injects the visitor can be correlated with the artist's guilt as a white Afrikaans South African man. This part of his identity implicates him in the violence of apartheid, which he inevitably bears and through which his subjectivity has been formed. "I am guilty!" Geers has written. "I cannot hide my guilt as it is written all over my face. I was born guilty without being given the option" (Geers, quoted in Kerkham 2000, 31). The artist "carries the specter of being oppressor" through his inherited past as a white South African (Enwezor 1997, 204).

The installation passes this sense of guilt on to the visitor, regardless of whether she has committed bad deeds or has a guilty conscience. As subjects, we cannot but perpetuate the violence of the discursive structures that have formed us. The Magistrate in Coetzee's novel—and, through him, Coetzee himself—was also struggling with the same guilt. Neither Althusser's guilt that transforms us into subjects through ideology nor the guilt that Geers carries as a white South African is (necessarily) linked to conscious choices or direct actions, yet is constitutive of a subject's identity.

If the guilt the installation confers on us is not a conscious choice, then how we deal with it certainly is. The installation calls the visitor to respond to this guilt. It challenges us to think of ways to transpose guilt into a critical stance and a creative mode of being instead of a predicament that imprisons us in a paralyzing state of waiting in the present. Thus, while the installation stages the entrapment of the subject in ideological structures, it also offers the tools to unsettle these structures. Two ways in which this is accomplished are (1) the visibility and materiality of its structure and (2) the installation's effect of haunting. By elaborating these factors, I will show how they lead up to what I identify as the work's main barbarian operation.

The title of the work may cultivate the expectation of a presence inside the labyrinth. As soon as we realize that the installation is empty, we turn our gaze to the labyrinth's structure. The installation's frame—fences crowned with barbed-wire—suddenly becomes visible. As Geers said in a conversation with Nicolas Bourriaud, every object in his art embodies an ideological structure: "Whether it's a broken bottle or a security sign or a border fence, the object is the material manifestation of an ideological system" (Bourriaud, Buren, and Geers 2005, 154). The labyrinth in *Waiting for the Barbarians* becomes a visual metaphor for ideology.

Ideology, however, is by definition invisible. As Althusser writes, "Ideology never says, 'I am ideological'" (1984, 49). Its power and efficacy pertain as long as it remains hidden.[7] If the labyrinth is a visual metaphor for ideological structures, by drawing attention to its frame, Geers's work makes ideology shed its invisibility, from which it draws its power. By becoming visible, an ideological structure becomes vulnerable. By making the visitor aware of the ideological structures in which she is implicated, the installation gives her the option to face them critically. Even though the visitor remains implicated in these structures (she is still positioned inside the labyrinth), turning her attention to the labyrinth's fences may trigger a critique of the terms through which she is subjectivized.

Unlike most typical labyrinths, this one is made of fences, allowing a better view of the labyrinth's different paths. The visitor feels imprisoned but also exposed. The labyrinth's disorienting effect makes the subject vulnerable but also creates the possibility for a repositioning of the subject in relation to the discursive structures that shape her. The labyrinth is porous from every side—a permeability that is in certain ways reminiscent of the porous wall in Kafka's "The Great Wall of China." The partial transparency of the fences generates a different experience than that of a labyrinthine structure made of concrete walls. Its permeability increases our determination to find a way out, although nothing guarantees that the outside would be a safer or better place.

Waiting for barbarians suggests a stagnant, passive state, wherein the (civilized) subject appears impotent, without agency, hoping for an external intervention. Geers's installation challenges the visitor to quit waiting for barbarians and focus on the structures that shape and constrain our subjectivity instead. In so doing, it urges the visitor to come up with the means to deal with the non-arrival of the other. Finding another "kind of solution" to the barbarians' absence requires questioning the structures that made us dependent on the notion of the barbarian.

Haunted by History

The image of the labyrinth is also central in Coetzee's *Waiting for the Barbarians* and constitutes one of the most conspicuous links between Geers's and Coetzee's works. The Magistrate uses the labyrinth as a metaphor for his entrapment in the discursive structures of the Empire. Searching for a way out, he first sees the barbarian girl as "the only key" he has "to the labyrinth" (Coetzee 2000, 95). When he realizes that the girl is not another Ariadne who will lead him out of the maze, he resorts to a vision he believes will help him escape the labyrinth. He envisions a world in which the Empire has ceased to exist and all its violent marks have been erased and replaced by nature and peaceful human activity: "Be patient, one of these days he [Colonel Joll] will go away, one of these days quiet will return: then our siestas will grow longer and our swords rustier, . . . the mortar will crumble till lizards nest between the bricks and owls fly out of the belfry, and the line that marks the frontier on the maps of Empire will grow hazy and obscure till we are blessedly forgotten" (149). This contest of human civilization with nature, from which the latter will eventually come out the winner, dissolving arbitrary border divisions, is also part of Geers's vision in his *Waiting for the Barbarians*.

In the introductory text placed at the entrance of Geers's labyrinth, we read (in German): "Nature can and will reclaim here its territory."[8] Although it is announced as a permanent installation, Geers's labyrinth— and the violence of artificial borders that it signifies—is ephemeral, as this statement seems to suggest. It will inevitably be swallowed up by nature. As stated in the catalogue text, the artist planted ivy along the fences after completing the installation's setup. This climbing plant, which is growing today around the labyrinth's fences, was meant to envelop and eventually drown the construction.

But is nature's ability to erase the signs of barbarism and divisive violence the "message" the installation or the novel tries to convey? I argue that this is not the case. The Magistrate's fantasy of a return to a peaceful life in nature, devoid of the Empire's marks, is succeeded by the sudden realization of the utopian nature of this vision: "Thus I seduced myself, taking one of the many wrong turnings I have taken on a road that looks true but has delivered me into the heart of a labyrinth" (Coetzee 2000, 149). This labyrinth is the reality of the present, with which the Magistrate must struggle. Nature can function as a reminder of the transitoriness of every human construct and system—as it does in Geers's installation. But it can also feed escapist tendencies and become a path to historical oblivion.

Neither the novel nor the installation allows this oblivion. On the contrary: the ivy Geers planted around the installation's fences manifests the inescapability of violence, which also lurks in nature itself. As opposed to the labyrinth's structure, which makes violence visible and thus problematizes it, nature—in the form of the climbing plant drowning the installation—violently tries to efface the traces of the installation from the present, and thereby also its ability to act as a reminder of violence and artificial divisions. Nature may thus harbor more violence than the labyrinth itself.

The installation underscores the omnipresence of violence in the present and the past. Therefore, it performs two of the functions that according to Bal distinguish contemporary political art: "the affective—albeit oblique—engagement with the present" and "the refusal to excise the past from that present" (2011, 3). For Bal, the implication of the past in the present takes place through a transformation of perception into memory. In the following discussion, I use the figure of the ghost as a theoretical concept in order to show how the installation changes our perception of the here and now and unsettles our sense of self by introducing strands of historical memory in the present.

Although the installation is empty, the visitor senses invisible forces in it. These forces, which can be momentarily mistaken for the barbarians the visitor may be looking for, can be described as specters of history. The way the installation activates historical memory can be described in the terms of Jacques Derrida's practice of hauntology. In *Specters of Marx*, reflecting on the fate of Marx's "spirit" after the fall of communism, Derrida yields an image of the present as inhabited by specters and conceptualizes the relation between present, past, and future through a practice of hauntology. Playing with its near homonym, ontology, hauntology challenges the priority of presence and of being through a figure that hovers between presence and absence, life and death: the ghost (Davis 2005, 373). Hauntology proposes a conception of history as a perpetual coming back. A specter, Derrida says, "is always a revenant. One cannot control its comings and goings because it begins by coming back" (1994, 11). History as a spectral phenomenon does not move forward but appears and recedes, changing its shapes and claims on the present. Consequently, as Wendy Brown points out in her discussion of Derrida's hauntology, the past is not an objective account but what lives on from past events in the present, how these events "occupy the force fields of the present," how they grasp us and affect our visions of the future (2001, 150).

Geers's installation becomes an arena for an intersection of spectral forces. The allusion to Coetzee's novel and Geers's South African background evokes the context of apartheid. But apartheid violence is not the only specter the installation conjures. The labyrinth has religious overtones too, as we can view it as a symbol of the road to redemption. Nevertheless, the position of Geers's violent labyrinthine construction outside a Catholic monastery strikes a discordant note in the peacefulness of monastic life. Moreover, its evocation of borders and violent exclusions clashes with the inclusive ideal of Christianity.[9]

The tension this discordance creates may incite the visitor to seek other associations between the installation and the monastery. The out-of-placeness of the installation and its violent impression in the religious atmosphere of the monastery evoke associations between religion—or, better, its institutionalization by the church—and barbarism. The visitor senses the ghosts of torturers and Inquisitors, executioners in the name of religion, crusaders and burning martyrs, religious wars of the past, and the intifadas of the present and their brutal repressions. Under the impact of these spectral forces, the contradiction between barbarism and religion ceases to be so convincing.

The wider region of the installation has been marked by battles, military and political conflicts, and territorial changes, such as the battle of the Teutoburg Forest or the Peace of Westphalia. The specters of these border divisions are summoned by the image of Geers's barbed-wire fence and remind us that the seemingly peaceful landscape that hosts the installation has been subjected to divisive violence throughout history.[10]

The installation also haunts the visitor with specters of twentieth-century barbarism. Along the path leading from the railway station of Hörstel to the monastery, there is a monument to World War II. Next to the memorial stone are aerial photographs of the area before and after the World War II bombardments. Although nature has concealed the signs of this destruction with the passing of time, as we walk by this monument, we are made aware of the violence and barbarism that lurk in unexpected sites. The installation's haunting effect alerts us to such sites of barbarism.

Situated in a German province largely destroyed during World War II, Geers's *Waiting for the Barbarians* evokes the specter of one of the most blatant instances of barbarism in modern history: the Holocaust. The fences allude to concentration camps.[11] The material of the labyrinth— the barbed wire that crowns the fences—also functions as a trigger of historical memory. As Alan Krell (2002) explains, barbed wire has become a symbol of modernity in its function as an instrument of oppression, territorial expansion, and border protection. It has been seen in various contexts, among which Kitchener's blockhouses in the Boer Wars and, later, apartheid in South Africa, the barb-wired no-man's-land of World War I, the electrically wired fences of Nazi concentration camps, and, today, detention centers for asylum seekers.[12]

The choice of a South African artist to situate this work in Germany does not seem arbitrary. Both the German and the South African context are invested with historical guilt, which is transmitted to the visitor. The work's concurrent evocation of the specter of Western colonialism (through its affiliation with Coetzee's novel and South Africa) and of the Nazi regime conjoins two of the most striking strands of barbarism in modern Western history through the image of barbed wire. This encounter is not without consequences for our understanding of these contexts. If "the idea of barbarism has been central to intellectual debate about fascism," Brett Neilson remarks, "it has played a lesser role in the study of imperialism" (1999, 90). By evoking the specters of both Nazism and colonialism, the work places them under the common denominator of barbarism. The cohabitation of the two specters transfers the indignation associated with Nazism upon the colonial regime. It thus enables an understanding of the Holocaust as a form of imperialism without a "civilizing mission."[13]

The setup of the installation in 2001 and its continuing presence today turn it into a reminder of barbarism both in the past and present. The work encourages us to seek invisible forms of violence and exclusionary practices in our supposedly borderless, postpolitical world.

If nature has concealed most traces of past violence in the area— marks of border divisions, battles, bombings—the installation reexposes those traces and invites us to revisit the historical narratives attached to them. As we are haunted by specters of the past, nothing seems peaceful or innocent anymore. The beauty of nature and the serenity of the monastery seem deceptive, as if hiding something barbaric. Through this operation, the artwork itself becomes a "barbarism": a strange, incongruous element in this location, which brings out the violence in its surroundings by conjuring specters that do not allow this violence to pass into oblivion.

Notably, specters are summoned through the installation's aesthetic of *absence*. Geers's emphasis on absences and irresolute traces has been read as an example of what art critic Ralph Rugoff calls a "forensic aesthetic." According to this aesthetic, the work invites the viewer to become a "forensic anthropologist" forced to "speculatively piece together histories that remain largely invisible to the eye" (1997, 62). However, a "forensic" reading of the artwork requires a sober, disengaged look that would allow the viewer to assemble the pieces of an invisible puzzle. To my mind, this is at odds with one of the main effects of Geers's work: It implicates the visitor in those invisible traces of history that form a force field at the installation's site. By engaging the visitor in historical memory on a physiological, visceral level, the work proposes an affective understanding of history as it is constantly being rewritten in the present.[14] Experiencing the past as it makes its claims on the present is crucial in understanding our own position in the here and now. Thus, the installation urges the visitor to be more a "clairvoyant" than "forensic anthropologist": alert to the spectral presences that shape, produce, and claim our present.

For Derrida, hauntology is not just a theoretical model but a practice of living. "Learning to live" can happen only "between life and death," and this "between" entails learning "to live with ghosts," in "the upkeep, the conversation, the company, or the companionship" of those others that oscillate between existence and nonexistence and are never fully present (Derrida 1994, xviii). For Derrida, this "being-with specters" requires a responsibility before the ghosts of the dead and the unborn (xix). Learning to live with ghosts would mean learning how to give them speech and listen to them rather than be unaware of them or try to exorcize them (47, 176).

Listening to specters does not offer the viewer of Geers's work the comfort of a safe interpretation. Ghosts do not yield clear-cut knowledge. We can try to listen to them, but, as Derrida argues, the spectral can make no promises. Specters signal a "being-there" of something absent or departed that "no longer belongs to knowledge" (6). Living with ghosts also means learning to cope with this unknowability. Ghosts address the living with voices of the past or with not-yet-formed possibilities for the future (Davis 2005, 378–79). How we interpret their address and act on it is our responsibility. In this precarious space between the knowable and the unknowable, power and impotence, lie the visitor's agency and responsibility as a historical subject to be mindful of the complex operations of the past in the present, as she tries to envision the future.

By introducing the logic of haunting in our present, the work enables the coexistence of antithetical states. The visible and the invisible, presence and absence, the knowable and the unknowable, come together in the figure of the ghost, forming an unstable space that questions the rigid borders the installation so forcefully inscribes. Geers's installation makes us distrust our here and now and question its familiar messages. By urging us to listen to ghosts around us, the installation yields a precarious view of the present, whereby things we took for granted acquire a strange aftertaste. The political space shaped by the installation is no longer a safe and familiar location but a space wherein the visible—that is, what we are used to seeing in a certain way—becomes suspect and unreliable. This displacement of the familiar captures one of the work's "barbarian operations."

The topos of *waiting for the barbarians*, as already suggested, implies a mode of living in the present that has its eyes turned to the future but is simultaneously immersed in an enervating guilt that stems from the past. This guilt may be repressed and forgotten but nonetheless manifests itself in the present in the form of inertia and stagnation: the subject is condemned to wait for a deus ex machina and seeks salvation in forces outside its own space—outside the labyrinth. Geers's empty installation encourages us to stop focusing on the absence of the other as the structuring principle of the present and listen to the specters that intrude on our seemingly empty present with their half-presence. The focus is neither on absence nor on presence but on invisibility, half-presence. What the installation adds to Cavafy's topos is the insight that the barbarians are not necessarily fully absent but may still be around, haunting the civilized. Their effect on us is therefore very real. The barbarians are not there to lead us out of the labyrinth of our system, but in our search for another "kind of solution," it might help to listen to the specters of history around us.

Geers's labyrinth introduces a disjoined quality of time: history not as a straight line but as a constant "coming back." The work thereby makes history a living part of the present. Specters, as Fredric Jameson argues, make us aware of the fact that a self-sufficient notion of the present cannot exist (1999, 39). The present is always noncontemporaneous with itself, never identical to itself. Derrida's emphasis on the disjunction of the present from itself collapses the absolute separation between present, past, and future. Specters show us how the identity of the present to itself is breached and how the present is a "spectral moment" that already contains the past and the future.

This disjoined identity of the present may help us conceptualize the subject in a slightly different way. If Althusser's subject affirms its self-identity through self-incrimination, the figure of the ghost, I argue, signals the possibility of another mode of being. As Butler argues, the existence of the "I" in Althusser is dependent on a blind complicity with the law, which compels individuals to respond to the hailing by incriminating themselves. But if acceptance of the law is necessary for the "I" to exist, then how, Butler asks, can the subject ever critically interrogate the law? A critique of the law and of the terms by which we are called into being as subjects cannot happen "unless the one who offers that critique is willing, as it were, to be undone by the critique that he or she performs" (Butler 1997b, 108). Butler considers that there may be other possibilities for being that would produce a different response to the hailing of ideology and resist "its lure of identity" (130). "Being," Butler suggests, should be read as a potentiality that cannot be exhausted by any interpellation and thus holds the potential to undermine the workings of ideology (131)."A failure of interpellation," according to Butler, "may well undermine the capacity of the subject to 'be' in a self-identical sense, but it may also mark the path toward a more open, even more ethical, kind of being, one of or for the future" (131). This different mode of being would allow us to question the labyrinth's incriminating structures.

The ghosts that accompany the visitor bring us closer to such a different mode of being, which is not an affirmation of self-identity but a negation of the oneness of the self with itself. Althusser's subject needs to say "here I am" at the cost of pleading guilty and thus submitting to the law. The ghost, on the other hand, is able to say at the same time "here I am" and "here I am not." Self-negation is necessary for questioning the law and ideology because it frees us from the need to affirm our subjectivity through guilt and submission. This partial self-negation challenges the process of interpellation as a restoration of self-identity through the linguistic consolidation "here I am." The ghost undoes the self-identity of the present because it brings into it the past and the future. Similarly, it unsettles the subject's self-identity because it points to a mode of being between presence and absence, identity and non-identity. Therefore, by allowing specters to touch our subjectivity, we also open ourselves to the potentiality of an ethical mode of being as (historical) subjects. This mode is not grounded in guilt as a means of preserving the law but may turn this guilt into a responsibility toward the past as well as the future.

Staring Encounters: Graciela Sacco's *Esperando a los bárbaros*

Our own undecidable meaning is in the irreducible figure that stands in for the eyes of the other.
—Gayatri Chakravorty Spivak, *Death of a Discipline*

Esperando a los bárbaros (1996) by Graciela Sacco also takes up the challenge of seeking another "kind of solution" to the waiting. Just like Geers's labyrinth, Sacco's installation does not present any barbarians. However, the encounter with the viewer in Sacco's work takes place on different terms than in Geers's labyrinth and suggests another way out of civilization's aporia.

Born in 1956 near the city of Rosario in Argentina, where she still lives, Sacco is a visual artist, photographer, and video and installation artist with international acclaim.[15] Her work *Esperando a los bárbaros* is a billboard-type installation comprising a hundred eyes printed on paper, each of them framed between pieces of rough wood. The work is created with the heliographic technique, which Sacco brought to the forefront of contemporary art. Heliography describes the "chemical action of light on emulsified photosensitive surfaces."[16] Her heliographic technique allows the transferring of photographic images onto a heterogeneous group of supports, such as paper, leather, wood, stone, glass, plastic, and metal. The capacity of the heliographic process to make the most illusory shadows fixed yet diffuse creates the impression that the artist "'writes and unwrites' in light" (Damian 2005; Kartofel 2006).

In *Esperando a los bárbaros* the use of the heliographic technique for printing eyes on paper produces the effect of dozens of eyes looking at the viewer from the wall of the gallery.[17] Their framing in wood conveys the impression that the subjects to whom these eyes belong are behind a wooden fence, trying to peek at the other side. The wooden pieces seem to hinder their vision, denying them access to what lies beyond this wooden barrier.

Just as in the analysis of Geers's work, my postulated viewer of this artwork, as well as the collective "we," is part of the discursive system we may call "the West"—even if the viewer resists it. The eyes in Sacco's installation, disembodied and disconnected from their context, function as metonymies of individuals, for which any clues to their appearance, race, ethnic origin, culture, age, and gender are missing. Without the face, a safe guess about the identity of these people is impossible. Faces function as cues to our roots and histories and enable our identification with social or ethnic groups (Garland-Thomson 2006, 176). If faces are sites of identification and communication, the eyes in Sacco's work, separated from the face, at first glance seem to forestall any contact with the viewer based on recognition.

Faced with dozens of staring eyes, the viewer may experience the discomfort of being observed by anonymous viewers. Because these observers

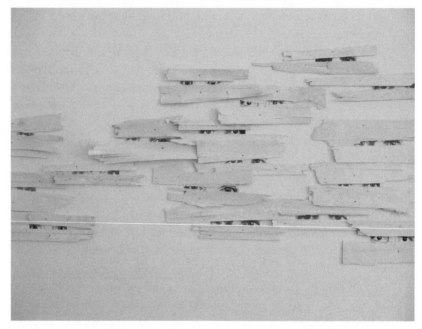

FIGURE 6.4 Detail of the installation *Esperando a los bárbaros*, by Graciela Sacco (1996). Heliography on paper and wood, variable dimensions. Photograph by the author, taken at Museum Morsbroich, Germany, where the installation was part of the exhibition "Radical Shift: Political and Social Upheaval in Argentinean Art since the 1960s," March 13–May 22, 2011. Photo reproduced by permission of the artist.

are hidden behind a fence, they are likely to be perceived as enemies who can strike at any moment. Therefore, in this first episode of the encounter between viewer and image, the eyes may feed the paranoia of the civilized subject, who sees evil others everywhere.

This paranoia is particularly pertinent since the terrorist attacks on September 11, 2001, which produced the "terrorist" as the primary enemy of the "civilized world." The distinctive feature of this new type of enemies is their anonymity and *lack* of distinctive features. As Arjun Appadurai remarks, the increase in terrorist actions since September 11 has induced uncertainty regarding the agents of such violence: "Who are they? What faces are behind the masks? What names do they use? Who arms and supports them? How many of them are there? Where are they hidden? What do they want?" (2006, 88). Though created in 1995, Sacco's installation speaks to the contemporary amplification of anxiety regarding these others, about which little is known. Even if the viewer's first response is marked by suspicion, the installation, I contend, does not exacerbate our fear of unidentified others. Rather, it counterpoints this fear with the challenge of a different response, without having to know the other's name, status, and even facial features.

In an attempt to make the eyes intelligible, the viewer may seek to frame the image in an existing narrative. She therefore latches on to the only textual indication: the title. *Esperando a los bárbaros* is a Spanish translation of Cavafy's "Waiting for the Barbarians." As Sacco informed me, the source text for her choice of title was Cavafy's poem. The installation—just as Geers's work does—constitutes a transcultural and intersemiotic translation of the topos of *waiting for the barbarians*.[18] The precise mode of interaction between the visual and textual aspects of Sacco's installation deserves further elaboration.

The Viewer as Civilized

In order to probe Sacco's redeployment of Cavafy's narrative, we can follow (at least) two interpretive courses, depending on whether or not the viewer sees the eyes in the installation as the barbarians in the narrative of its title. If those eyes belong to the barbarians for which the viewers-as-civilized-subjects are waiting, then the absence of barbarians in the Cavafian narrative is contradicted in Sacco's work by a minimal presence of the other through the synecdoche of the eyes. However, the installation does not offer a full-fledged version of barbarians that would enable the viewer to appropriate them within a Western representational regime. There are simply no bodies or faces on which our culturally constructed fantasies of the other can be projected. Thus, the work calls for an eye-to-eye encounter with others without the interference of cultural prejudice and before any process of labeling can be set forth.

To articulate the terms of this encounter, I use the concept of the "stare." Various vision-related concepts are regularly employed in visual analysis. The most popular are probably the "look" and the "gaze." The gaze has been used to describe a hierarchization between the viewer and the object of viewing, which produces, as Rosemarie Garland-Thomson puts it, "an asymmetrical power relation between a largely predatory viewer and victimized viewed" (2006, 189).[19] Since the title of Sacco's installation suggests a hierarchical division between civilized and barbarians, with the latter presumably functioning as the object of the "civilized gaze," the concept of the gaze might seem the obvious choice for approaching Sacco's installation. However, I argue that the artwork triggers a different kind of relationship with the viewer, which the concept of the gaze falls short of capturing.

As opposed to the gaze, the stare stresses the potential productive mutuality of a visual encounter. According to Garland-Thomson, we stare at something because it interrupts comforting narratives and certainties by embodying something baffling, contingent, unfamiliar, and yet strangely recognizable (2006, 174).[20] Of course, staring could also be perceived as an act of objectification grounded in a voyeuristic impulse. However, the concept has another side as well: it denotes a kind of looking that demands a response. Especially in the case of face-to-face staring, the power relation between the subjects involved is not predetermined and does not register a clear subject-object distinction. Staring can thus be a dynamic visual exchange due to its open-ended aspect, which creates a space of unpredictability (181).

The eyes in Sacco's installation invite such a staring encounter if we get past the fear they initially induce. Staring at another person certainly differs from staring at an artwork, since the viewer's stare cannot actively affect the eye images in the installation. Although the viewer is the only one who can register the effect of the staring encounter, the staring takes place nonetheless, because we experience the eyes staring at us just as we stare at them. Since the eyes refuse to yield markers of identification, there is no clear social frame for the viewer's confrontation with them. Therefore, the viewer is neither in full control of the encounter nor in a superior position, as one would perhaps expect from an encounter of a civilized subject with barbarians. The absence of the other's face sabotages this operation of binarization. The eyes alone are not enough to make us register the "owners" of the eyes as "barbarians" in a conclusive manner. In this way, the eyes refuse to validate the dichotomy projected by the linguistic part of the installation—its title.

If we often look at others in order to confirm our own self-image and strengthen our position in the social world, then staring at Sacco's installation does not gratify this desire. The viewer becomes vulnerable instead of achieving self-identification through the other. Our encounter with the eyes does not enable us to measure ourselves against any recognizable barbarians. However, by withdrawing the safety of familiar representational systems, the work makes the outcome of our confrontation with the other open and unpredictable. The narrative of *waiting for the barbarians* thereby receives a twist. The artwork suggests that the solution to the predicament of civilization will come neither from a "constitutive outside" nor from inside civilization (as Geers's installation partly seems to suggest) but through the formation of a zone of contact between inside and outside.

The illegible eyes in Sacco's installation refuse to be fully translated yet create a zone between self and other, wherein a relation can be established on another basis. To give in to the experience of this encounter, we have to give up part of our deep-rooted fantasies of barbarians and confront others not as evil enemies but as adversaries. Chantal Mouffe proposes the notion of the "adversary" as an alternative to the category of the "enemy" and the violence the latter implies. When we turn enemies into adversaries, Mouffe argues, we cease to perceive the "they" as a threat to the identity and existence of the "we." Instead, we acknowledge the legitimacy of the other (2005, 15–16, 20). As a result, the "they" is not an enemy to be eliminated but a legitimate opponent whom we can face in a "common symbolic space" (20). Taking up Mouffe's notion of the adversary, Bal argues that this notion transforms the "they" into a "you" (2011, 12).[21] This entails a transition from an "us versus them" dialectic to a relation between an "I" and a "you," which, I argue, takes place in the viewer's encounter with Sacco's work: the other ceases to be a barbarian when everything else fades away and we focus only on the eyes.

The eyes in Sacco's work suggest a possible way out of the aporia of Cavafy's poem. Even if the barbarians do not exist in the ways the civilized have constructed them, the work draws attention to human beings outside the walls of our alleged civilization, to whom we can relate differently, by leaving stereotypical representations "out of sight." As a result, the narrative of the Cavafian intertext is revised: the categorical distinction between barbarians and civilized loses its force through this eye-to-eye contact, which promises another kind of relationality that emerges from the mutual staring.

The Viewer as Barbarian

Another way of relating Sacco's work to Cavafy's poem is based on the reverse hypothesis, that the eyes in Sacco's installation do not belong to the barbarians of the title but are the apprehensive eyes of the civilized waiting for the barbarians. Following this postulation, the role of the title's barbarians is assigned to the viewer. Supposing that as (Western) viewers we have internalized the label of the "civilized," the realization that we must be the barbarians of the narrative occasions a reversal of perspective. We are suddenly the objects of the look of the civilized (the eyes). Forced to assume, even momentarily, the position of the barbarian, we feel interpellated. The eyes place us in a guilty position or invest us with evil qualities, as is the case with the common demonization of the barbarian in civilizational discourse.

The wooden planks that close off the eyes in Sacco's work index a fence. A parallel can be drawn here with Geers's labyrinthine fence. The fence in Sacco's work is possibly meant to protect civilization by barricading civilized subjects against the projected danger of others. Civilization is thereby presented as a self-enclosed construct that wards off alterity—as is also the case with Geers's labyrinth. We can also imagine the wooden planks as nailed across the windows of a house. Architectural constructs, according to Deleuze and Guattari, function like faces (1987, 191). Thus, the civilized looking through the planks would appear to be trapped in a house, whose windows—its "eyes" to the outside world—are "blinded" by planks nailed across them. However, just as the barbed-wire fence in Geers's labyrinth does not completely hinder our view of the outside, the "blinds" that the wooden planks set up leave crevices through which the subjects behind them can look and be looked at. These crevices expose the civilized "prison house" to its outside.

But to what kind of solution to the predicament of civilization do these openings point? The title suggests that the eyes of the civilized are waiting for us—the barbarians—and thus see in us the solution to the waiting. If we are, indeed, the barbarians they are waiting for, our role comes with a sense of responsibility. Instead of posing as the victimized object of the civilized gaze, the viewer can try to redefine her role as a barbarian and invest it with creative functions. Instead of "where are the barbarians?" the challenging question for the viewer could be "what could I do to fulfill my barbarian task?" The viewer is called to become, as it were, the solution to the waiting. The search for the whereabouts of the barbarians gives way to a performativity of barbarism.

The dislocation of the viewer-as-barbarian also underscores the relative nature of the barbarian: the eyes become visual inscriptions of the fact that the barbarian is in the eye of the beholder. This realization does not necessarily entail a relativist approach to the barbarian, which would circumvent the power relations permeating the term. The artwork foregrounds these power relations through its title and simultaneously debunks them by deessentializing the barbarian. Instead of being-barbarian in an absolute sense, the viewer is incited to perform constructive barbarian acts, which may hold the promise for exiting the state of waiting.

Cultural Translation

The title pluralizes the work's interpretive possibilities and directs it from a local to a transcultural context. Graciela Sacco's art, despite its international acclaim, is often framed by critics within the political and cultural context of Argentina and Argentine art. In an article on Sacco in the *New York Times*, characteristically entitled "Bringing Argentina out of the Shadows" (July 9, 2000), Lyle Rexer presents Sacco's work in the context of the emerging art scene in democratic Argentina and views her artistic production in relation to the Argentine sociopolitical climate in the last decades. Although Sacco "began making art at the end of the most dangerous and difficult period of recent Argentine history," according to Rexer, the current "transformed political climate" in Argentina "has made her art a calling card for a nation that might once have prohibited it, or worse." Her task is therefore to rescue Argentina from "artistic oblivion" and bring the nation, artistically speaking, "out of the shadows."

There is nothing wrong, of course, with representing one's nation in the international art scene. Nor do I wish to downplay the significance of the political and cultural context in which Sacco's work is produced and the complex ways in which it informs her work. Nevertheless, I am particularly interested in how the title *Esperando a los bárbaros* contributes to making the work's local context part of a transcultural, intertextual network.

The fact that in *Esperando a los bárbaros* Sacco chose a foreign, non-Argentine point of reference—Cavafy's poem—is significant, if we consider that Argentina has a long tradition in the dialectic of civilization versus barbarism. The work that introduced this tradition was *Facundo: Civilization and Barbarism* (*Facundo: Civilización y barbarie*, 1845), written by Argentina's great intellectual, writer, president, and political innovator Domingo F. Sarmiento.[22] *Facundo* proposed the dialectic between civilization and barbarism as the central conflict in Latin American culture and society (Echevarría 2003, 2). For Sarmiento, civilization was linked to European Enlightenment and identified with modern Western ideals and practices. He located civilization in the culture of the metropolitan city, whereas barbarism represented for him the backwardness and brutality of the countryside (12). Sarmiento turned this dichotomy into a prominent theme in Latin American literature and used it to give Argentina a national discourse, "through which the country could think itself" (Sorensen Goodrich 1996, 6; Echevarría 2003, 10).

It is likely that Sacco's work stages an implicit dialogue between Cavafy's theme and Sarmiento's employment of the "barbarism versus civilization" dichotomy. Although the precise mode of interaction of these works is not explored here, Sacco's choice to refer to Cavafy could imply a reversal and critique of the premises of Sarmiento's book. Whereas Cavafy's poem underscores the dependence of the civilized on the barbarians they are waiting for, *Facundo* describes the reverse situation: "barbaric" Argentina waiting for the European civilization to save it. Several questions arise from the intertwining of the two contexts. More than one and a half centuries after *Facundo* was written, can Argentina still identify the West as the ideal marker of its future and seek its salvation in Western culture? Or has the role of the West today as a social imaginary and an object of desire for societies beyond the West begun to fade? What is the fate of Sarmiento's dichotomy in contemporary Argentina, and how does Cavafy's topos relate to Argentina's tumultuous political history? By raising such questions, Sacco's reference to Cavafy does not pose as an escape from her own national context. Through Cavafy, the installation also interrogates Argentine national discourse. Thus, Sacco's work goes beyond the artist's national context in order to go back to it and address it from another, foreign perspective.

The interaction of the work with its *parergon*—the title—makes it a testing ground for transcultural translation. The work translates "waiting for the barbarians" in Spanish and relocates this topos in a Latin American context, enriching it with new perspectives through a new context and medium. The narrative's "original" context is shown as unsaturated and open, as all contexts are (Spivak 1992, 783).

Apart from the tension created between the local and the global, the installation and its title also stage a comparative confrontation between two artistic paradigms: modernist and contemporary relational art. The theme of *waiting for the barbarians* found its first literary expression at the outset of modernism (Cavafy's poem appeared in 1904). The poem's narrative is injected with the teleological vision of modernity, while it is also critical of modernity's "grand narratives." The expectation of the barbarians' arrival can be read as the utopian reality to which modernist art often aspired. The people in Cavafy's poem have turned away from reality and have invested their hopes for salvation in a utopia that will be realized when the barbarians arrive. Sacco's work breaks with this utopian vision. It leaves the future direction of its title behind in order to focus on relations in the present. Instead of waiting for barbarians, the work shapes a space of interaction between self and other in the here and now of the encounter with the viewer.

In *Relational Aesthetics*, art critic Nicolas Bourriaud argues that with artworks today it "seems more pressing to invent possible relations with our neighbours in the present than to bet on happier tomorrows" (2002, 45). Bourriaud considers relationality—or what he calls "relational aesthetics"—as the distinctive feature of contemporary art.[23] Relational art is not just destined for aesthetic consumption but engages the sphere of interhuman relations and creates new models or relationality with viewers (28). Unlike modernist art, relational art does not seek to represent or form utopian realities but stays in the present and tries "to construct concrete spaces" (46). Thus, Sacco's installation and its title stage the tension between two artistic paradigms: a modernist art that endorses utopianism and strives for a total transformation of reality (the narrative of waiting for barbarians), and a relational art that produces artworks as "relational microterritories" (31).

Sacco's work enacts a surpassing of its modernist past and, in this sense, an overcoming of the futile waiting that typifies modernist narratives. Nevertheless, the title accompanies the work as a reminder that the discourse that produced the narrative of our salvation by barbarians is still active in our political realities. Therefore, the relationality Sacco's work proposes becomes even more meaningful when measured against a discourse still active in the present. The narrative of *waiting for the barbarians* is a critical reaction to this discourse as well as an acknowledgment of its pervasiveness.

In Sacco's work, the role division between the viewer and the eyes along the lines of "civilized" and "barbarians" is useful for exploring the viewer's response to the artwork, especially for probing the relation to its title. However, the roles the title suggests are projected and enacted so that the artwork can eventually overcome them. Sacco's installation transcends the barbarian/civilized dichotomy by proposing an alternative relationality in the event of its encounter with the viewer—a relation that unravels between an "I" and a "you."

Looking Elsewhere—a Detail

One element in Sacco's work that might escape attention at first is that on closer look, it becomes clear that not all the eyes are staring at us. Some are looking *through* us rather than *at* us: they seem distracted or vacant, looking into the void. Others look up, excluding the viewer from their visual field. This observation adds a new dimension to the work.

What we see as "the others" of Western civilization—if that is what we take those eyes to be—do not always seek to be defined in relation to Western cultural norms. Many cultures are assumed to look up to the West as a superior model or to have their eyes turned to Western powers in need of help—financial or military. Sarmiento's *Facundo* also projected European civilization as an ideal toward which Argentine society and culture should progress. In this context, those eyes in Sacco's work that turn away from the (Western) viewer may be refusing to validate the viewer's gaze. They may be refusing to be compared to Western standards and be found inadequate or inferior. They may be refusing to look at Western culture as the broker of cultural and moral values. The eyes that look away decenter the viewer as civilized subject. They suggest that the world does not permanently have its eyes turned westward. As a result, the viewer may experience a deterritorialization—she is not the center on which the eyes of the world are focused. Our center disseminates into multiple smaller centers, at least as many as the eyes on Sacco's heliography.

This multiperspectivism challenges the dual logic of barbarian versus civilized. The multidirectionality of the eyes hints at the complex ways in which cultures influence each other and challenges practices of crosscultural comparison along the lines of a reductive West–non-West divide, with the West functioning as the normative center of comparative practices. The European tradition, as Natalie Melas argues, often functions as "an implicitly universal form from which theoretical models can be generated" and subsequently applied to the "raw" comparative material of other cultures (2007, 32). In the face of this tradition, the disorienting eyes in Sacco's work make the "sovereign authority of a single perspective" inadequate and untenable by signaling the presence of diverse sites of enunciation away from the metropolitan centers (36). Therefore, from the margins of the West, Sacco's installation performs a critique of Western comparative practices.

The work refuses to reaffirm Western traditions of comparativism based on a universalist perspective. Following Melas's distinction, the work does not stand "for the world"—just as it does not stand for a universal narrative of *waiting for the barbarians*—but stands "in the world," in a complex relation to the irreducible extensiveness of a global cultural network (36). It constitutes, in Edouard Glissant's terms, a relational and comparative "degeneralized universal" (quoted in Melas 2007, 36). In these ways, *Esperando a los bárbaros* performs and proposes alternative comparative practices.

Two Alternatives to Waiting

Geers's and Sacco's artistic stagings of the topos of *waiting for the barbarians* forward two different visions for a solution to civilization's aporia. Geers's labyrinth focuses on the violence within civilization and brings out the barbarism in our familiar, naturalized, civilized surroundings. By activating violent memories from the history of Western civilization—recast as a history of Western barbarism—Geers's work confronts us with our implication in the structures of civilization. In so doing, it entertains the possibility for change from within the discursive structures we inhabit. This change from within, however, may still involve the intervention of the other. This intervention comes from the impact of the specter, which unsettles our perception of the present and our identity as historical subjects. While Geers's work makes us painfully aware of the barbarism around and inside us, it also points to the possibility of another mode of being with specters. This mode of being may turn our guilt as historical subjects into a more productive sense of responsibility to be alert to the shifting echoes of the past in our present as we move toward the future.

Sacco's vision for a solution takes shape in a zone of contact in which the self and the other confront each other on equal terms. The eyes stage a game of hide-and-seek with the viewer. This elusiveness enhances the work's affective force: the viewer has the opportunity to relate to the eyes before deciding what the image means, before posing the question of whom these eyes belong to, and before assigning to them preconceived distinctions of civilized and barbarians. Even when—under the influence of the title—the viewer is tempted to assign such discursive categories to the image, the unclear status of the eyes confuses these categories: it makes their assigning ambiguous and problematic (who are the civilized, and who are the barbarians?).

In Sacco's work, the waiting for the other is transformed into the immediacy of an unpredictable encounter in the present. Thus, unlike Geers's labyrinth, Sacco's work does not ponder a solution from within our discursive structures but from a confrontation between self and other, reconfigured as an "I" and a "you" in the immediacy of a dialogic exchange.

Neither Geers's nor Sacco's installation provides a recipe for another "kind of solution" to the futile waiting. They take civilization's aporia as a testing ground on which they experiment with possible alternatives. Their proposed alternatives emerge through their staging of tensions on different levels. Geers's installation performs the tension between conflict-ing versions of the past and their resonance in the present, between the serenity of nature and its violent side, between visibility and invisibility, and between guilt and responsibility. Sacco's artwork performs the tension between an oppositional thinking in terms of barbarians and civilized and an alternative relationality, in which the other is seen as a legitimate "you" instead of an objectified third-person enemy.

As a result, both artworks become political not by transmitting a straightforward message but by producing complex narratives that cap-tivate and confuse us. They engage their viewers "without dictating in what way viewers will be affected" (Bal 2011, 3). According to Bal, this kind of affective engagement is a distinguishing feature of contemporary political art. In these artworks, unresolved tension and confrontations are not sources of stagnation but precisely what propels the state of waiting toward an active engagement that makes these works active in the present.

New Barbarians

We now turn to an artistic visualization of "new barbarians" as they take shape in the photo-performance portfolio "The New Barbarians" (2004–6) by performance artist and writer Guillermo Gómez-Peña and his troupe La Pocha Nostra.[1]

As discussed previously, Geers's labyrinth confronts the visitor with the absence of barbarian others, which draws attention to the barbarism in civilization's structures. The foreign presences conjured by the installation are specters, which modify our perception of the surroundings and ourselves as historical subjects. Sacco's *Esperando a los bárbaros* offers metonymical traces of the other by bracketing the body and the face through a close-up on the eyes. By visually staging the invisibility (Geers) or minimal presence (Sacco) of the other, neither of these works brings an end to the waiting by offering representations of barbarians. The absence of barbarians in these two works is counterpoised by their ostensive presence in Gómez-Peña's project. "The New Barbarians" overwhelms the viewer with an overload of cultural signs in provocative combinations on the bodies of performance personas. If the "waiting" in Geers's and Sacco's titles contains the promise of arrival, Gómez-Peña's "New Barbarians" seem to materialize that promise. The form this materialization takes, however, falls short of the expectations of the civilized imagination.

Born in Mexico City, Guillermo Gómez-Peña moved to the United States in 1987, where he established himself as a prominent performance artist and writer based in San Francisco. In his art projects, performances, and books, he addresses issues of cross-cultural and hybrid identities, migration, globalization, the politics of language, border cultures, border crossings, and the interface between North and South (especially the US-Mexican border) and between mainstream US and Latino culture. His performances, essays, and experimental poetry—in English, Spanish, or "Spanglish" (a combination of English and Spanish)—stage confrontations and misunderstandings between cultures, races, ethnicities, and genders by using various media and technologies.[2] In the "ever-evolving manifesto" of his performance troupe La Pocha Nostra, Gómez-Peña describes his troupe as a "transdisciplinary arts organization" that crosses borders "between art and politics, practice and theory, artist and spectator" (2005, 93).

"The New Barbarians" is a large body of work, which, in the artist's words, intends to "explore the cultural fears of the West after 9/11."[3] It includes the following photo-performance portfolios: "Ethno-Techno," "Post-Mexico en X-paña," "The Chi-Canarian Expo," "The Chica-Iranian Project," "Tucuman-Chicano," and "Epcot-El Alamall."[4] These photo-performances also developed into a real-life performance in the format of a fashion show entitled "The New Barbarian Collection," which premiered in November 2007 at Arnolfini in Bristol. For "The New Barbarian Collection," Gómez-Peña, his troupe, and a number of European-based artists set up what they called "an X-treme fashion show," through which they engaged the audience with "fashion-inspired stylized performance personas stemming from problematic media representations of foreigners, immigrants, and social eccentrics, as both enemies of the state and sexy pop-cultural rebels." This is part of the show's description on the artist's Web site: "The show is about politicized human bodies far more than clothing. What is actually being 'sold' is a new designer hybrid identity and the human being as a product. The performance also explores the bizarre relationship between the post-9/11 culture of xenophobia and the rampant fetishization of otherness by global pop culture."[5]

The photo-performance portfolios composing "The New Barbarians" are expressions of the same rationale. They feature hybrid personas in provocative costumes and props, partly inspired by stereotypical media representations of "new barbarians." By constructing alternative versions of new barbarians, the project challenges the typecasting of others as bar-barians in the West after 9/11. This strange fashion shoot results in pho-tographic portraits with characteristic titles such as *Androgynous Guest, Guerilla Supermodel, Islamic Immigrant, Generic Terrorist, Hybrid Gang Banger, Supermodelo zapatista, Turista Neo-Victoriana,* and *Aristócratas nómadas.*

As the only materialization of the figure of the new barbarian I look into, Gómez-Peña's project occupies an important part in this book. His project engages the theme of barbarism through what I call a "barbarian aesthetic." I here examine how this aesthetic can contribute to a "barbar-ian theorizing"—to borrow Walter Mignolo's term—from the periphery of the West.[6]

Specifically, this chapter starts with a brief survey of linguistic bar-barisms in Gómez-Peña's work through an analysis of samples from his bilingual writing practices and then explores how *visual* barbarisms are at work in "The New Barbarians": elements that do not allow the viewer to synthesize the images into coherent narratives. Gómez-Peña's personas form a visual "barbarian grammar" based on elements from heterogeneous discursive fields and theoretical idioms. This visual grammar takes up, appropriates, but also questions popular theoretical concepts and frame-works. By overloading the viewer with cultural references, Gómez-Peña's barbarians tempt us to engage in the game of their theorization, while they simultaneously confound our attempts to theorize them.

By conversing with theory, Gómez-Peña's barbarians perform their "barbarian theorizing" through and against existing theoretical idioms. This theorizing should not be imagined as a visual demonstration of popular theoretical views. The photo-performances in "The New Bar-barians" do not support a theoretical discourse by functioning as post-dictions and making the theory "pre-dictive metaleptically" (Spivak 1992, 776). In other words, they do not just illustrate theoretical proposi-tions but become agents of a visual mode of theorizing. This theorizing, I argue, is based on an attitude of non-seriousness, the implications of which I chart.

These barbarian figures are also compared with other positive con-ceptualizations of new barbarians, particularly in Walter Benjamin and in Michael Hardt and Antonio Negri's *Empire.* Finally, by unpacking the artistic interventions of Gómez-Peña's barbarians in relation to Geers's and Sacco's installations, I pose the question of these works' relation to the political, as it ties in with their aesthetic performance.

The Barbarisms of Bilingualism

> I am not interested in . . . legitimizing the global by reversing it into the local. I am interested in tracking the exorbitant as it institutes its culture.
> —Gayatri Chakravorty Spivak, "Acting Bits/Identity Talk"

Gayatri Spivak argues that what we call "culture" stands for "an unacknowledged system of representations that allows you a self-representation that you believe is true" (1992, 785). Following this logic, Spivak continues, US culture is "the dream of interculturalism: benevolent, hierarchized, malevolent, in principle homogenizing, but culturally heterogeneous" (785). As this hegemonic system is taking over the globe, however, people tend to forget that the word *American* accompanies every manifestation of US interculturalism—as in "African-American," "Mexican-American," "Muslim-American" (885). This suggests that in US interculturalism there is still an overarching cultural authority, a hegemonic center, toward which all cultural forces are drawn. This kind of hierarchized interculturalism accommodates minor identities and (sub)cultures as long as they conform to the homogenizing normative principles of US culture and acknowledge the English language as the global language of communication—a lingua franca.

In his writings and performances, Gómez-Peña expresses his fear of English becoming the only language in an authoritarian state. The following quotation from one of his performances is characteristic:

> I dreamt the US had become a totalitarian state controlled by satellites and computers. I dreamt that in this strange society poets and artists have no public voice whatsoever. Thank God it was just a dream. In English. English only. Just a dream. Not a memory. Repeat with me: *Vivir en estado del sitio* is a translatable statement; to live in a state of siege *es suseptibile de traducción*. In Mexican in San Diego, in Puerto Rican in New York City, in Moroccan in Paris, in Pakistani in London. Definitely, a translatable statement. (Gómez-Peña, quoted in Spivak 1992, 791).

Against the totalitarian impact of the English language, Gómez-Peña describes and performs a counter-suggestion: speaking simultaneously in multiple languages, mixing linguistic codes, and creating new idioms, in which the English language loses its hegemonic force, as it is made to coexist and interact with different languages. *"Vivir en estado del sitio* is a translatable statement; to live in a state of siege *es suseptibile de traducción."* The repetition of the first phrase in reverse translation pleads for the equal standing of the languages participating in this sentence.

However, Gómez-Peña here does not advocate an absolute trans-latability according to which every utterance could be transferred into another language without any change or loss. If that were the case, there would be no point in resisting the idea of a lingua franca. Gómez-Peña's writings and artistic practices probe issues of (un)translatability. He often speaks or writes in Spanglish and inserts foreign words and phrases (primarily Spanish) into his English texts. This practice is in accordance with Chicano language, which consists of a version of American English with elements of a pseudo-Mexican slang.[7] The following piece is part of a performance text from 2004, "To Those Who Are As Afraid of Us As We Are of Them":

> I speak therefore I continue to be a part of "us"
> To the shareholders of monoculture
> I say, we say:
> We, bilingual, polylingual, cunilingual,
> Nosotros, los otros del mas allá
> del otro lado de la linea y el Puente
> We, rapeando border mistery; a broader history
> We, mistranslated señorrita,
> eternally mispronounced
> We, lost and found in the translation
> lost and found between the layers of this text
> We speak therefore you cease to be
> even if only for a moment
> I am, US, you sir, no ser
> Nosotros seremos
> Nosotros, we stand not united
> We, matriots and patriots
> We, Americans with foreign accents

We, Americans in the largest sense of the term
(from the many other Americas)
We, in cahoots with the original Americans
who speak hundreds of beautiful languages
incomprehensible to you
We, in cahoots with dozens of millions of displaced
Latinos, Arabs, Blacks and Asians
who live so pinche far away from their land
and their language
We feel utter contempt for your myopia
and when we talk back, you lose your grounds. (Gómez-Peña
2005, 231–32)

The poetic voice in this text is a collective "we," explicitly addressing a "you." The "we" and the "you" seem to delineate a distinction between a heterogeneous, multicultural, polylingual group vis-à-vis the monolingual "shareholders of monoculture." The latter group most likely refers to mainstream US culture and its use of English as a lingua franca.

Although the multilingual "we" is clearly opposed to the "you," it does not stand outside it. The we includes "Americans" but "with foreign accents" and "in the largest sense of the term / (from the many other Americas)." It would perhaps be more accurate to say that the we is situated at the margins of the you. This plural, marginal we poses a threat to the monoculture of the you. This threat stems from the incomprehensibility of the we to the you: the "hundreds of beautiful languages" we speak are "incomprehensible to you." If power and control over the other are based on knowledge, then the barbarian languages of the we confuse the you and deprive it of its sense of control over its marginal others. As a result, the we threatens the very grounds of the existence of the you: "We speak therefore you cease to be," "and when we talk back, you lose your grounds."

What I find most fascinating about this performance piece is not its propositional content as such—the idea that the margins can challenge the center through their difference and linguistic pluralism—but the way this idea is performed in language. This central idea is enacted through a series of linguistic barbarisms, through which the challenge of the polylingual margins to the monolingual center materializes in language.

The piece is bilingual, with several Spanish verses, phrases, or words interrupting the flow of the English text. There is no strict division between the English and the Spanish: the two languages interfere not only within the same verse but sometimes even within the same word. This mutual interference takes different forms, including neologisms, unorthodox word combinations, errors, misspellings, surprising alliterations, puns, and wordplays. New words are devised based on common English words. For instance, the neologism "matriots" is placed near the word "patriots" in a juxtaposition that denaturalizes the latter by drawing attention to its etymology and, through it, to its patriarchal origins.[8] Similarly, the word "cunilingual" is modeled after "bilingual" and "polylingual."

Apart from neologisms, there are also Spanglish phrases and words, such as "rapeando," in which the English verb "rap" is adjusted to the Spanish conjugation for present continuous. In the same verse, the juxtaposition of "border mistery" and "broader history," and the striking alliteration and rhyming it produces, acoustically creates a broadening of borders from lines into spaces (border–broader). On these border spaces, "history" is not a fixed account but still a "mistery" and can thus be rewritten to include the histories of border cultures and of "Americans in the largest sense of the term." "Mistery" is misspelled, perhaps under the influence of the "i" of "history." Another linguistic error follows in the next verse: "We, mistranslated señorrita, / eternally mispronounced." Here, the poetic voice slightly misleads the reader: while "mistranslated" and "mispronounced" urge the reader to look for mistakes in translation or pronunciation, the actual error lies in the spelling of the word "señorrita," wrongly spelled with a double r.

In the verse "I am, US, you sir, no ser," alliterations and the mixture of languages generate different semantic possibilities. Starting with the English "I am," the verse ends with the Spanish "no ser" (not to be). The negation of existence implied in "no ser" puts the English "I am" into question and implicitly refers to the verse "We speak therefore you cease to be." The Spanish "no ser" functions as a barbarism that haunts the identity of the mainstream culture, confidently affirmed by the phrase "I am" with "US" right next to it. In the second part of the verse, "you sir, no ser" sounds very similar to the phrase "yes sir, no sir," which holds connotations of servile obedience and subordination.[9] These connotations are at odds with the overall function of this verse, which triggers *in*subordination to the dominant language through linguistic barbarisms and thereby questions the authority of the "US" and the English "I am." The submissiveness of the "yes sir, no sir," acoustically hidden within the more insurgent "you sir, no ser," reminds us, however, that no act of contestation is permanent. A barbarism with a destabilizing function within a certain context may also turn into a confirmation of, or an act of subordination to, the dominant culture.

This observation also suggests that marginal groups and border cultures—the poem's "we"—do not by definition contest the dominant simply by occupying the margins. In fact, marginal groups often try to impose their own "universal" truths and hegemonic positions or imitate the mechanisms and power structures of the mainstream culture.[10] Thus, the margins should also be under critical scrutiny. This is also suggested in one of Gómez-Peña's "Activist Commandments of the New Millennium": "Confront the oppressive and narrow-minded tendencies in your own ethnic- or gender-based communities with valor and generosity. The 'enemy' is everywhere, even inside ourselves" (2000, 93).

Through its barbarisms, Gómez-Peña's performance text shows how the heterogeneous, polylingual, mistranslated, misspelled, mispronounced, misunderstood "we" threatens the premises of the "shareholders of monoculture." The polylingualism of those other Americans is perceived as a threat precisely due to the mainstream culture's insistence on unity. In the face of the patriotic motto "united we stand, divided we fall," commonly used in US political speeches and popular culture, Gómez-Peña writes in the same performance text: "Nosotros, we stand not united." The gist of the former motto is that as long as people stay united, they cannot be easily destroyed. Here, this message is revised. When unity becomes a homogenizing principle of consensus that distrusts and marginalizes foreign elements, this artificial unity is not as strong as one may think. Such a unity suppresses the tensions, conflicts, and agonistic elements that arise at the borders between "languages," where different idioms, ideas, practices, and cultures rub against and into each other. These tensions come alive in Gómez-Peña's performance text. The tensions between languages need not be a threat to their respective unity but can form political sites of contestation. In this way, Gómez-Peña turns the non-unity of a multilingual, heterogeneous "we" into a source of empowerment.

The barbarisms Gómez-Peña inserts in this piece, as well as in other of his writings, challenge the reader to operate in two linguistic systems simultaneously. As one system is measured against the other, their limitations, problematic aspects, and power relations are also brought to the foreground. The foreign words and phrases that interrupt the flow of the English demonstrate the impossibility of an absolute transference of meaning through translation. It is impossible to replace them by English words and still retain the same meaning and effect.

"*Vivir en estado del sitio* is a translatable statement; to live in a state of siege *es suseptibile de traducción.*" Rereading this statement by the artist, I cannot "translate" it as a naïve endorsement of translatability but as staging the possibility of transforming the dominant language when we place it next to another language. This transformation is possible even when one lives "en estado del sitio"—under the suffocating influence of an Anglo-dominated culture. "To live in a state of siege" is a translatable statement, and the linguistic reversal that takes place in its translation suggests that the content of the statement is also reversible. A way of reversing the tyranny of monolingualism is by infusing the dominant language with barbarisms. This is a common practice in Gómez-Peña's performance texts, but what happens to this practice when we move from the textual to the visual realm?

From Visual Mimicry to a Babelian Performance

Gómez-Peña's practice of using two (or more) languages simultaneously and inserting barbarisms into dominant idioms finds a parallel in his visual strategies. In "The New Barbarians" different visual codes interact and clash with each other. The barbarian personas borrow elements from diverse sources: media representations of "evil others," bits and pieces from American popular culture (fashion shows, movies, TV, comics, rock and roll, hip-hop), border and Chicano culture, Western high art, the history of the visual and performing arts, religious imagery, journalism, anthropology, and pornography. Oversaturated signs from these sources form unorthodox combinations, constructing an array of eccentric barbarians.

Typologies of barbarians in contemporary Western media and politics belong to a strictly coded representational regime. Although the tag of the barbarian is conferred on diverse "others," the media-construed personas of these others bear fixed features, which ensure their recognizability by the public. By distorting a repository of stereotypes, Gómez-Peña's barbarian personas perform and parody the West's fear of others, especially since 9/11.

These personas are located at the US periphery and at the interface between mainstream Western and non-Western cultures (mainly Latino and Middle Eastern). With this in mind, one can argue that Gómez-Peña's "New Barbarians" employs the strategy Homi Bhabha calls "colonial mimicry," a strategy of appropriating colonial discourse in a way that produces "its slippage, its excess, its difference," resulting in the disavowal of its authority (1994, 122–23). Colonial mimicry reads Western narratives in unconventional ways or employs them for purposes not foreseen by the dominant culture (Bhabha, presented in Moore-Gilbert 1997, 131–32).

Certain photographic performances in "The New Barbarians" enact a visual mimicry of Western classical themes. For instance, *Piedad postcolonial* from the portfolio "Post-Mexico en X-paña" is a postcolonial appropriation of a classic subject in Christian art, the pietà, which depicts the Virgin Mary in grief, cradling the dead body of Christ.[11] In Gómez-Peña's *Piedad* the role of the Virgin Mary is performed by a man, dressed as a Native American from the waist up, and in drag from the waist down, wearing a long black skirt.[12] The man is holding an ax in his left hand, and with his right arm he is supporting a naked dead body. Instead of showing grief or meditative sorrow—as the Virgin Mary does in the Western tradition—this Native American is looking away from the dead body and has an austere expression. The exposed breasts and genitals of the dead body supported by his arm suggest that the Christ figure is female (unlike the body of Christ, covered with a loincloth in the classical pietà). Nevertheless, the body structure looks somewhat masculine. The head is shaved, which confuses the viewer's attempt to assign a sexual identity to this persona. The facial characteristics are partly indistinct, as the largest part of the face is painted red, as if wearing a mask. This queer body has one stereotypically recognizable racial feature: the eyes suggest that the figure playing the dead Christ is of Asian descent.

Hardly any of the elements in the classic pietà theme remain intact in this staging, apart, perhaps, from the position of the dead body. The participating figures—a Native American (played by Gómez-Peña) and (possibly) an Asian—are foreign to classical Western culture. The gender roles of the pietà are also confounded, with the Virgin Mary as male and the body of Christ as female and queer. The stern expression of the Native American figure and the ax he holds suggest that either he has killed the person he is holding or he is determined to avenge her death. The violent connotations of the ax and the man's defiant expression turn the Christian narrative of the grieving mother upside down. The association of Christianity with violence unsettles this narrative. The image strongly evokes the role of Christian Europe in the annihilation of the Native American population. If the dead body is a visual synecdoche for this annihilation, then we can read the man's expression as grief and anger, and his ax as a pledge for revenge.

The suggestion that Christianity has committed worse crimes against Europe's others than the crime staged in the pietà robs the Christian narrative of its sanctity. The new *Piedad* casts a critical eye upon its Western "original," but it also contains visual ambiguities—barbarisms— that prevent us from categorizing it as a straightforward anticolonial narrative. The Asian features of the dead body, for example, could be a hitch in such a narrative. Other confusing elements are the gender of the Christ figure, as well as the hybrid costume of the man, combining caricatural Native American and drag elements. These elements turn the image into a complex intersection of cultural, gender, queer, (anti- and post-)colonial, historical, religious, and racial discourses, which deter us from situating it within a singular framework.

"The New Barbarians" project includes two more translations of the same Western theme: *La piedad intercontinental* and *La piedad intercontinental (invertida)*, both from the portfolio "Chi-Canarian Expo."[13] Other photo-performances that appropriate Western religious themes are *La dolorosa* (from the portfolio "Chi-Canarian Expo") and *Sagrada familia* (from the portfolio "Post-Mexico en X-paña"). *Sagrada familia* stages a comparable "blasphemous" recasting of the religious theme of Joseph, Mary, and baby Jesus, staged by three very unlikely figures: a weighty Arab man holding a gun (Joseph), a Muslim woman covered with a black burka but with her legs exposed in a seductive pose (Mary), and a third figure wearing an oxygen mask and underpants with the Superman logo—a parody of the "almighty" Jesus.

FIGURE 7.1 Guillermo Gómez-Peña, *Piedad postcolonial*, 2005. From the portfolio "Post-Mexico en X-paña." Photograph by Javier Caballero (original photo in
color, reproduced here in black and white). Courtesy BRH-LEON editions.

As performances of colonial mimicry, these images turn Western iconography and religious narratives against themselves. In doing so, they uncover the contradictions that inhere in Western culture itself, such as that of a religion proclaiming love and mercy and instigating brutal wars and barbarism.[14] The association of Christianity with barbarism was also brought forth by Geers's installation. This association suggests that contemporary Western condemnations of Islam as a barbaric religion turn a blind eye to the barbarism committed in the name of Christianity in history.

The unlikely personas featuring in these restagings of Western high art also allude to the non-Western origins of Western art and its influences from other cultures. By exposing these interconnections with other cultures, as well as the internal contradictions in Western discourses, Gómez-Peña's barbarians manage to pluralize the West itself. The West is barbarized and emerges as a collective heritage, constituted by various non-European influences.

By critically recasting Western narratives, Gómez-Peña's barbarians do not impose a new authoritative narrative in the place of the one they rewrite. Although they project alternative histories from the margins, the bits and pieces of these histories do not add up to a coherent account issued from a uniform perspective. They draw from diverse ethnic, racial, cultural, and gender discourses and unravel their critique by mobilizing various theoretical perspectives—queer, anticolonial, postcolonial, posthuman—without pledging dogmatic allegiance to any of them. The photo-performances in "The New Barbarians" do not propose a unified anti-Western narrative but a syncretic, barbarian visual idiom, which contradicts the very possibility of a homogeneous cultural narrative. Their visual grammar does not fit within a singular representational framework or theoretical discourse.

The confrontations that "The New Barbarians" stages between diverse discourses expose the inconsistencies and blind spots in these discourses. Things normalized within a certain cultural framework—the burka in Muslim communities, an ax or saw in the hands of a carpenter, a cross in the hands of a priest, sexy lingerie on female bodies on Western billboards and in commercials, machine guns in the military, red feathers on Native Americans in American westerns—are transformed into

FIGURE 7.2 Guillermo Gómez-Peña, *Generic Terrorist.*
Photograph from "The Chica-Iranian Project" portfolio (original photo in color, reproduced here in black
and white). Photograph by James McCaffrey. Source:
Gómez-Peña et al. (2006, figure 4, p. 20). Reproduced
by permission of Sage Publications.

ex-centricities. They lose their reference to the center that issues their normalization because they are integrated in foreign visual idioms: a burka
covering a woman with fully exposed legs (*Islamic Immigrant*), a cross next
to a gun in the hands of a "gang banger" (*Hybrid Gang Banger*), or a bandit
figure from a western (*El Spaghetti Greaser Bandit*), women's lingerie on a
male body (*Androgynous Guest*) or on a military cyborg (*Ciborg miliciana*),
a machine gun held by a neo-Victorian/Native American female tourist
(*Turista Neo-Victoriana*), and red feathers on the head of an Amazonian

FIGURE 7.3 Guillermo Gómez-Peña, *Hybrid Gang Banger*. From "The Chica-Iranian Project" portfolio (original photo in color, reproduced here in black and white). Photograph by James McCaffry. Source: Gómez-Peña et al. (2006, figure 7, p. 23). Reproduced by permission of Sage Publications.

Indian in drag, occasionally posing as the Virgin Mary (*El indio amazonico, La piedad postcolonial*).

Thus, these images often exceed the practice of colonial mimicry and engage in what we could call—borrowing Jacques Derrida's term—a "Babelian performance": a performance that demands and simultaneously forbids translation by projecting the unfeasible univocity and transparency of signs.[15] This visual Babelian performance invites translation into a familiar narrative and simultaneously makes this translation impossible. These personas speak a barbarian language, which plunges the

FIGURE 7.4 Guillermo Gómez-Peña, *Islamic Immi-grant*. From the "Tucuman-Chicano" portfolio (origi-nal photo in color, reproduced here in black and white). Photograph by Ramon Treves. Source: Gómez-Peña et al. (2006, figure 8, p. 24). Reproduced by permission of Sage Publications.

center's dream of a lingua franca into a sea of errors, cacophonies, and incongruities.

The aspirations of the United States to establish English as a com-mon language and to "translate" the difference of minorities in the domi-nant discourse could be visualized as the dream of a contemporary Tower of Babel. The performance of Gómez-Peña's barbarians impedes the construction of this tower by showing what happens when the translating impulse goes mad. These barbarians reap stereotypical images out of their usual context and make cultural signs coexist with signs from different visual orders and typologies of others. As a result, the letters that make up the Western visual alphabet are rearranged in a barbarian visual grammar, although the images may still remind us of things we have seen on TV. Gómez-Peña's troupe sees itself as "a virtual *maquiladora* (assembly plant) that produces brand-new metaphors, symbols, images, and words to explain the complexities of our times" (Gómez-Peña 2005, 78). Their language contains barbarisms—elements used in improper ways, which contaminate the imagery we have internalized as citizens of the West. The name of Gómez-Peña's troupe, La Pocha Nostra, is a Spanglish neologism and thus itself a barbarism, while it also *signifies* barbarism (in the sense of foreignism or contamination): one of the possible translations of La Pocha Nostra, as we read in the troupe's manifesto, is "our impurities"; another is "the cartel of cultural bastards" (78).

Recasting the Stereotype

"The New Barbarians" may be interpreted as expressions of the dream of a transcultural world, wherein people exchange identities and construct themselves as they please. Nevertheless, I argue that their vision of identity is of a different kind. Melancholic, apathetic, perplexed, or distant, most of these personas do not look like happy citizens of a hybridized world.

What kind of vision of identity does "The New Barbarians" act out? And what do these barbarians do with stereotypical images of barbarian others? "The Chica-Iranian Project" is a good theoretical object for probing these questions. In "The Chica-Iranian Project," Gómez-Peña and a group of mainly Chicano and Iranian artists "exchange" and alter each other's identities. They create twelve barbarian personas in "ethnic drag," which incorporate Hollywood and media typecasting and stereotypes of Middle Eastern terrorists, Latino "gang bangers," and other "evil others" from these two cultural spaces. As we read on Gómez-Peña's Web site, the resulting photo-performances are meant to visualize the dangers of ethnic profiling in the post-9/11 era. The subtitle of the project—"Orientalism Gone Wrong in Aztlan"—hints at the confusions and "mistranslations" that take place in this Oriental/Latin American mix.[16]

The presentation of this portfolio on Gómez-Peña's Web site takes place through an interactive game with the viewer, entitled "Test Your Ethnic Profiling Skills." The viewer is asked to match the names of the participating artists with the performance personas they have constructed. The underlying question of the game is, "Can the US differentiate between Mexicans and Iranians? Between 'Latinos' and 'Middle Easterners'?" The game sets a trap: The viewer will most probably fail this classification exercise. Guessing the artists' "real" ethnic affiliations (Chicano, Iranian, and, in the case of one artist, Hapa/half-Japanese) behind their ethnic personas is not easy. In most cases the artists' personas deviate from their own ethnic affiliation. The *Typical Arab Chola* is played by a Chicana artist, *El Spaghetti Greaser Bandit* by an Iranian artist, *Palestinian Vato Loco* and *Generic Terrorist* by Gómez-Peña, who identifies himself as Post-Mexican, *La Kurdish llorona* by a Hapa/half-Japanese artist, and so on.

The probable failure of the viewer to win this guessing game brings out the misconceptions involved in ethnic profiling. As Gómez-Peña remarks elsewhere, ethnic profiling has become an accepted practice after 9/11, and the category "Arab-looking" includes most Latinos and brown people as well. As a result, all these ethnic others have "become an ongoing source of anxiety and mistrust for true 'patriotic' Americans" (2005, 274). Staged as an interactive game, "The Chica-Iranian Project" makes the viewer/player complicitous with practices of ethnic profiling and the resulting "misunderstandings" that turn people into victims of hate speech, violence, and discrimination.

Although cultures and ethnicities mix more and more as a result of globalization, people still cling to simplistic representations in order to make sense of the chaotic realities around them. Stereotypes offer a secure point of identification for social groups, assisting them in defining themselves against their reductive representations of others. Although the stereotype itself, as Ruth Amossy and Therese Heidingsfeld argue, is "necessarily reductive," it does not always have to be involved in "reductive enterprises" (1984, 700). They suggest a functional approach to stereotypes, focusing on their shifting operations in the interaction between text and reader (or image and viewer) (700).[17] In *Declining the Stereotype*, Mireille Rosello suggests that it could be more useful to ask, "What can I do with a stereotype?" instead of trying to eradicate or oppose it (1998, 13). "The Chica-Iranian Project" probes precisely this question. It acknowledges the power and ineradicability of stereotypes, and instead of trying to eliminate them, it plunges into our preconceptions in order to perform them otherwise.

The project does not replace stereotypes of Middle Eastern and Latino others with positive and more true-to-life representations of these groups. Instead, it interrogates the economy of the stereotype itself. A stereotype, according to Amossy and Heidingsfeld, is a hyperbolic figure of a cultural model, which exacerbates the general rule and presents itself "in the margin of excess where forms become fixed and hardened" (1984, 690). However, there is ambivalence at the heart of a stereotype: it oscillates between something already known and taken for granted, and something that must be constantly and anxiously reconfirmed through repetition (Bhabha 1994, 95). This suggests that the "known" in the stereotype is not as securely established as the rhetorical force of the stereotype might suggest (Moore-Gilbert 1997, 117). Stereotypes must be repeated in order to maintain their force. This repetition also makes shifts in their pervasive functions possible.

The project makes use of this ambivalence by reproducing stereotypical images of Latinos and Middle Easterners with a twist. The barbarisms inserted in the images unsettle the homogeneity of stereotypical patterns. Such barbarisms are the message written on the naked chest of the *Generic Terrorist* that reads "Pleez do not liberate me," the American flags that form the pattern of the burka in *Afghani Immigrant in Texas*, or the cloth with an Arab script that the *Cigar Shop Indian Chief* is holding.

Whenever a stereotype is reproduced, Amossy and Heidingsfeld argue, elements that happen to disturb the pattern of the stereotype are "relegated to the level of 'remnants'" (1984, 693). The reader or viewer is trained to disregard those remnants by viewing them as details that individualize a stereotypical image or add to its reality-effect (693). This, however, happens on the condition that these remnants "be neither completely heterogeneous nor visibly contradictory" (695). "The Chica-Iranian Project" does not meet this condition. The "leftovers"—the elements not recognized as part of the stereotype—are very hard to neutralize or ignore because they are in stark contrast to the narratives each stereotypical image evokes. They stand out as unfitting intrusions, sabotaging the reassuring déjà-vu effect that stereotypes produce (695).

The *Generic Terrorist*, for instance, reproduces the figure of the Arab suicide bomber. But it is the message "Pleez do not liberate me" on the chest of this figure that becomes the crux of the image. Instead of being neutralized by the image's stereotypical elements, it attracts the viewer's attention because it carries a different narrative. Where we would perhaps expect a message praising the glory of Allah or proclaiming "death to infidels," this message ironizes the Western conviction that nonliberal societies are waiting for the West to save, liberate, and enlighten them by imposing democracy and liberal values on them. Thus, this deviant element prevents the stereotype of the Middle Eastern terrorist from being unproblematically recuperated.

The barbarians in "The Chica-Iranian Project" do not make claims to a true, essential identity by trying to set a "wrong" representation "right." The contamination of ethnic stereotypes in this project performs the impossibility of articulating stable ethnic or cultural identities. As Rosello argues, stereotypes imply a theory of identity and can thus be employed "to exclude, to police borders, to grant or deny rights to individuals" (1998, 15). If stereotypes help draw clear-cut ethnic distinctions, then the barbarian ethnic others in "The Chica-Iranian Project" try to blur these lines. They infuse stereotypes with barbarisms—elements that confuse, as Spivak puts it, "the possibility of an absolute translation of a politics of identity into cultural performance" (1992, 782). As a result, they blur the identities of minority voices "without creating a monolithic solidarity" (782).

In his article "The New World (B)order" Gómez-Peña writes about new identities in the contemporary world:[18] "This new society is characterized by mass migrations and bizarre interracial relations. As a result new hybrid and transitional identities are emerging. . . . The bankrupt notion of the melting pot has been replaced by a model that is more germane to the times, that of the *menudo chowder*. According to this model, most of the ingredients do melt, but some stubborn chunks are condemned merely to float" (1992/1993, 74). In these reflections,

Gómez-Peña sees models of cultural assimilation—the concept of the "melting pot"—as a failed and outmoded experiment. In proposing the "menudo chowder" model, he focuses on its stubborn chunks: the elements that cannot be translated in the dominant idiom.[19] In his discussion of Gómez-Peña's "menudo chowder" model, Bhabha sees these "chunks" as the basis of cultural identifications, which take place through performative operations. According to Bhabha, these chunks are spaces "continually, *contingently,* 'opening out,' remaking the boundaries, exposing the limits of any claim to a singular or autonomous sign of difference—be it class, gender or race" (1994, 219). In the performance of "The New Barbarians," the chunks that refuse to go away can be identified as visual barbarisms: discordant elements that prevent the viewers from synthesizing the elements of the image into a coherent narrative.

The visual incommensurabilities in Gómez-Peña's personas give expression to the internal contradictions in Western visual narratives. The persona entitled *Islamic Immigrant* is a case in point. The image features a woman sitting on a chair with her legs crossed in a seductive pose. The woman is holding a rifle and wearing a black burka that cloaks her face and upper part of her body, revealing only the eye area. Her legs, however, are exposed and attract attention due to the sexy pantyhose and high-heeled shoes. The background is covered by wallpaper with a military camouflage pattern. In this image, the female Islamic immigrant is portrayed as a hooker, a religious fundamentalist, and a terrorist: an outrageous condensation of stereotypes in one image. Her portrait contains all the contradictory ingredients of the stereotypes of Oriental peoples, especially Muslims: she embodies a rampant sexuality; she follows strict religious prescriptions that restrain this sexuality; she looks enigmatic, erotic, and treacherous; and she poses a violent (possibly terrorist) threat. This threat is suggested not only by the rifle and the military-patterned wallpaper but also by the juxtaposition of the gun and the burka—a connection reminiscent of the practice of Muslim women during anticolonial struggles to carry guns under their burkas. The interlacing of all these stereotypes highlights the inconsistencies and absurdities in popular representations of Islamic women immigrants and undercuts the credibility of these representations. Since the image does not add up, the reality-effect of its stereotypical elements is put under suspicion.

The personas in "The New Barbarians" become visual metaphors of an irretrievable "reality." The designation "barbarians" here refers to a set of highly stylized figures. I argue that the theatricality and hyperbolic performance of these overtly fabricated figures underscore the *catachrestic* nature of the name "barbarian": the fact that this name does not correspond to a real presence but is a "concept-metaphor without an adequate referent" (Spivak 1993, 60).[20] Defined as a name applied "to a thing which it does not properly denote," a catachresis is always an approximation, a misfit, an improperly used word "for which there is no *adequate* literal referent."[21] The concept of catachresis is crucial in Spivak's thought as a reminder of the perils of transforming a name to an actual referent (156).[22] Against this essentialist tendency, catachresis points to the breach between a name and its referent, while it recognizes the inescapability of using this name—though always with the awareness that its use is *improper*.[23]

Gómez-Peña's barbarian figures embody the impossibility of literalizing the metaphor of the "barbarian." The cultural references and discursive fields that permeate them make them anything but "literal." Just as these figures deliberately fail to represent "real barbarians," any attempt to attach the term "barbarian" to real human beings can never fully succeed. In this way, these personas contribute to the perpetuation of the "waiting" for barbarians, seen as the desire for an inaccessible presence. They point out that we can never match the name "barbarian" to a literal referent because that referent does not exist outside discourse. The name "barbarian" is always a misuse; it may be applied to bodies of others, but it cannot grasp them through this designation. Therefore, Gómez-Peña's personas point to the dangers of using this appellation. Its use is accompanied by the violence of a misuse, suggested here by the improper and mismatched combinations of signs on the bodies of "The New Barbarians."

A Non-serious Theorizing

In this time and place,
what does it mean to be "transgressive"?
What does "radical behavior" mean after Howard Stern,
Jerry Springer, Bin Laden, Ashcroft, Cheney,
six-year-old serial killers in the heartland of America,
. . . .
what else is there to "transgress"?
Who can artists shock, challenge, enlighten?
—Gómez-Peña, from "Post-Script: Millennial Doubts"

The hyperbolic performance of Gómez-Peña's barbarians creates a distance from the viewer. This distance is enhanced by the way these personas lay bare the act of acting: everything, from the general setup of the images to the posture of the barbarians, indicates that we are dealing with a staged, highly stylized performance, with no pretensions to subtlety or realistic representation. Their performance can be articulated in terms of the Brechtian approach to acting: the actor maintains a certain distance from the role, which may be perceived as "coldness and haughtiness" (Jameson 1998, 75). This attitude also marks the acting of the barbarian personas. The performance artists create a distance not only from the roles they embody but also from the viewer. In a Brechtian vein, they provoke the viewer without inducing empathy and identification, inviting viewers to think and reflect rather than relate to them.

The ironic distance these personas take from the viewer allows us to watch images with disturbing, confrontational, and violent elements. These include no less than dead animals (e.g., *El chamán travesti*, *Super-modelo zapatista*); dead people (e.g., *La piedad postcolonial*, *La piedad intercontinental*); knives, axes, pistols, and machine guns (e.g., *Sin título*, *Alianzas aleatorias*, *Ciborg miliciana*, *Unapologetic Evil Others*); naked bodies in bondage with their heads and faces covered or with their limbs attached to instruments of torture (e.g., *Desencuentro total*, *Re-enactment*), people wrapped up in barbed wire (*Abu Ghraib Reenactment*), and so on. The emotional impact of the violence staged by Gómez-Peña's barbarians is in my view dampened by means of their excessive, staged, non-serious character.[24] The viewer is unable to identify with them because they are far removed from our subjectivity. In Brecht's theory, this distancing is a necessary ingredient of the *Verfremdungseffekt* (defamiliarization or estrangement-effect).[25] The action must be alienating in order to shatter the illusion that what we see is real. By obstructing emotions based on identification, Gómez-Peña's barbarians invite reactions that do not rest on sentimentalism or sympathy but on the shock of nonidentification. This shock is part of the critical thinking these barbarians trigger—a thinking that manages to be politically engaging through its distance.

One political ramification of the theatricality of these barbarians is the antiessentializing of the barbarian. The "barbarian" becomes an array of staged roles rather than an inherent quality of certain subjects. In these performances, it is as if civilization dresses up its others in barbarian costumes and has them perform their role as "evil others." The projection of the barbarian as a series of staged roles has further implications. As Jameson argues, the Brechtian performance not only foregrounds the act of acting but wants to show to the audience "that we are all actors and that acting is an inescapable dimension of social and everyday life" (1998, 25). Gómez-Peña's barbarians highlight acting as an indispensable aspect of social life. But how does this Brechtian insight, in the way the barbarian personas perform it, function in a contemporary context?

On one level, the theatricality of the barbarians brings out the theatricality in contemporary US culture—a culture wherein, as has so often been claimed, spectacle is indistinguishable from reality. American performance culture permeates everyday life but also the realms of politics, war, and torture. Describing his reaction to a photograph of a prisoner tortured by the US army, Slavoj Žižek remarks: "When I saw the well-known photo of a naked prisoner with a black hood covering his head, electric cables attached to his limbs, standing on a chair in a ridiculous theatrical pose, my first reaction was that this was a shot from the latest performance-art show in lower Manhattan" (2009, 146). Žižek argues that as opposed to torture practices carried out in other cultures and nations, which are executed in secret, US army tortures tend to record the prisoner's humiliation with a camera, making it part of a performance. "The very positions and costumes of the prisoners," Žižek continues, "suggest a theatrical staging, a kind of tableau vivant, which cannot but bring to mind the whole spectrum of American performance art and 'theatre of cruelty'" (146).[26] Viewed in this light, the excess and theatricality of Gómez-Peña's barbarians do not seem foreign to American culture.

Nevertheless, the barbarian personas add a second layer of distance from the American "theatre of cruelty." This distance draws specific attention to the theatrical aspects of US culture. For example, the photo-performances that thematize torture overemphasize the staging of the scene. In the image *Abu Ghraib Reenactment*, shot in black and white, two men stand next to each other, both wrapped in barbed wire. The man on the left is holding a machine gun, pointed at the other man. The man on the right has a serene facial expression, his eyes closed, perhaps awaiting his execution. He is wearing a shirt full of holes and covered in what seems to be blood, and underneath he is wearing pantyhose—an allusion to the sexual humiliation of prisoners by US soldiers in Abu Ghraib. What strikes me in this image is that neither of these men is looking at the other. They both turn to the camera: the prisoner with his eyes closed and the torturer with his eyes wide open. It is thus an explicitly staged scene, confirming Žižek's assertion about US army torture that it is performed not simply in front of a camera but, first and foremost, *for* the camera.

However, there is a crucial difference between the effect of this photo-performance and that of the photos of army torture Žižek describes. The personas in *Abu Ghraib Reenactment* do not have the same affective impact as recorded scenes of torture. They do not emulate pain, agony, or humiliation but enact the *staging* of pain and agony. The viewer's empathy is further diminished by the knowledge that these are not recordings of real torture. As a result, what the barbarians communicate to the (Western) viewer may seem to be this: It is not our fault you cannot identify or sympathize with us. Even if you are not aware of it, you are used to keeping this distance from others in everyday life, because real pain and violence reach you as a spectacular performance. But our staged performance bothers you because we make you aware of your own distance from things or other human beings.

The pervasiveness of the culture of spectacle in our lives does not prevent us from experiencing things as "real." On the contrary, as Žižek argues, there is an "underlying trend to obfuscate the line that separates fiction from reality" (2005, 147). We do not give up on reality but try to create a sense of reality in everything, without the dangers "the Real"

FIGURE 7.5 Guillermo Gómez-Peña, *Abu Ghraib Reenactment*, 2006. From "The Chi-Canarian Expo" portfolio (original photo in black and white). Photograph by Teresa Correa. Courtesy BRH-LEON editions.

entails. As a result, the taste of reality we get today comes from products, situations, or actions deprived of their substance:

> In today's market, we find a whole series of products deprived of their malignant property: coffee without caffeine, cream without fat, beer without alcohol. . . . And the list goes on: what about virtual sex as sex without sex, the Colin Powell doctrine of warfare with no casualties (on our side, of course) as warfare without warfare . . . up to today's tolerant liberal multiculturalism as an experience of Other deprived of its Otherness (the idealized Other who dances fascinating dances . . . while features like wife beating remain out of sight . . .)? (Žižek and Daly 2004, 105)

This describes a process that yields "reality itself deprived of its substance": "Just as decaffeinated coffee smells and tastes like real coffee without being real coffee" (Žižek 2002, xxvi). As a result, Žižek claims, the "twentieth-century passion to penetrate the Real Thing (ultimately, the destructive Void) through the cobweb of semblances which constitute our reality thus culminates in the thrill of the Real as the ultimate 'effect'" (xxvi–xxvii).

Reality TV is one example of this trend: these shows sell "real life," but in fact people are still acting, playing themselves. Gómez-Peña's barbarians bring about the reverse effect: they incite us to see things as constructed, fictional, unreal. They reintroduce a distance between performance and real life—it is impossible to view those personas as real people. Thus, they bring fiction back into our sense of reality. In other words, they do not put the caffeine back into our decaf coffee, but they make us taste decaf coffee as not real coffee.

The barbarian personas make us experience our realities as less than real by refusing to take themselves too seriously. The *non-serious theorizing* they develop carries significant political ramifications. As cultural anthropologist Johannes Fabian argues in "Culture with an Attitude," humor, irony, and parody can function as strategies of defiance and negation, which allow us to counter false expectations of congruity in culture (2001, 97). Fabian proposes a strategy of negativity in our approach to culture, which he describes as "a critical mode of reflection that . . . negates what culture affirms" (93). In our theorization of culture, he argues, we need to challenge "those ideas that make us so terribly positive and serious" (98). In the performance of Gómez-Peña's barbarians, the redeployment of stereotypes turns into such a strategy of non-serious negation. By using reflexivity, irony, and self-deprecating humor, and by "being unserious about culture" (98)—all ingredients of Fabian's strategy of negativity—Gómez-Peña's barbarians unsettle the seemingly rational structures of Western society and tease out its irrational underbelly.

The non-serious attitude of the barbarian personas is aimed not only at culture but also at theory. By keeping an ironic distance from themselves, they also distance themselves from the theoretical discourses that could claim them. The titles of photo-performances such as *La piedad postcolonial, Hybrid Gang Banger*, or *Aristócratas nómadas*, for example, contain explicit references to postcolonial discourses, theories of cultural hybridity, and (intellectual) nomadism, respectively. The references to popular theoretical concepts in the titles are, I contend, not a manifestation of the theoretical allegiances of "The New Barbarians." Rather, they constitute a strategy through which they avoid being appropriated by theory—be it postmodern, postcolonial, poststructuralist, or humanist—by making it part of their ironic critique.

By refusing to take themselves too seriously, the barbarian personas avoid reduction to theoretical commonplaces. They explicitly thematize several currently popular issues, including borders, identities, race, gender, violence, the West and its others, the role of the media, and the relation of the margins to the center. Thus, they appear as perfect examples to use for studying multiculturalism, globalization, border crossings, the postcolonial condition, alternative histories, cross-culturalism and (cultural) translation, hybridization, queer identities, posthumanism, and so on. The theoretical references of their performance—complemented by Gómez-Peña's theoretical writings—are impossible to miss. Surrounded, as it were, by theory, the barbarians make it hard for their viewers not to look at them through a preconstructed theoretical lens.

Do their theoretical allusions make these barbarian personas predictable, convenient, and obedient case studies for theorists? I argue that this is not the case. Thematizing theory can be seen as part of their non-serious attitude and aesthetic of excess. The barbarian personas are not just overloaded with props, makeup, and costumes but also with popular issues, concepts, and theories. The latter are also part of the cultural baggage they recycle. By performing an overload of theory, they point to the oversaturation of certain theoretical concepts and views, which have become buzzwords within self-authenticating theoretical discourses. Thus, by making theory part of their non-serious theorizing, the barbarians plead for a constant revision of theoretical concepts and reclaim the "edge" of theory. The critical potential of concepts is not to be taken for granted, because concepts may turn into empty fashionable terms. Therefore, by not taking theory seriously, Gómez-Peña's barbarians urge us to take theory more seriously than we often do.[27]

In borrowing tools from different theoretical "toolboxes," Gómez-Peña does not commit to a theoretical discourse. In one of his "Activist Commandments of the New Millennium," he writes: "Be an 'outsider/ insider,' a temporary member of multiple communities" (2000, 94). This practice of multiple provisional belongings does not necessarily entail lack of true engagement. By shifting alliances and belonging to different communities, we become aware of the blind spots in our principles and discursive frameworks. In this spirit of antidogmatism, it is perhaps slightly contradictory that Gómez-Peña has often formulated his artistic and theoretical principles in the form of commandments and manifestos. However, even in these prescriptive texts he makes sure to insert self-undermining "barbarisms." Thus, among his "Activist Commandments of the New Millennium" we read: "Question everything, *coño*, even these commandments" (2000, 93). The same commandments end with a subversive postscript: "P.S.: And one more thing—don't make the mistake I am making in this text and take yourself too seriously" (94). Moreover, the manifesto of La Pocha Nostra is entitled "An Ever Evolving Manifesto," which underscores its provisional character (2005, 78).

Although the barbarian personas flirt with different theories of identity and difference, they do not commit fully to any of them. This attitude hints at one of the main tasks of the "new barbarian" they propose: to offer a critique of existing discourses not by seeking to construct a new dominant discourse and, through it, a new center of power but by creating a language able to generate its own barbarisms. Such a language would question and renew itself before its signs turn into stereotypes.

Other New Barbarians

Just as Kendell Geers's and Graciela Sacco's installations participate in a transcultural and intermedial network through their title, "The New Barbarians" converses with works that engage with the figure of the "new barbarian." There are parallels between Gómez-Peña's barbarians and Hardt and Negri's "new barbarians," laid out in *Empire* (2000). Hardt and Negri's "new barbarians" are a "new nomad horde," a "new race" invested with the task of invading, evacuating, and bringing down Empire (213). The authors view the new barbarians as the answer to Nietzsche's famous question in *The Will to Power*: "Where are the barbarians of the twentieth century?" (quoted in Hardt and Negri 2000, 213). Hardt and Negri see Nietzsche's barbarians, for example, in the multitude that brought down the Berlin Wall in 1989. However, the new barbarians, the authors argue, should not only cause destruction; they must also create an alternative global vision. This would be the "counter-Empire," which the authors identify with a "new Republicanism" (214). Taking up Benjamin's notion of positive barbarism and his vision of the "destructive character," they contend that "the new barbarians destroy with an affirmative violence and trace new paths of life through their own material existence" (215).

According to Hardt and Negri, barbaric deployments that can trace such new paths often appear in "configurations of gender and sexuality": bodies "unprepared for normalization" "transform and mutate to create new posthuman bodies" that subvert traditional "boundaries between the human and the animal, the human and the machine, the male and the female, and so forth" (215–16). In this delineation we recognize the transgressive and posthuman bodies of Gómez-Peña's barbarians, which accommodate not only different identities but also incongruous life-forms, matter, and modes of being. Among them, we find half-naked cyborgs with machine guns and robotlike masks (*Ciborg miliciana*); actors in a soap opera with alien heads (*Telenovela española*); figures in drag with shields, high heels, and Indian feathers, holding dead chickens and supporting themselves with crutches (*El chamán travesti, Alianzas aleatorias*); and various queer bodies defying borders of normality. Such corporeal mutations constitute for Hardt and Negri an "anthropological exodus," which is crucial in the struggle of republicanism (read: barbarism) "'against' imperial civilization" (215). They conclude that "being republican today" (for them a synonym for the "new barbarian") means "struggling within and constructing against Empire, on its hybrid, modulating terrains" (218).

Although Hardt and Negri's conclusion finds support in Gómez-Peña's barbarians, the two visions are not a perfect match. Hardt and Negri's project of building a counter-Empire has, in fact, hegemonic aspirations. Through their critique of Empire, Hardt and Negri unwittingly reveal their own imperial project, the "New New Empire," or, as they call it, "New Republicanism"—a project that, as Mihai Spariosu argues, does not really "offend the sensibilities of democratic Western society" (2006, 92). By contrast, Gómez-Peña's barbarians do not aspire to replace a dominant discourse with a new doctrine. Rather, they decentralize dominant discourses by assuming a multiplicity of positions and testing several aesthetic and theoretical strategies, without committing to them dogmatically.

Gómez-Peña's barbarians could also be seen as embodiments of a twenty-first-century version of Walter Benjamin's barbarian. As argued previously, Benjamin's barbarians in "Experience and Poverty" share most of the qualities of Benjamin's "destructive character." Gómez-Peña's project differs considerably from Benjamin's. Each project responds to different social and political realities. In 1933, Benjamin's barbarians are invested with the potential to create something radically new through destruction of the old, in order to "to make a new start; . . . to begin with a little and build up further" (2005b, 732). Gómez-Peña's barbarians do not begin with "a little" after having erased the old. They construct their barbarian grammar out of the excess of the existing culture, by devouring and contaminating its saturated modes of expression. In their performance, the existing culture is parodied, restaged, and reinvented.

However, the common denominator in Benjamin's and Gómez-Peña's barbarians lies in their readiness to question existing structures and replace them with something new, whether this newness emerges from the ashes of the old (in Benjamin) or from its excess (in Gómez-Peña). Moreover, although Benjamin's and Gómez-Peña's projects spring from a different historical moment, they share a similar starting point: the overload of culture, which Gómez-Peña's barbarians perform and exploit, is also what triggers Benjamin's proposal for a new kind of barbarism.

The poverty of experience that Benjamin diagnoses emerges from an excess of ideas and styles. People, Benjamin says, "have 'devoured' everything, both 'culture and people,' and they have had such a surfeit, that it has exhausted them" (2005b, 734). Benjamin seeks new expressive forms to counter this excess. Gómez-Peña exploits this excess and turns it against the culture that has produced it. His barbarians expose the excess of capitalist US culture and simultaneously reclaim this excess in ways that cannot be captured by the norm or the stereotype. Whereas the overload of culture Benjamin describes in 1933 is a sign of bourgeois decadence, in the beginning of the new millennium, Gómez-Peña's barbarians turn this overload into a force of contestation of dominant narratives. In this way, they propose a new *Barbarentum*, based not on a destruction of the old (as in Benjamin) but on a cannibalistic aesthetic that devours everything and spits it out in new configurations.

Benjamin's and Gómez-Peña's barbarians share an openness to self-contestation. To Gómez-Peña's motto "question everything, *coño*, even these commandments" we could juxtapose Benjamin's principle: "always radical, never consistent" (Gómez-Peña 2000, 93; Benjamin 1994, 300).[28] This prevents their positive barbarism from turning into another version of the "old" or the dominant. "The destructive character sees nothing permanent," writes Benjamin in "The Destructive Character," and this includes his own methods and beliefs. He "has no interest in being understood. . . . Being misunderstood cannot harm him. On the contrary, he provokes it" (2005b, 542). Gómez-Peña's barbarians also invite self-questioning and misunderstandings through their "non-serious theorizing." Safeguarding the openness of one's own statements or performances becomes an indispensable feature of the new barbarian, either of the twentieth or of the twenty-first century.

From Absence to Excess: Three Ways to Political Art

If Geers's labyrinth is empty and Sacco's installation withholds every trace of the other besides the eyes, Gómez-Peña's barbarians appear full-fledged before the viewer. Yet they are just as confusing as the eyes in

Sacco's work. Although we can analyze the individual signs that each persona comprises, when trying to lead our analysis to a coherent interpretation, we are often at a loss.

The barbarisms that constitute Gómez-Peña's visual grammar are part of an aesthetic of excess. In stark contrast with Gómez-Peña's project, Kendell Geers's *Waiting for the Barbarians* and Graciela Sacco's *Esperando a los bárbaros* adopt an aesthetic of invisibility and suggestiveness, respectively. Compared to Geers's and Sacco's works, Gómez-Peña's barbarians reveal too much instead of too little. However, precisely this extreme visibility and theatricality of their performance discourage the viewer from relating to them as human beings. The inability to relate to these figures, however, has a political function. It compels the viewer to experience the dehumanization that takes place in constructing the other as barbarian. Moreover, it projects the catachrestic character of the designation "barbarian" by suggesting that this name has no proper meaning and literal referent.

Geers's and Sacco's works play with traces, absences, or elusive signs. Gómez-Peña's barbarian bodies are overly representational, so much so that they question the very possibility of representation, seen as an intelligible correspondence between a certain reality and an image of this reality. The constellation these three artworks form through their engagement with barbarism and barbarians is marked by a movement from an aesthetic of absence and invisibility (Geers) to minimal presence and suggestiveness (Sacco) to excess and visual overload (Gómez-Peña). The figures of otherness that emerge through these aesthetic visions—absent barbarians, invisible specters, half-hidden others, and ex-centric new barbarians—cast a critical eye on the barbarians Western discourses have constructed in the past but also in the twenty-first century.

Although the works' aesthetic visions differ, the critical operations performed by Geers's, Sacco's, and Gómez-Peña's works are comparable. Geers's and Sacco's installations show more by showing less: their affective operations are mobilized by the things the viewer can imagine and experience because of (partial) invisibility or absence. Gómez-Peña's barbarians show less by showing more: despite their semiotic overload, they remain inaccessible and distant and refuse to represent any "real barbarians." This play between visibility and invisibility, excess and inaccessibility, distance and proximity makes us question the kind of straightforward knowledge our vision supposedly produces. In all three works, what we think we know (and control) by seeing is put in doubt. We simply cannot trust our eyes. Neither the eyes in Sacco's installation, nor the spectral forces in Geers's labyrinth, nor the personas in Gómez-Peña's "New Barbarians" offer us the ease of recognition that familiar faces and objects guarantee.

The explicit political content of "The New Barbarians"—its critique of mainstream US culture—enhanced by the theoretical essays that accompany the portfolios, raises the question of the relation of the aesthetic to the political. Does the work's aesthetic become an auxiliary means of serving an activist agenda of resistance to the mainstream? Although Gómez-Peña's barbarians practice a kind of activism through art, it is not so much their political agenda that makes them political art. Their political interventions unravel through the barbarian aesthetic they create. Western imagery is inflated, cut, and pasted in such a way that its own severed parts are unrecognizable yet strangely familiar. The political is thus played out in the tensions they stage between different cultural registers and representational regimes—tensions often suppressed by a "monolingual" culture of consensus. Their political force is in line with Chantal Mouffe's definition of the political. According to Mouffe, "the political" captures the agonistic dimension that she takes to be "constitutive of human societies" (2005, 9). It describes a "vibrant 'agonistic' public sphere of contestation" that acknowledges the "conflictual dimension of social life" as a necessary condition for democratic politics (4).

Gómez-Peña's, Sacco's, and Geers's aesthetic strategies carry political investments. The aesthetic of these works is not a vehicle for an extractable political message but creates political spaces, charged with the kind of agonistic relations that, according to Mouffe, typify the political. Their aesthetic strategies—showing too much or too little—oppose a visual economy of excess to an economy of debt and withholding. Despite their divergent strategies, however, they all resist reduction to illustrations of a theoretical and/or political position. Instead, they become agents of a barbarian mode of theorizing. Their political potential emerges from showing "the kinds of critical thinking that images can make possible" (T. Clark 2006, 185).

Gómez-Peña's personas enact a nightmarish version of popular images of barbarians. At the same time, as the enigmatic eyes in Sacco's *Waiting for the Barbarians* and the spectral forces in Geers's labyrinth, they may be viewed as the ugly caterpillars that bear the promise of a better alternative to the binary logic of "civilized versus barbarians." These figures turn the "barbarian" into a marker of ambiguity and confusion. This barbarian challenges "the barbarian" of dominant Western discourses, who poses as the inferior part in a predetermined comparison with a "civilized" standard. The new barbarian is a genuinely comparative figure, functioning in the margins of dominant discourses and inviting open-ended encounters between two (or more) subjectivities, objects, languages, or discourses, foreign to each other.

The confrontation of the viewer with Geers's, Sacco's, or Gómez-Peña's works could also be seen as an instance of comparison, when the viewer's sense of self and preconceptions are tested against the artworks' performance. The openness of this comparison entails the risk of reconstituting dominant discourses. Thus, a certain viewer might still fill in the missing gaps of Sacco's eyes with images of threatening barbarians behind the wooden fences, ready to invade our space. This could reinforce this viewer's conviction that the borders of civilization should be closed for immigrants. Likewise, Gómez-Peña's exposure of the internal contradictions within Western representational systems need not have subversive effects on all viewers. As Bhabha argues, internal contradictions always exist and do not necessarily make powerful discourses less effective (1994, 134). Some viewers may perceive the performance of "The New Barbarians" as too "unserious" and estranging to be worth engaging, or as a form of activist resistance that can be anticipated and absorbed by the dominant. The kind of agency "The New Barbarians" assumes might thus end up reconstituting the mainstream. In political art, such risks are part of the unresolved tensions artworks set up, but they are risks certainly worth taking.

Afterword

The future can no longer be thought of as the "defense of Western civilization," constantly waiting for the barbarians. As barbarians are ubiquitous (they could be in the plains or in the mountains as well as in global cities), so are the civilized. There is no safe place to defend and, even worse, believing that there is a safe place that must be defended is (and has been) the direct road to killing.
—Walter Mignolo, *The Idea of Latin America*

As the constellation of cultural objects in this book shows, barbarian operations and constructive sites of barbarism can be found everywhere: inside, outside, and at the interstices of the walls of civilization; on a microscopic level, in the smallest details of texts; on a macroscopic level, in the travels of an object through different texts, media, and cultural contexts; on a kaleidoscopic level, in normative or subversive citations and repetitions; in mistranslations and in allegorical readings; within ourselves; inside the labyrinth of Western civilization or at the other side of a fence; in the overload of culture; in visual excess or in suggestive absences; in the interaction between readers or critics and the cultural objects they engage.

On the shifting ground on which the operations of barbarism unfold, a barbarian mode of theorizing may be envisioned. The notion of barbarian theorizing pertains to the question of *how* (else) we could do what we do as scholars, artists, cultural theorists, or students. Connected to the *how* is the perhaps even more significant question of *why*. The latter question concerns the practical value of an affirmative recasting of barbarism in relation to actual subjects in the world: people marginalized, excluded, or subject to processes of barbarization and othering by dominant groups. What is the point of theory, even a barbarian theory, if it has no impact on constructions of others as barbarians and the violence against them? Where do these others and their bodies fit in this talk about barbarian theorizing?

Although language is constitutive of our realities, it is important to maintain a distinction between the other as a *linguistic construction* and *actual others*, on which linguistic categories of otherness are imposed. Categories of otherness are certainly involved in very material ways in forming subjectivities. Nevertheless, trying to maintain such a distinction makes us more alert to inconsistencies in the ways others are discursively constructed: it allows us to recognize cases in which linguistic constructions of otherness are strikingly at odds with the actual conditions and practices of their material referents. Those construed as barbarians, for instance, may in reality be our neighbors—people we happen to have a lot in common with and who may be quite similar to us.

An absolute conflation of "linguistic" and "real" others may result in the full identification of a linguistic category of otherness with specific groups of people. The label "barbarian" becomes indistinguishable from specific subjects, which suffer the violence of this essentialist practice. Nevertheless, adopting a *radical* division between linguistic and real others also contains certain pitfalls. The theoretical propensity to radicalize the distinction between linguistic categories of otherness and real others is often motivated by the desire to protect subjects from the violence of an essentialist conflation of the linguistic and the real. Theories premised on an ethics of the Other, for example, have often endorsed the notion of an absolute Other, which always remains foreign and unintelligible in its alterity and thus cannot (and should not) be appropriated (and controlled) by the self and its discourses. Despite the political and ethical merits of this theoretical stance—meant to protect subjugated others and minorities from violent acts of othering or control—when tested on sociopolitical realities, such an approach may sabotage the possibility of communication and contact with others. The idea of an inaccessible Other that cannot and should not be "translated," violated, and appropriated by discourse often assumes in practice a form of respect toward real subjects, which is premised on distance rather than proximity. In order not to risk doing violence to others, one misses the chance to engage with them in potentially transformative encounters.

In language, the difference between self and other constitutes a strict dualism. As a result, we often conceptualize actual encounters with others in binary terms and consequently construct relations of absolute difference between self and other—relations of one to zero. In practice, the difference between self and other is not a relation of one to zero but a difference in degree, whereby the other may differ from, but also resemble, the self, without being reduced to it. Therefore, addressing and interrogating the problematic relation between linguistic categories of otherness and the people on which they are conferred may form a basis for productive encounters between interlocutors or adversaries instead of barbarian enemies.

This basis does not guarantee easy dialogues. Cross-cultural communication and exchange is not a smooth process. But focusing on the tension between similarity and alterity, communication and miscommunication, we become more sensitive to those barbarisms that enter the discourse of the self, triggering operations of self-*alter*ation. Barbarism, as this book shows, is a disruptive element within the self: a constant reminder of the fact that we can never own what we think belongs to us, including our languages, our cultural practices, our own selves. Barbarians are dangerous because they threaten to expose the self to the inconsistencies of its own language—its internal barbarisms. This exposure brings about a disappropriation of one's own language and culture, a self-dispossession that may be uncomfortable, even painful. But it also contains a promise for discovering new ways of relating to our home and cultural "belongings," ways that are more inclusive, less focused on ownership and authority and more on acts of hospitality. The language of the civilized self is not homogeneous and univocal, as it always contains the sound of the other—but this other need not be a barbarian or an absolute Other. It can simply be *an* other, an interlocutor, an adversary, or our next-door neighbor.

The strategies, operations, and analyses in this book will certainly not give clear-cut solutions or put an end to the violence against others in the name of civilization, liberalism, religious fundamentalism, or other interests and ideologies. The applicability or potential impact of an affirmative recasting of barbarism in our sociopolitical and cultural realities might thus seem far-fetched—and in a certain sense it is. However, significantly, the construction of barbarians and thus also the violence against them (symbolic or physical) starts with the performative act of naming. Naming barbarians creates barbarians. At the same time, "barbarian" is an exceptionally mobile category. The criteria and features that make us "recognize" others as barbarians change in each context and period, according to the interests and defining standards of the self. Viewed as such, "barbarian" is an overarching, versatile category of otherness—almost a passkey for constructing subjects as dangerous or inferior. This makes its violence more pervasive and real, since it could be applied to virtually any subject under specific circumstances. Remarkably, the category "barbarian"—the most persistent other in Western history—has all the more material effects because it is purely discursive. However, it is precisely its discursive character that makes the barbarian suitable for resignification and subversive, critical operations.

Consequently, in regard to barbarism and barbarians, the distance between theory and practice, words and acts, symbolic and physical violence is not as vast as one might think. Small shifts in the ways we conceive and use "barbarism" and the "barbarian" in language or in visual representations could have a tangible impact on the ways we tag, construct, and treat others as barbarians in domestic and international politics and in everyday life. The distance between an either/or logic—the logic of "you're either with us or with the barbarians"—and a pluralized, performative, counterintuitive, creative conception of barbarism and the barbarian, could also make the very real difference between a barbaric war against the West's "new barbarians" and, in Cavafy's words, another "kind of solution."

Notes

INTRODUCTION

1. When using the term "theory" in this book, I usually refer to the kind of theory primarily developed and practiced within literary studies in the last few decades. "Theory" was mainly associated with poststructuralism and particularly with an operation of formalism, the "uncovering of the structural conditions and features of a text" (Butler, Guillory, and Thomas 2000, viii). However, the term "theory" in the last twenty years has taken a more political turn within academic discourse. Redeployed in "legibly 'political' contexts" and "politically invested arenas" such as race, colonialism, gender, and sexuality, it involves what is also known as postcolonial theory and cultural studies (ix).

2. Foucault's use of the term "operation" often refers to discursive acts involved in, or coinciding with, the production of knowledge and power in a given discursive formation. He also employs the term to refer to processes that enable action to "speak" by turning it into language (see, for example, Foucault 2002, 69, 80, 116, 172, 347; 2000).

3. The term "constitutive outside" is used by Judith Butler to refer not to an absolute outside that exceeds the limits of discourse but to "that which can only be thought—when it can—in relation to that discourse, at and as its most tenuous borders" (1993, 8). The term was proposed by Henry Staten in his discussion of Derrida's thinking (1984, 16, 20, 24). The aim of the notion, according to Mouffe, is to underscore the fact that "the creation of an identity implies the establishment of a difference, difference which is often constructed on the basis of a hierarchy." Since every identity is relational, "the affirmation of a difference is a precondition for the existence of any identity, i.e. the perception of something 'other' which constitutes its 'exterior'" (2005, 15).

4. Derrida elaborates this process through the notion of the "double mark." Every name or concept is involved in the "structure of the double mark." Although it is caught in "the closed agonistic, hierarchical field of philosophical oppositions," a concept also retains "its old name" in order to "destroy the opposition," to which it "has never quite yielded" (2004, 4, 5). Every concept receives "one mark inside and the other outside" the system of binaries and can thus

generate a "double reading": it sustains an opposition but can also critique and disorganize the traditional binary to which it belongs (4). Inevitably, putting "old names to work" involves the risk of "regressing into the system that has been, or is in the process of being, deconstructed" (5). But to do away with old names and thus "cross over," as Derrida calls it, "into the outside of the classical oppositions," is missing the opportunity to intervene in the system—here, the binary system that produces the barbarian and the civilized. In the process of using old names for new purposes, we should not forget that the system to which they belong is not "a sort of ahistorical thoroughly homogeneous table" but instead a "hierarchically ordered space whose closure is constantly being traversed by the forces . . . that it represses" and expels (5).

5. On the double sense of meaning as "to mean to" (intend) and "to mean" (signify) and the implications of this ambiguity, see Bal (2002, 271–72).

6. As Derrida argues, the iterability of every utterance—the fact that it performs differently in its every use—"leaves us no choice but to mean (to say) something that is (already, always, also) other than what we mean (to say)" (1988, 62). This gap between intention and meaning guarantees the fundamental undecidability of all utterances—literal, serious, fictional, literary, and so on.

7. Here, I take my cue from Mieke Bal's concept-based methodology in which she argues that "interdisciplinarity in the humanities must seek its heuristic and methodological basis in concepts rather than methods." She proposes a methodology that uses concepts in order to understand the research object better and on its own terms (2002, 8).

CHAPTER I

1. The story was probably written in 1917 and published in 1931, seven years after Kafka's death. The English translation I am using is by Willa and Edwin Muir (Kafka 1999).

2. Deleuze and Guattari argue that in Kafka there is no "infinite hierarchy belonging to a negative theology" but a *"contiguity of desire* that causes whatever happens to happen always in the office next door" (1986, 50). In the story, this contiguity of desire manifests itself in the narrator's desire for answers to his inquiries about the wall's construction. All his answers slip away and are succeeded by new questions. This produces a mercury-like effect: whenever the reader thinks the narrator has provided the answer to a question, the answer slips out of the reader's hands, disappearing through the gaps in the story's wall.

3. Deleuze and Guattari's views discussed in Réda Bensmaïa (1986, xi). In their reading, Deleuze and Guattari distance themselves from symbolic, allegorical, or mythical interpretations of Kafka's work and suggest a literal reading of his work. As a result, they are less interested in interpretation—digging

beyond the surface of the work—but read his work as "an experimental machine" for effects (xi). In my view, reading Kafka literally does not rule out the reader's desire for allegorization, to which the stories appeal. In Kafka's account of the wall of China, we find the literal and allegorical, just like the mythical and the real, on the same discursive level, without one having priority over the other.

4. In his essay "Franz Kafka: On the Tenth Anniversary of his Death," Benjamin also notices that in Kafka each experience "gives way and mingles with its opposite"; "the very possibility of the third alternative puts the other two, which at first seemed harmless, in a different light" (1999b, 126).

5. This discontinuity, Deleuze and Guattari argue, appears in Kafka especially when power manifests itself as a "transcendental authority, as a paranoid law" imposing "a discontinuous distribution of individual periods, with breaks between each one, a discontinuous repartition of blocks, with spaces between each one" (1986, 72). Moreover, they argue that the blocks in Kafka's writing do not distribute themselves around a circle with discontinuous arches but "align themselves on a hallway or a corridor" along an unlimited straight line (73). On this line, each block has doors far from the doors of other blocks, but it also has connecting back doors, through which the blocks become contiguous. "This is the most striking topography in Kafka's work, and it isn't only a 'mental' topography: two diametrically opposed points bizarrely reveal themselves to be in contact" (73).

6. Levine makes this observation about Kafka's stories in general.

7. For the idea of teaching and pedagogy as an "undoing" of what has been established by education, see Felman, "Psychoanalysis and Education: Teaching Terminable and Interminable" (1987).

8. In the English edition of Kafka's stories I am using (Vintage, 1999), this fragment (translated by Tania and James Stern), added right after "The Great Wall of China," is perceived by the reader as a postscript—an adjunct to the main story about the wall. However, this fragment is not formally part of "The Great Wall of China." In other editions of Kafka's stories that include "The Great Wall of China," such as the German edition edited by Paul Raabe (1970), this fragment is left out.

9. "Babel" is the name of God the father. It is thus a proper name, and as such it remains untranslatable. But it is simultaneously a common noun, signifying "confusion." As God delivers his punishment, Derrida argues, the proper name of God is divided in people's different foreign tongues, spreading and signifying "confusion." Therefore, according to Derrida, translation becomes necessary (due to linguistic confusion) but impossible, since a proper name is untranslatable (1985, 173, 177–78). For another detailed analysis of the myth of Babel in relation to language and translation, including an analysis of Derrida's "Des tours de Babel," see de Vries, "Anti-Babel" (2002, 211–92).

10. The narrator is condescending toward this theory, underscoring its irrationality: "There were many wild ideas in people's heads at that time—this scholar's book is only one example" (Kafka 1999, 239).

11. In his reading of Derrida's essay on Babel, Stathis Gourgouris considers the myth and deconstruction of Babel in terms of a desire of diaspora. The "Babelian performance" (the myth and deconstruction of Babel), Gourgouris argues, is "the origin of a desire that has scattered its traces all over history, a diasporic desire that has plunged history into confusion—after all, Babel is also the mythical *archē*, the governing principle, of diaspora" (2003, 303).

12. For Deleuze and Guattari's notion of desire, see "The Desiring Machines" (1984); on desire in relation to Kafka's work, see "Immanence and Desire" (1986, 143–52).

13. Deleuze and Guattari discussed in Bensmaïa (1985, xiii–xiv).

14. Perhaps the anonymous scholar's proposal for the convergence of the two projects is implicitly reformulated by Kafka himself in one of *The Zürau Aphorisms*: "If it had been possible to build the Tower of Babel without having to climb it, that would have been sanctioned" (2006, 18). This other tower, which one would not have to climb, could take the form of the wall. In Kafka, the Tower of Babel is not only transfigured into a horizontal construction (a wall) but also takes an earthbound direction. In the spirit of reversal, one of Kafka's very short stories introduces "The Pit of Babel" (Der Schacht von Babel) (1961, 34–35).

15. The term "paradox-object" has been used by art theorist Boris Groys to refer to objects of contemporary art. For Groys, the field of contemporary art can be viewed as "an embodiment of paradox" (2008, 3): "Already in the framework of classical modernity, but especially in the context of contemporary art, individual artworks began to be paradox-objects that embody simultaneously thesis and antithesis" (3). Particularly since World War II, we find, for example, paintings that can be seen as abstract and realistic, documentary and fictional, or objects that can be described as both "traditional sculptures" and as "readymades" (3). Groys argues that our difficulty in making sense of, and dealing with, modern art "consists in our unwillingness to accept paradoxical, self-contradictory interpretations as adequate and true" (4). Seen as a paradox-object, barbarism is in tune with Groys's vision of contemporary art.

16. In my reflections on the relation between the positive and the negative in this paragraph, I take my cue from Felman's exposition of "radical negativity" (2003, 101–5).

CHAPTER 2

1. A transcript of Tony Blair's statement can be found at http://news.bbc .co.uk/2/hi/uk_news/politics/1538551.stm .

2. A transcript of Tony Blair's statement at the G8 summit meeting can be found at www.g8.utoronto.ca/summit/2005gleneagles/blair_blasts050707.html.

3. Joschka Fischer's statement can be found at www.dw.de/dw/article/0,,1201023,00.html.

4. See Mamdani (2004, 18). According to Mamdani, this "culturalization" can be credited to Bernard Lewis's 1990 article "The Roots of Muslim Rage" and Samuel Huntington's 1993 article "The Clash of Civilizations?," which he developed into a book (1996).

5. According to Huntington, the other great threat to Western civilization comes from China.

6. While Huntington views multiculturalism as a domestic threat, he also concedes that the world is inevitably "multicultural" and thus a "global empire" is impossible (1996, 318).

7. In the 1990s, when Huntington's study was written, these phenomena included a "global breakdown of law and order," "increasing anarchy," "a global crime wave," "mafias and drug cartels," a "weakening of the family," and "ethnic, religious, and civilizational violence" (1996, 321). The almost apocalyptic tone of Huntington's diagnosis reflects the tendency to regard one's present era as unique and unprecedented.

8. Bernard Lewis introduced the phrase "clash of civilizations" (1990).

9. From Bush's "Speech to Employees at the Federal Bureau of Investigation," September 25, 2001 (2003, 22).

10. For example, in his presidential address to the nation on September 11, 2001, he quotes from Psalm 23: "Even though I walk through the valley of the shadow of death, I fear no evil, for You are with me" (Bush 2003, 3).

11. From the "Presidential Address to a Joint Session of Congress," September 23, 2001 (Bush 2003, 15–16).

12. The first quotation is from Bush's "Speech to the Employees of the Department of Labor," October 4, 2001; the second, from "Presidential Radio Address to the Nation," October 6, 2001 (Bush 2003, 30, 32).

13. From the presidential address to a joint session of Congress, September 23, 2001 (Bush 2003, 16).

14. The first quotation (about Nicholas Berg's decapitation) is from "President Thanks Military Personnel and Families for Serving Our Country," December 7, 2004, and "President's Radio Address" May 15, 2004, http://georgewbush-whitehouse.archives.gov/news/releases/2004/12/20041207-2.html. The second is from an interview with *Al Arabiya*, May 5, 2004, http://abcnews.go.com/Politics/story?id=120660&page=1. Parts of these statements are also quoted and discussed in Brown (2006, 159).

15. One example among many is the study by Israeli historian Élie Barnavi (2006), in which he seeks the origins of terrorism in religion.

16. From "President's Remarks at 'Congress of Tomorrow' Lunch," February 1, 2002, quoted in Brown (2006, 179).

17. Žižek goes even further to argue that the real problem with capitalism does not lie in its "secret Eurocentric bias" but in "the fact that it *really* is universal, a neutral matrix of social relations" (for the way he develops this argument, see 2009, 132–34).

18. Fish's essay appeared in an issue of the journal *The Responsive Community* dedicated to the question "Can Postmodernists Condemn Terrorism?"

19. See Rothstein, "Moral Relativity Is a Hot Topic? True. Absolutely," *New York Times*, July 13, 2002, http://pascal.iseg.utl.pt/~ncrato/Recortes/EdRothstein _NYT_20020613.htm.

20. The book was first published in French in 2004 as *Le choc des barbaries: Terrorismes et désordre mondial.*

21. Another noteworthy reversal is performed by Terry Eagleton, "Culture Conundrum," *The Guardian*, May 21, 2008, in which he elaborates the claim that "culture is the new barbarism." See also Eagleton (2009, 154–60).

22. Todorov's study was first published in French in 2008 as *La peur des barbares.*

23. Todorov develops his position by arguing against a kind of relativism that shies from judgment of other cultures and, in Todorov's view, may lead to nihilism. But he also declares to be equally opposed to a dogmatism based on ethnocentrism, whereby the "we" is the holder of the true and the just (2010, 13–14). He thus pleads for a more nuanced approach, which should focus on the complexity of every situation, instead of sweeping judgments based on black-and-white distinctions (10).

24. The translator of Todorov's book (2010) sometimes translates the French *barbarie* as "barbarity" instead of "barbarism." For reasons of consistency with the terminology used in this chapter, I use the term "barbarism" in my discussion of Todorov's study (except when quoting from Todorov's book).

25. In Todorov's account, "civilization" is an absolute and single notion, and the permanent opposite of barbarism. Where others—such as Huntington—use "civilizations," Todorov uses the word "culture" in the plural to signify historical formations and groups of people with common ways of life and thinking, common traditions, and so on. In order to avoid semantic confusion, Todorov reserves the word "civilization" only for those absolute values that are the opposite of barbarism. In his definition, civilization is an exclusively moral category (2010, 26).

26. Todorov devotes a part of his book to the defense of what he considers as the true heritage of Enlightenment and its humanist values against what he views as misconceptions and abuses of the legacy of Enlightenment today (2010, 28–31).

CHAPTER 3

1. Scott makes this argument for categories of gender, such as femininity, masculinity, sex, homosexuality, and heterosexuality.

2. Although there are many studies of the barbarian in specific periods in Western history, there is to my knowledge no comprehensive, systematic genealogical study of this notion. A popularized genealogy of the barbarian can be found in the study by French philosopher Roger-Pol Droit (2007). Also, Mark Salter (2002) gives an overview of the discourse on barbarism and civilization since the Middle Ages.

3. The word "savage" comes from the Latin word for "wood" (*silva*) and was first employed for men who lived in the German forests without an organized society (Salter 2002, 20).

4. The trope of the "noble savage" was used by the Romantics to formulate a critique of European civilization. See White, "The Noble Savage Theme as Fetish" (1978).

5. *Gaijin*, literally meaning "outside person," is the Japanese word for a foreigner and was especially used for Westerners (European travelers and merchants) visiting Japan. It refers to difference in ethnicity or race (Buckley 2002, 161–62).

6. The figure of the barbarian has had a very central place in the Chinese imaginary. The Chinese resisted cultural influences from the West. Within this ideology of self-sufficiency, perceived by Westerners as xenophobia, peoples outside the Chinese borders, Westerners in particular, were viewed as barbarians. For an exploration of barbarians in Mandarin culture, see Cameron (1970).

7. A typical example of the importance of language in differentiation in the Hebrew tradition is the word *shibbōleth*. In Judges 12:4–6, the pronunciation of the word was used as a test for nationality, to distinguish Gileadites from Ephraimites (*Advanced Learner's Dictionary*, 1998). The word's pronunciation thus marked some people as insiders and others as foreigners. The word is still used as a word, phrase, or principle that distinguishes a particular class, nation, or group of people (*Concise Oxford Dictionary*, 2001).

8. Religion was also central to the Hindus' opposition between themselves and non-Hindus, *mlechhas*. See Diamond (1974, 125); and E. Hall (1989, 5).

9. Although the specific construct we call "the West" has only been in use in the last two centuries, there are of course older uses of "west." See Sakai and Morris (2005, 372); and Williams (1985, 333).

10. As Ella Shohat and Robert Stam argue about the relation between West and non-West, "the two worlds interpenetrate in an unstable space of creolization and syncretism" (1994, 15). However, the discourse of purity of the European civilization was premised on exclusions of other cultural influences, such as the influence of Egypt on Greek civilization, of Africa on the Roman Empire, and

of Islam on Europe's economic, political, and intellectual history (58; Robinson 1983, 4). One of the best-known (and most controversial) attempts to revise the Eurocentric construction of the West is by Martin Bernal (1987).

11. In her study on ethnic stereotypes, Rosello takes the "reluctant witness" as "an emblematic figure" that can be very helpful in addressing issues related to ethnic stereotyping. The "reluctant witness," she argues, "knows that there is no outside, especially if two speakers share the same language, the same linguistic crucible where stereotypes have slowly formed over centuries of intertextual references" (1998, 1).

12. We should not forget that the notion of one Greek language, even in the classical period, is contestable, since Greek was a "collection of myriad regional dialects." Thus, in many cases, communication among Greeks of different regions would have been just as difficult as between Greeks and non-Greeks (J. Hall 2002, 116–17).

13. For extensive analyses of the use of the barbarian in Greek drama, see E. Hall (1989); Long (1986); Colvin (1999); and Bacon (1961).

14. All these examples are presented in Munson (2005, 65–66).

15. The philological and conceptual history of "culture," as well as the history of its relation to "civilization" and "barbarism," are too complex to be accounted for adequately in this typology. My account is limited to a selection of characteristic historical constellations that bring out the transformability of their interrelation.

16. In this sense, the term "civilization," more than "culture," is almost automatically conceived in opposition to an outside and a barbarian other. Hence, "civilization" seems to need the figure of the barbarian for its self-definition more than "culture" does.

17. In the ancient world, the specific term "culture" is of course not used as such, but the idea of it is expressed through other related concepts.

18. Isocrates was also a fierce proponent of a strict opposition between Greeks and barbarians and saw the barbarians of Asia as the natural enemies of the Greeks (Long 1986, 149). For Isocrates, Hellenicity was identified with Athenian education (J. Hall 2002, 209).

19. However, not every barbarian was a potential Roman citizen. There were conquered barbarians within Roman borders: those were the groups that could potentially share the benefits of *Romanitas*. But there was also a barbarous exterior of savagery, aggression, and lack of organization (Goffart 1981, 280). This external *barbaricum*, which was defined in more absolute terms, contributed to the self-perception of the Roman Empire as the order that warded off chaos from the civilized world (280).

20. For a discussion of Schiller's views on the relation between ethics and aesthetics, see J. Bennett (1996).

21. The Dada movement, which started in Zürich during World War I and reached its peak from 1916 to 1922, was a movement in art, literature, theater, and graphic design (Kreuter 2006, 41). Surrealism began in the early 1920s, and many surrealists were initially involved in the Dada movement.

22. Both communism and Marxism have been identified with "barbarism." Bernard-Henri Lévy's *Barbarism with a Human Face* (1979) is a fierce attack on communism as well as on Marxism and the "Sovietophilia" of left intellectuals. The group Socialisme ou Barbarie presents an interesting intervention in this divide between capitalism and communism. Founded in France in 1949 by Cornelius Castoriadis and Claude Lefort, Socialisme ou Barbarie was a revolutionary political group, which also produced a journal under the same name, still circulating in the mid-1960s. The group, with Castoriadis as its main representative, advocated an alternative position both to Western capitalism and to the Soviet Union. "Barbarism" in Socialisme ou Barbarie is represented by Western capitalism and Soviet communism, as well as the new class of bureaucrats to which they had both given rise, albeit in different forms. Castoriadis's socialist alternative to this barbarism was an *autonomous socialism* "based on the self-rule of factories by workers" and on the "assertive free development of the critical individual living in equality with others" (Bronner 1999, 214; Curtis 1992, xix).

23. The political foundations of the opposition are also played out in Aeschylus's *Persae*, which dramatized the repercussions in Persia of the Persian defeat by the Athenian fleet in Salamina. In this tragedy, it is suggested that the Persians were defeated because they were prone to despotism, slavishness, and excess, whereas Athenian greatness was based on equality, freedom, and democracy and therefore destined to last through the centuries (E. Hall 1989, 10).

24. Admittedly, the functioning of the Athenian Empire differs from that of other large empires in Western history. It was based on a democratic political system and sought economic and cultural domination not so much over foreign (barbaric) nations but over other Greek nation-states.

25. The concept of empire pervades and extends over several of the civilizational standards laid out in this chapter, such as ideology, economy, politics, gender and sexuality, race, and culture.

26. When talking about modern European empires, we could distinguish two periods: the colonization of the Americas (1492 to the 1830s); and the colonization of Africa, Asia, and the Pacific (1730s until after World War II). Both periods generated strict oppositions between the European (Spanish, British, French) self and colonized others, drawn along diverse lines, such as geography (Europeans versus non-Europeans), religion (Christians versus infidels), culture and progress (civilized versus savages or barbarians), race, and so on (Mills 1997, 21).

27. The figure of the barbarian is particularly foregrounded in Euripides. In his tragedies, the projection of typical barbarian qualities such as foolishness,

cowardice, and injustice enhanced the audience's perception of the opposite virtues—wisdom, courage, and justice—as typically Greek/Athenian (J. Hall 2002, 177–78).

28. Elias writes on the threshold between the civilized and the barbaric: "The greater or lesser discomfort we feel towards people who discuss or mention their bodily functions more openly . . . is one of the dominant feelings expressed in the judgment 'barbaric' or 'uncivilized.' Such, then, is the nature of 'barbarism and its discontents' or, in more precise and less evaluative terms, the discontent with the different structure of affects, the different standard of repugnance which is still to be found today in many societies which we term 'uncivilized'" (2000, 51).

29. For the relation and opposition between "human" and "animal," see Agamben (2002).

30. The complex genealogy of the concepts of the human, humanity, and humanism, and the precise ways by which they produce their outside, exceeds the scope of this study.

31. For one analysis of encounters between European civilization and indigenous civilizations of America, and the cultural confrontations to which these encounters led, see Todorov (1984).

32. This quotation is by Eusebius, one of Porphyry's great adversaries, who here indignantly reports what he claims were Porphyry's own words (G. Clark 1999, 127).

33. For a detailed exploration of Byzantine writers' perception of the West as barbarian, see Goffart (1981); see also the entry *barbaros* in Liddell and Scott (1996).

34. In 1537, Pope Paul III issued a bull that condemned as heretical the opinion that the American Indians could not receive the Christian faith, although this had a very limited effect on the behavior of the conquistadores (Jahoda 1999, 16).

35. According to Manning Marable, race, unlike ethnicity, is a passive affiliation (presented in Shohat and Stam 1994, 20).

36. For the definition of ethnicity, see Murji (2005, 112); for the definition of nation, see Abbé Sieyès (1789), quoted in Hindess (2005, 232).

37. Herodotus also questions Hellenicity as resting on a homogeneous ethnicity (J. Hall 2002, 190–91). In his conception of Hellenicity, cultural criteria (including language and religion) are promoted "to the same level as kinship" (193).

38. Plato's views are expressed through the voice of the "Stranger" in the dialogue.

39. Despite Plato's relativism in this passage, his other writings contain contradictions on this matter, which have led commentators to adopt different interpretations of his position. According to Julius Jüthner, for instance, Plato did

maintain a belief in racial purity, which created an unbridgeable gap between Greeks and barbarians (Jüthner, presented in J. Hall 2002, 213).

40. Remarkably, in 1869, the English cultural critic Matthew Arnold uses the term "barbarian" as a positive signifier to refer to the aristocratic classes. He contends that all the qualities of the barbarians have been inherited by the aristocracy in his present-day England. He views the barbarians as a source of life and vigor for Europe, and as the true ancestors of the British:

> The Barbarians, to whom we all owe so much, and who reinvigorated and renewed our worn-out Europe, had, as is well-known, eminent merits; and in this country, where we are for the most part sprung from the Barbarians, we have never had the prejudice against them which prevails among the races of Latin origin. (1966, 100)

Among the merits and qualities he ascribes to the barbarians (and thus to English aristocracy) are personal liberty and individualism, the care for the body and for manly exercises, vigor, good looks, chivalry, self-confidence, "high spirit," and "choice manners." The only flaw he finds with the barbarian disposition lies in the fact that barbarians have an "exterior culture," not much concerned with the "powers of thought and feeling" (101).

41. The quotation is from "Beyond the Black River" (Howard, quoted in Miller 2006).

42. The quotation is from "Queen of the Black Coast" (Howard, quoted in Miller 2006).

43. E. Hall makes this point in her discussion of Aeschylus's *Agamemnon* (1989, 205–6).

44. For the intersection of gender, sexuality, and race in the colonies, see McClintock (1995); and Stoler (1995).

45. For the sexual metaphors of penetration and conquest, which were used to describe the attitude of Westerners vis-à-vis the Orient, see also Said (2003, 44).

46. Some progressive models mentioned in this section could also be called "evolutionary." "Evolution" is most notably inscribed in the discourse of the life sciences, and it is from evolutionary processes as understood by biologists that the concept has been transferred to the social sciences (Rose 2005, 117). What is implied in both "progress" and "evolution" is the idea of a gradual progression toward an improved state. This also suggests that historical change follows a logic of steps or stages and does not follow from radical breaks or revolutions (117).

47. The views of these historians on this issue are discussed in Hartog (2001, 80–81).

48. Narratives of progress from savagery, primitivism, and barbarism to civilization were very popular in the eighteenth and nineteenth centuries. Such

models were, for example, formulated in France by d'Holbach in 1770 and Diderot in 1776, or in England by Ferguson in 1767. The latter describes the progress of humanity as a movement from "rudeness" to civilization (Todorov 2010, 28).

49. A critical elaboration of this perception of indigenous peoples is developed by Fabian (1983).

50. In *Persian Letters*, which is both a critique of Europe and a reaffirmation of the otherness of the (non-European) barbarian, Montesquieu elaborates the ambivalent relation of the "barbarian" to Europe. On the one hand, the barbarian hordes threaten Europe; on the other hand, the barbarians have also been seen as "a source of innovation, strength and vigour" (Montesquieu, presented in Salter 2002, 22). For a detailed analysis of Montesquieu's *Persian Letters*, see also Boer (2004, 49–74).

51. In the Hellenistic period we encounter several challenges to, or reversals of, the opposition between Greek and barbarian, for instance, in Agatharchides of Cnidus (second century BCE) and Posidonius of Apamea, a Stoic philosopher and ethnographer of the first century BCE (Hartog 2001, 100–101). Such views are comparable to the ideals attached to the figure of the "noble savage," which became popular in the eighteenth century.

52. Of course, one cannot generalize all attempted reversals as ultimately Eurocentric and unable to radically question European civilizational discourse. Each reversal needs to be examined separately.

53. White focuses on the notion of the "wild man." Although the image of the wild man differs from that of the barbarian, many of White's observations on the wild man can be extrapolated to the barbarian. White also discusses the similarities and differences between the two concepts (1972, 19–21).

54. White sees the interiorization of the wild man as a remythification, because it still functions as a projection of repressed anxieties and desires (1972, 7).

55. Freud, presented in Brown (2006, 163).

CHAPTER 4

1. The first version of the review-essay "Rigorous Study of Art" was written between July and December 1932, and a second version was published in *Literaturblatt der Frankfurter Zeitung* in July 1933. The essay is translated by Thomas Y. Levin (2005b).

2. Benjamin's essay is a review of the first volume of *Kunstwissenschaftliche Forschungen*—a collection of art-historical essays from scholars of the Vienna school, which Benjamin saw as introducing a new method for the study of art. Benjamin perceived this method as a translation of his own critical project into art-historical practices (Levin 1988, 81).

3. On this point I agree with McLaughlin, who does not see a systematic theory of barbarism deriving from Benjamin's uses of the concept in various contexts in his writings (2006, 5).

4. "Erfahrung und Armut" was written between spring and autumn 1933.

5. In my exploration of the notion of "experience" in this chapter I refer to the concept of *Erfahrung* in Benjamin, not *Erlebnis*. Benjamin elaborates the distinction between the two notions in "The Storyteller" (1936) and "On Some Motifs in Baudelaire" (1940). Although they are both usually translated in English as "experience," when Benjamin differentiates the two, he presents *Erlebnis* as a kind of immediate experience, lived through momentarily, while *Erfahrung* is something that has taken place as well as an ongoing kind of experience that enables new modes of reflecting, knowing, and understanding to emerge. The latter kind of experience is tied to the possibility of sharing and communicating, and it is precisely this experience and its communicability that have been lost with modernity, particularly after World War I.

6. According to the argument in "The Storyteller," this recent poverty of experience has made storytelling a craft of the past.

7. Benjamin makes this point in relation to the work of Paul Klee, Adolf Loos, and Paul Scheerbart, who for him embody this creative, forward-looking spirit. It is noteworthy that Loos, whom Benjamin counts among the "good barbarians," is also for Theodor Adorno an example of barbarism, but in a negative sense. According to Adorno, the merging of aesthetic beauty and real purposiveness (what he calls the "literalization" of art), as he sees it take place in the architectural theory of Loos, is barbaric: "Das Barbarische ist das Buchstäbliche" (The barbaric is the literal) (1970, 97, quoted in McLaughlin 2006, 7). Buildings built to serve nonartistic purposes are not aesthetically significant to him. In this context, barbarism for Adorno becomes synonymous with functionality in architecture. What Adorno sees as barbaric is barbaric for Benjamin too, but in a positive sense: this functionality is the source of aesthetic innovation (McLaughlin 2006, 7).

8. Van Alphen mentions, for example, Charles Baudelaire, Rainer Maria Rilke, and Paul Celan (2007, 341–42). On the same issue, see also Baer (2001).

9. The first version of the essay "Das Kunstwerk im Zeitalter seiner Technischen Reproduzierbarkeit" was written between autumn and December 1935. The second version was composed between the end of 1935 and the beginning of February 1936. The third and last version is dated between spring 1936 and March/April 1939.

10. For the issue of distraction (in Benjamin and others) and its significance in modernity, see van Alphen (2007).

11. On this point, see also Cadava (1997, 47); and Düttmann (1994, 36).

12. The aesthetization of war finds its literary expression in the movement of futurism, especially in Marinetti's manifesto on the Ethiopian colonial war—an

ode to the beauty of war, parts of which Benjamin quotes in the epilogue to his essay "Work of Art." The reasons for the fascist beautification of war, however, are not purely aesthetic. According to Benjamin, the actual reasons lie in the fact that war "can set a goal for mass movements on the largest scale" and "makes it possible to mobilize all of today's technical resources" while in both cases maintaining "the traditional property system" (1999b, 234).

13. In major German dictionaries, the most common entry for *barbarism* is *Barbarei*, which is generally defined as the opposite of civilization or culture. The second most common entry is *Barbarismus* (a mistake or foreign element in language). *Barbarentum* is relatively uncommon in contemporary German and has an archaic sound to it. According to the 1997 edition of Schulz and Basler's dictionary, beginning at the end of the eighteenth century *Barbarentum* was used to denote the amount and distribution of foreigners in an area. Later in the nineteenth century, *Barbarentum* was used to signify primitivism, or, in the context of progressive models, a less-advanced state or social formation. Finally, in early twentieth-century usage the word was a synonym of *Barbarei*, signifying "tyranny" (*Gewaltherrschaft des politischen Gegners*), and, in particular, the dictatorship of the national socialists (Schulz and Basler 1997, 125). This could suggest that Benjamin opposes his positive *Barbarentum* not only to *Barbarei* but also to this particular use of *Barbarentum*. I do not have any evidence on how common this use of *Barbarentum* was at the time. However, considering the established use of *Barbarei* in German to refer to Nazi violence, and given that in the rest of Benjamin's writings the barbarism associated with Nazism is expressed with the term *Barbarei*, I contend that his *Barbarentum* more likely counters the term *Barbarei*.

14. The barbarism within culture is pointed out in *The Arcades Project* (fragment N5a, 7) from a slightly different perspective: "Barbarism lurks in the very concept of culture—as the concept of a fund of values which is considered independent, not, indeed, of the production process in which these values originated, but of the one in which they survive. In this way they serve the apotheosis of the latter [word uncertain], barbaric as it may be" (Benjamin 1999a, 467–68) (Die Barbarei steckt im Begriff der Kultur selbst: als dem von einem Schatze von Werten, der unabhängig von dem, in welchem sie entstanden, aber unabhängig von dem, in welchem sie überdauern, betrachtet wird. Sie dienen auf diese Weise der Apotheose des letz[t]ern [?], wie barbarisch der immer sein mag; Benjamin 1991, 6:584). The statement is cryptic, especially because it is fragmented and lacks context. Benjamin seems to find barbarism in the alienation of values from the production process in which they are being consumed at a specific historical moment. *Barbarei* here appears to refer to the refusal to critically reflect on the values that one has internalized in a social system. As a result, values become reified within a culture that greets them as unchanging possessions instead of

mobile entities, dependent on the changing context of their production and consumption. The same quotation from *The Arcades Project* is somewhat reformulated in Benjamin's essay "Eduard Fuchs, Collector and Historian" (1937). The term *Barbarei* is not used in that quotation, but the same condition is ascribed to the concept of *Kultur*: "The concept of culture—as the embodiment of creations considered independent, if not of the production process in which they originate, then of a production process in which they continue to survive—has a fetishistic quality. Culture appears reified" (2006a, 267). In the context of the latter essay, it becomes clearer that Benjamin sees barbarism in the reification of culture—in "the disintegration of culture into goods" that become objects of possession (267). The barbarism of this bourgeois fetishism prevents people from having any form of genuine experience.

15. Another use of the concept of barbarism, which bears similarities with the way Benjamin describes *Barbarismen* in "The Work of Art," appears in *The Origin of German Tragic Drama* (*Ursprung des deutschen Trauerspiels*, 1928). In his preface, *Trauerspiel* is labeled as "strange or even barbaric" (1985, 49–50; for the German, see Benjamin 1991, vol. 1, bk. 1, 230). Scholars see *Trauerspiel* as a "caricature" or a "misunderstanding" of classical tragedy, whereas Benjamin sees it "according to the peculiar logic of 'renewal or rebirth in decline'" (quoted in McLaughlin 2006, 11). In "The Work of Art," Benjamin places *Barbarismen* in art in the same context of decadent epochs. It is particularly during decadent or critical times that "the extravagances and crudities of art" (*Barbarismen*) thrive and give rise to new and revolutionary artistic forms (1999b, 230).

16. For the creative force of language in Benjamin, see Benjamin's "On Language as Such and on the Language of Man" (2004); Bracken (2002); and Menninghaus (1980). In "On Language as Such" Benjamin connects the creative nature of language with the creative act of God in Genesis and argues that at its origin language was meant to produce, not just describe. In Genesis, Benjamin contends, the creation of man seems to be the product of language as such: "In this 'Let there be' and in the words 'He named' at the beginning and the end of the act, the deep and clear relation of the creative act to language appears each time. With the creative omnipotence of language it begins, and at the end language, as it were, assimilates the created, names it. Language is therefore both creative and the finished creation; it is word and name" (2004, 68). For an analysis of Benjamin's "metaphysics" of language, see de Vries (2002, 266–75).

17. Benjamin's call for "mobilization" echoes Ernst Jünger's concept of "total mobilization," which Benjamin explicitly refers to in his essay "Theories of German Fascism" (2005a, 318). Jünger, an intriguing and controversial figure in German literature and social theory, wrote the essay "Total Mobilization," which first appeared in the anthology *Krieg und Krieger* (War and warrior), edited by Jünger himself in 1930. The essay studies the relationship between society, war,

and technology and can be seen as a prefiguration of totalitarian societies. It attracted critical reactions both from traditional conservatives and left-wing critics (such as Benjamin). John Armitage remarks that for Jünger the "total mobilization of the state's military and social resources" that typified the post–World War I period "in Jünger's terms . . . firstly caused the end of nineteenth century limited war and what might be termed 'partial mobilization,' that is, of rigid demarcations between civilianization and militarization, and secondly brought about the downfall of the old European monarchies" (Armitage 2003, 194–95; Jünger 1993, 125).

18. Benjamin's image of World War I soldiers returning from the front in silence illustrates this impotence of the language of experience.

19. Benjamin's ideas on the mobilization of language in "Experience and Poverty" also echo Jünger's famous work *Der Arbeiter* (The worker), published in 1932, shortly before Benjamin wrote "Experience and Poverty." In it, Jünger sought to explain the crisis of the postwar bourgeois society from a nationalist, right-wing perspective. The crisis of European civilization after World War I was intensified by total disorder brought about by the destructive force of technology (Werneburg and Phillips 1992, 48). Jünger saw technology as the only force not subject to crisis and disintegration. Since he saw no alternative to technological civilization, he pleaded for an assimilation and utilization of the forces of technology for a "revolutionary nationalism" (47). In this context, Jünger's figure of the "total work-character" embodies social transformation and even a new form of humanity, consisting of highly functionalized and nonindividualized, nondifferentiated human beings (Jünger 1932, 100; Werneburg and Phillips 1992, 48–49). Jünger's ideas here come close to Benjamin's thoughts in "Experience and Poverty," although it is certainly not the same "revolutionary nationalism" that Benjamin has in mind when he proposes a "mobilization" of language. If technology is given the right to participate in the act of naming—which is an act of creation—Benjamin hopes that the new humanity will not be Jünger's automated nonindividualized workers but perhaps more like Scheerbart's "completely new, lovable, and interesting creatures." Benjamin goes along with Jünger's idea of mobilization but aspires to subvert Jünger's desired outcome.

20. Cf. terms like "brotherhood," "sisterhood," "parenthood," or the communal sense in "neighborhood."

21. There are Nietzschean echoes in Benjamin's figure of the destructive character. Cf. the following quotation from *Thus Spake Zarathustra* (*Also Sprach Zarathustra*, 1885): "New paths do I tread, a new speech cometh unto me; tired have I become—like all creators—of the old tongues. No longer will my spirit walk on worn-out soles" (2008, 71) (Neue Wege gehe ich, eine neue Rede kommt mir; müde wurde ich, gleich allen Schaffenden, der alten Zungen. Nicht will mein

Geist mehr auf abgelaufnen Sohlen wandeln; 1994, 84). The fact that Nietzsche's prophet-philosopher refers to himself as a "creator" brings him closer to Benjamin's "barbarian" (in "Experience and Poverty"), who, unlike the "destructive character," destroys the old in order to create something new.

22. Hegel's words are quoted in Benjamin's essay "Eduard Fuchs, Collector and Historian" (2006a, 270; also quoted in Wohlfarth 1994, 163). Benjamin quotes this sentence from Hegel to refer to the "eristische Dialektik" (eristic dialectic) (Benjamin 1991, vol. 2, bk. 2, 481).

23. For the relation of the collector with tradition, see Arendt (1999, 48–49).

24. Wohlfarth argues that Benjamin is not against "authentic" traces but rather pleads for the destruction of their secondary substitutes, the dreadful accumulation of which can be seen in the artificial paradise of the bourgeois interior (1994, 172). Based on that, one may argue that the barbarian destroys the secondary traces, while the collector gathers authentic ones.

25. For the notions of tradition and destruction in Benjamin, see Düttmann (1994, especially 54–55).

26. Here Benjamin crosses paths with Martin Heidegger, who also envisions a "tradition that does not give itself up to the past, but thinks of the present" (Heidegger 1962, 8; translated and quoted in Arendt 1999, 50).

27. The term *Umwerthung* makes its first appearance in Nietzsche's *Beyond Good and Evil*. Thereafter, it is used in *The Antichrist, Genealogy of Morals, Twilight*, and *Ecce Homo* (Large 2010, 5).

28. In his "Letter to Gershom Scholem on Franz Kafka," Benjamin writes about Kafka's relation to tradition in a way that captures his own relation to tradition, not as a transmission of doctrines or clear-cut knowledge but as a practice of listening and capturing "snatches of things"—indistinct elements that are reinvented in the present: "Kafka listened attentively to tradition. . . . This listening requires great effort because only indistinct messages reach the listener. There is no doctrine to be learned, no knowledge to be preserved. What are caught flitting by are snatches of things not meant for any ear. This points to one of the rigorously negative aspects of Kafka's work. (This negative side is doubtless far richer in potential than the positive)" (2006a, 326).

29. The term "illocutionary force" belongs to J. L. Austin's speech act theory and refers to the performative force of an utterance—the "performance of an act *in* saying something"—as opposed to the "locutionary aspect" of an utterance that conveys meaning (1980, 94–108, particularly 99).

30. I primarily take my cue from Venuti (1996b, 1994, 1995).

31. Venuti borrows the notion of the "remainder" from Lecercle (1990) to refer to the irreducible and untranslatable difference left behind by the translation (Venuti 1996a, 91).

32. Jacobs notes in relation to "The Task of the Translator" that the essay demands a "violent translation of every term promising the key to its definition" (1993, 129).

33. It is noteworthy that a similar formulation can be found in the concluding verse of C. P. Cavafy's poem "Waiting for the Barbarians" (1904), the subject of the following chapter. As the barbarians fail to show up while everyone is waiting for them, the poem ends with the words: "And now, what's going to happen to us without barbarians? / They were, those people, *a kind of* solution" (translated by Keeley and Sherrard 1992, 19; emphasis added). This indeterminate formulation—"a kind of"—is a crucial detail in the poem.

34. Translation, Venuti argues, particularly of conceptually dense philosophical discourse, "can never simply express ideas without simultaneously destabilizing and reconstituting them" (1996b, 25). On the same issue, see also Venuti (1995). On the relation of philosophy and translation, see A. Benjamin (1989); as well as Steiner (1975).

35. For this notion of critique in Benjamin, see Bracken (2002, 341).

36. Benjamin's motto in German reads: "Immer radikal, niemals konsequent" (1978, 1:425). Benjamin wrote this in a letter to Gershom Scholem on May 26, 1926, to describe his attitude to all things that matter.

37. Benjamin makes this comment in relation to the new schools of architecture, which try to transform bourgeois homes and their inhabitants.

38. Quoted in Arendt (1999, 52). For the original, see Benjamin (1978, 1:330).

39. There are many—mythical or historical—narratives from Greek antiquity in which the oracle's predictions are not fulfilled. These "misfires" are ascribed to a "wrong" interpretation of the oracle's words by those seeking consultation. The fact is, however, that the oracle's prophecies can be interpreted in contradictory ways, because their formulation usually is open to more than one interpretation.

40. "The Destructive Character" is not a "well-developed characterization" but a text full of fragmentary and provocative formulations. The style of writing causes misunderstandings "that it neither seeks nor avoids." Therefore, the text itself proceeds exactly in the same manner as the destructive character; it does not just describe this character but performs it by employing a "destructive style" (Wohlfarth 1994, 178).

CHAPTER 5

1. With the term "history" or "discourse of history" I refer to dominant academic conceptions of history in the West. To be sure, the term constitutes a generalization and an artificial abstraction from a complex network of heterogeneous narratives and modes of writing about the past. Although its use cannot

easily be avoided, I try to problematize it in this chapter. The same holds for the "discourse of civilization."

2. Although the theory of the performative is used throughout this study, it is here laid out in more detail due to its central role in this chapter in relation to iterability.

3. The terms "performative" and "speech act" in J. L. Austin's theory refer to an utterance that does what it designates (e.g., in the utterance "I promise to protect you," one performs the promise by uttering these words). Performatives are opposed to constative utterances, which describe, state, or represent something else. Although he distinguishes two categories of utterances—constative and performative—Austin concludes that all utterances, even constative statements, are to some degree performative. The constative and the performative can thus be considered aspects of the same utterance.

4. For a concise presentation of the travels of the notion of the performative in theory, see Culler (2000).

5. Words like "senators," "praetors," and "consuls" in the poem allude to ancient Rome.

6. See Haas (1982); and Savidis, "Cavafy, Gibbon and Byzantium" (1985, 96–97).

7. These three works are existentialist meditations revolving around the process of waiting, which becomes the crux of their plot. *The Tartar Steppe* tells the story of the slow and painful disillusionment of Lieutenant Giovanni Drogo, who is assigned to an old fortress on the country's frontier where the desert starts. The protagonist longs for military glory and spends years waiting for an attack by the Tartars, who in the old days were rumored to live in the desert. Nothing ever happens at the fortress, and Drogo wastes his life waiting for the enemy. In Beckett's absurdist play *Waiting for Godot*, two characters, Vladimir and Estragon, wait in vain for someone named Godot, whose arrival is (eternally) deferred. Gracq's *Opposing Shore* stages a mysterious atmosphere of a lurking menace between two imaginary Mediterranean nations that have been in a state of dormant warfare with one another for centuries. No frontal attack from the opposing shore takes place in the course of this novel.

8. In an anthology of poems inspired by Cavafy and edited by Nasos Vagenas (2000), fourteen of the selected poems respond to, or restage, Cavafy's "Waiting for the Barbarians." The poets of these fourteen poems originate from Argentina, Australia, Bulgaria, Canada, Egypt, Great Britain, Holland, New Zealand, Romania, Serbia, and the United States.

9. See O'Connell (2008) for O'Connell's poem and a discussion of its parallels with Cavafy's poem by O'Connell himself.

10. "Pakeha" are New Zealanders of European ancestry.

11. Felman relates the promise of proper meaning with the figure of the metaphor and traces the deconstruction of metaphor and its transfiguration into anaphora through a series of unkept promises in *Don Juan* (2003, 24–25).

12. Some critics argue that a "polyphonic" dialogue is at play in the poem: there are not just two but several people who pose and answer the questions. Savidis considers this option and rejects the idea of only two interlocutors, which, in his view, would mean that the questions should "be ascribed to a person of extremely low intelligence to which another person, endowed with infinite patience, replies" (my translation from an essay by Savidis [1985, 64]). Savidis eventually states his preference for a third line of interpretation, according to which the questions are uttered by the same person who answers them in the tone of an internal monologue. The latter view is also shared by Seferis (1974, 394–95) and Karaoglou (1978, 302). Tsirkas argues that although the entire dialogue takes place between two speakers, in the final two lines we hear the direct voice of "the poet" (1971, 326). My preference goes to the interpretive option of two speakers, which in my view embody the tension between two forces within the discourse of civilization: a force of questioning and critique (the first speaker) and a force of authority, repeating and confirming the Empire's "truths" (the second speaker).

13. For a metrical analysis of the poem, see Mackridge (2008, 287–89).

14. The first quotation is from Coetzee's novel (quoted in Spivak 2003, 22). The second is Spivak's (23).

15. The Magistrate also views the desert as a space in which his encounter with the barbarians takes place on equal terms. When he meets the barbarians in the desert and hands over the girl to them, he remarks, "I have never before met northerners on their own ground on equal terms" (Coetzee 2000, 78).

16. Saunders makes the same argument with regard to the status of the foreigner (2001, 218).

17. See, for example, Ryan (2002); Cohn (1999); Barthes (1981); Booth (1961); Ferguson (1997); Foucault (1995); Hayward (1994); Lamarque and Olsen (1994); and Herrnstein Smith (1978). Hayden White in *Metahistory* (1973) describes historical discourse not as an accurate representation of the past but as a series of creative texts structured by tropes, narrative strategies, and ideological underpinnings that form our historical understanding. White elaborated and nuanced his arguments in *Metahistory* in two collections of essays, *Tropics of Discourse* (1978) and *The Content of the Form* (1987).

18. The translation is mine. In this phrase that Lechonitis ascribes to Cavafy himself, the Greek phrase for what I translate as "historical poet" (ποιητής ιστορικός) could either be translated as "historical poet" or as "poet-historian."

19. The extreme attention to detail and love for historical precision in his poems; the extensive use of primary sources; his "archaeological" inspiration from inscriptions, ancient literary works, and objects; the full names and genealogical information for (historical or invented) characters; and precise chronological markers and indications of places are some of the ways in which Cavafy's historical sense manifests itself.

20. See, for example, Mackridge (2007, xxvi–xxvii). Cavafy is mainly interested in the post-classical era (Alexander's successor states and the Byzantine era) with its decadent empires—eras underrepresented in dominant historical accounts.

21. The poem was written in December 1898 but was not published and circulated by the poet until 1904.

22. For this contextual interpretation of "Waiting for the Barbarians," see Tsirkas (1971, 48–54).

23. Savidis suggests a possible historical connection of the poem with the Greco-Turkish War of 1897, a thirty-day war between Greece and the Ottoman Empire over the status of Crete (still under Turkish occupation), which Greece wished to annex. But Savidis also views the poem in a broader light, as thematizing the decadence of Western civilization (1985, 227).

24. For example, the poem is cited in the catalogue of Anthony Caro's sculpture exhibition "Barbarians" (2002). Edward Said's daughter recited it during his funeral as one of her father's favorite poems. The poem also gave its title to a collection of essays on Said, published after his death (Ertür and Sökmen 2008).

25. Critics such as Northrop Frye and Fredric Jameson have argued that every interpretation of a text can be considered allegorical, since it tries to make sense of textual images and events by attaching ideas to them. Frye's and Jameson's views on the matter are discussed by Attridge (2004, 36). Nevertheless, Attridge contends that a nonallegorical reading would still be possible. His example is Coetzee's reading of *Robinson Crusoe* in *Foe* (36).

26. Van Alphen prefers the term "affective reading" over Attridge's "literal reading" and convincingly argues that a literal reading can also be invested with meanings and ideas, just as an allegorical reading can (2008, 29–30). For van Alphen, an affective reading is attentive to textual elements and narrative techniques. However, it does not approach these as "'objective' textual structures" (as structuralism did) but is interested in how these elements transmit affects to the reader (27).

27. The emphasis on "war," "vengeance," and "justice" is in the original. The remaining emphasis is mine.

28. In her article, Saunders provides an elaborate discussion of the concept of the foreign in Coetzee's novel, which often pertains to that of barbarism.

29. Derrida notes that this freedom of literature is related to the modern idea of democracy in the West (1992, 37).

30. The distinction between "serious" and "non-serious" discourse can be traced back to Austin's *How to Do Things with Words* (1962) and the discussions that his views triggered among philosophers. Austin makes a distinction between "serious" or "ordinary" use of language and "non-serious" or "parasitic" use (of which typical examples are literary texts). He makes clear that his speech

act theory can be applied only to serious utterances. Non-serious use of language (including literature) is excluded from his theory (1980, 22). In "Signature, Event, Context" and *Limited Inc* Derrida performs a deconstructive critique of the serious/non-serious and normal/parasitic oppositions.

31. On the theme of torture in the novel, see the studies by Moses (1993) and Wenzel (1996).

32. With "uptake" Austin refers to the reception of an utterance by the audience.

33. White argues that the desire for the barbarian derives from the classical tradition (Greek and Roman), whereas the anxiety and fear for the other is more typical for theonomic traditions (the Christian and Hebrew) (1972, 10).

34. Renato Poggioli entertains the possibility of a third voice (that of the poet). He argues that the poet "looks at decadence not as an actor but as a spectator doubly removed, and hence able to afford both a sardonic and an urbane wit" (1959, 148). The possibility of a third voice reflecting on the preceding dialogue can be supported by the similar structure of other poems by Cavafy.

35. Decapentasyllabic verse is a common metric form in modern Greek poetry, comprising fifteen syllables in iambic verse. It has been the primary meter of traditional and folk poetry in Greece since the Byzantine period. Based on a metrical and typographic analysis of the poem, Mackridge argues that in the two final lines the voices of the first and second speaker come together, but he chooses not to personify the voices in the dialogue by ascribing them to either real or fictional characters (2008, 289).

36. My translation of Cavafy's own comments on the poem, published by Savidis in an interview, "O Kavafis ekfrazei ton meizona Ellinismo" (Cavafy expresses the greater Hellenism), in the Greek newspaper *Ta Nea*, April 23, 1983.

CHAPTER 6

1. I have not been able to determine the date of Linda Sutton's painting.

2. Ned Rorem's piece (for medium voice and piano) does not follow Cavafy's original text but an English translation of the poem.

3. The intellectual and performative power that van Alphen ascribes to art does not entail a personification of cultural objects. When I write about artworks in this study, it is not the works themselves that "speak" or "think." Rather, they trigger or inspire a mode of visual thinking or knowing that I try to capture and articulate, to the extent that it can be verbalized. As Attridge argues, when we ascribe consciousness or knowing capacities to works of art, what is really at stake is the staging of our pursuit of knowledge, and the work's refusal to "satisfy the thirst for knowledge that it generates" (2009, 32).

4. Geers has been described as a defiant artist, a "rebel," an "anarchist," a "responsible terrorist" (Neumaier 2001, 96); a "cultural terrorist" (Sans and Geers 2000, 270); the "thorn" or the "itch" in the institution (Geers, quoted in Neumaier 2001, 99). All these labels can be attributed to his controversial artistic and performative practices. These include throwing a brick through a gallery window, installing an electric fence in several group shows, placing texts with bomb threats in museums, and exhibiting a pornographic centerfold on which he ejaculated his semen (see, for example, Kerkham 2000, 30). Geers presents himself as a barbarian within the art world, trying to destabilize the system from within.

5. According to the Greek myth, the Minotaur devoured the Athenian youths and maidens sent regularly as a tribute to King Minos. With the help of the king's daughter, Ariadne, who gave him a ball of string, Theseus managed to kill the Minotaur and find his way out of the labyrinth.

6. Max Weber questions the Enlightenment's view of progress and happiness and views Western civilization as a highly rational and bureaucratically organized social order, an "iron cage" in which people are trapped (1999, 100–104).

7. On the invisible workings of ideology, see Barthes's seminal work *Mythologies* (1957).

8. My translation of the German "Die Natur kann und soll sich hier ihr Territorium zurückerobern."

9. Monastic life is, of course, rather exclusionary, as it seeks isolation and distance from worldliness. If we follow this line of thinking, the exclusionary character of the monastery is enhanced and negatively tinted by the exclusionary violence the labyrinth suggests.

10. The Teutoburg Forest, which is situated in the same area, has become the symbol of the famous battle, in which an alliance of Germanic tribes ambushed and wiped out a Roman army of three entire legions (9 CE). The battle established the Rhine as the boundary between Romans and Germans. As a result, the borders of the Roman Empire and its sphere of influence were limited to the territory below the Rhine. Another historical occurrence in the region, with significant consequences for the reordering of Europe's borders, was the Peace of Westphalia, which ended the Thirty Years' War in 1648 and led to the division of Europe into single sovereign states. For these historical allusions, see Winkelmann (2001).

11. In yet another association evoked by its location, the installation can be related to the division imposed by the "iron curtain" between Eastern and Western Europe. Notably, Geers initially wanted to place a border post from the Berlin Wall at the center of the labyrinth.

12. For a political history of barbed wire, see also Razac (2003); and Netz (2004).

13. The juxtaposition of colonialism and World War II also draws attention to practices of external and internal exclusion in Europe. Western civilization has identified its barbarian others both outside and within the European space. World War II—"this civil war fought by European civilization against itself"—is a case in point (S. Weber 1997, 92).

14. The effect of haunting as a constant "coming back" of history in the present is similar to what Mieke Bal has called "preposterous history": an act of reversal that "puts the chronologically first (pre-) as an aftereffect behind (post-) its later recycling" (1999, 6–7).

15. Sacco's work has appeared in several Biennales and other major exhibitions in museums and galleries worldwide, including Chile, Denmark, Argentina, Guatemala, Mexico, Brazil, Spain, England, and France. Sacco has also been a professor of twentieth-century Latin American Art at the University of Rosario in Argentina (see the artist's Web site, www.gracielasacco.net/).

16. Stephen Cohen Gallery, www.stephencohengallery.com/scg-archive/scg-2004.html. While heliography is commonly used in the development of architectural blueprints, Sacco developed her own anti-orthodox heliographic method in the 1980s, as she was looking for a way to print photographic images on a variety of surfaces. Sacco has also written a book in Spanish and English, *Escrituras solares: La heliografía en el campo artístico* (Sun writings: Heliography in the artistic field, 1994).

17. The installation has been exhibited at the 23rd International Biennial of Art of São Paulo (1996) and at the Massachusetts College of Art, Boston (2000). Recently, it was exhibited at Museum Morsbroich in Leverkusen, Germany, as part of the exhibition "Radical Shift: Political and Social Upheaval in Argentinian Art since the 1960s" (2011).

18. The term "intersemiotic translation" (or transmutation) was introduced by Roman Jakobson and refers to the "interpretation of verbal signs by means of signs of nonverbal sign systems" (1971, 429).

19. There are extensive theoretical discussions of the "gaze," from Sartre (2001) and Foucault (1975), to Silverman (1996), Bryson (1983), and Bal (1991, 2002).

20. For a more extensive theorization of the "stare," see Garland-Thomson (2009).

21. This kind of relation yields what Bal elsewhere calls a "second-person narrative" of an image—a narrative that can account for the agency of the image without falling back into the authoritarian elitist claims of the critic or into the pitfalls of ascribing intentionality either to the object or to its creator (2002, 281–82).

22. *Facundo* narrates the life of the gaucho Juan Facundo Quiroga, who terrorized provincial Argentina in the 1820s and 1830s. As Kathleen Ross points out, *Facundo* was also written to "denounce the tyranny of the Argentine dictator Juan Manuel de Rosas" (2003, 17). In the book, Facundo Quiroga is portrayed

as barbaric and opposed to progress because of his rejection of European ideals, which are identified with city culture, particularly that of Buenos Aires (Sarmiento 2003, 99). The book is not only a critique of Rosas's dictatorship but also a detailed exploration of Argentinian history and culture, read through this dichotomy. "Sarmiento's diagnosis is that Argentina is beset by the struggle between civilization and barbarism and that Rosas and his regime incarnate the latter" (Echevarría 2003, 12). Sarmiento poses the hope of civilization against the crude aspects of a brutal *caudillo* culture, which was dominant at the time. European immigration was for him the answer to the prevalent barbarism in his country (9).

23. "Contemporary art" at the time Bourriaud writes (2002) is the art of the 1990s, to which Sacco's installation also belongs. His argument, however, is also applicable to artistic practices of the new millennium.

CHAPTER 7

1. For the sake of brevity, in this chapter I refer to "The New Barbarians" as Gómez-Peña's project, even though several artists were involved in the making of these portfolios.

2. This information is drawn from Gómez-Peña (1996, 2000, 2005).

3. From the short description of the project on the artist's Web site, www.pochanostra.com/photo-performances/.

4. The first four of these portfolios are published on Gómez-Peña's Web site. A selection of images from the last three portfolios is published in Gómez-Peña et al. (2006). Images that are mentioned but not reprinted in this book can be accessed on the Web site of Gómez-Peña and his performance troupe, www.pochanostra.com/photo-performances/. These portfolios were created by Gómez-Peña and his troupe, in collaboration with other international performance artists and photographers. "Ethno-Techno: Evil Others and Identity Thieves" was shot in San Francisco with photographer James McCaffrey in 2004; "Post-Mexico en X-paña," in Madrid with photographer Javier Caballero in 2005; "The Chi-Canarian Expo" (in black and white), in Las Palmas de Gran Canaria with photographer Teresa Correa in 2006. "Tucuman-Chicano" was developed in the Argentine city of Tucuman with twenty Argentinian performance artists in 2005. "The Chica-Iranian Project" was created with four Chicano and three Iranian artists in San Francisco. "Epcot-El Alamall" was shot with photographer Ric Malone in 2004.

5. All information about "The New Barbarian Collection" performance in this paragraph is from the essay "The New Barbarian Collection Fall 2007" as published on the artist's Web site, www.pochanostra.com/dialogues/page/6/.

6. Mignolo (1998) develops this notion to refer to theory outside or from the margins of the West that challenges Western discourses.

7. The Chicano community, with whom Gómez-Peña is affiliated, is a syncretic border community of American-born and Hispanic-cultured peoples of Mexican descent. It has its own particular culture and language, which is a mixture of US elements with bits of a culture and language they imagine as Mexican, although they have not lived in Mexico themselves. Being Chicano thus implies the struggle of trying to be accepted in an Anglo-dominated US culture and at the same time maintaining a sense of identity in differentiation from mainstream US culture.

8. The word "patriot" derives from the ancient Greek *patris* (fatherland), which derives from *patēr* (father).

9. The phrase "yes sir, no sir, three bags full sir" has been used to describe an obedient, servile, or cowardly subordinate. It is attested from 1910 and used to be common in the British Royal Navy. The phrase is also found in the nursery rhyme "Baa, Baa, Black Sheep." See "Baa, Baa, Black Sheep," *Wikipedia*, http://en.wikipedia.org/wiki/Baa,_Baa,_Black_Sheep.

10. On this issue, see Butler (2000).

11. The subject of the pietà is primarily found in sculpture (with Michelangelo's version being the most famous) but has a long tradition in Western painting as well.

12. The same persona appears in several photo-performances in this project. In one of them, this figure (played by Gómez-Peña himself) is identified in the title as *El indio amazonico*.

13. *La piedad intercontinental* presents a half-naked woman, her chest pierced with nails, holding a dead black man with bandaged hands. *La piedad intercontinental (invertida)* is a reverse iteration of the previous image, with the black man in the role of Mary and the woman lying dead in his arms, with a crooked pair of scissors falling from her hand.

14. Gómez-Peña has referred to both Islam and Christianity as "two forms of dangerous fundamentalisms" (2005, 278).

15. Jacques Derrida first used the notion "Babelian performance" in "Des tours de Babel" (1985). In Derrida's use, "Babelian performance" describes the paradox in the "translatable-untranslatable" name of "Babel," which "at once translates and does not translate itself." "Babel" performs for Derrida the necessity and impossibility of translation (175).

16. Aztlan is the mythical place of origin of the Aztec peoples.

17. Amossy and Heidingsfeld (1984) focus on stereotypical representations in texts, but their views can be extrapolated in the study of stereotypes in visual material as well.

18. This article was developed into a book with the same title.

19. Menudo is a hearty, spicy Mexican soup, considered an effective cure for hangovers. Chowder is also a thick, hearty, chunky soup, usually with fish and potatoes.

20. For her use of "catachresis," see Spivak (1993, especially 29, 60, 71, 127–28, 137–39, 161, 298); see also Morton (2003, 34).

21. The first quotation is part of the *OED* definition of catachresis, quoted in Spivak (1993, 29). The second quotation is from Spivak (1993, 128).

22. "One of the offshoots of the deconstructive view of language," Spivak argues, "is the acknowledgement that the *political* use of words . . . is irreducibly catachrestic" (1993, 161). As a result, the task of a feminist political philosophy, according to Spivak, should not be to grasp the proper or true meaning of a name or to show how this proper meaning "always eludes our grasp" but "to accept the risks of catachresis" (161). The concept of catachresis could easily turn into a general position that acknowledges the catachrestic nature of all language. Spivak, however, warns against turning catachresis into a "totalizing masterword" (71).

23. In this sense, the concept of catachresis comes close to Spivak's notion of "strategic essentialism" as "a strategic use of positivist essentialism in a scrupulously visible political interest" (1996, 214).

24. Jill Bennett explores how animation is able to perform a similar operation: accommodating extreme, even unwatchable violence and simultaneously deadening the effects of this violence (2005, 116).

25. One of the origins of the Brechtian *Verfremdungseffekt* is the *ostranenie* (making-strange or defamiliarizing) of the Russian formalists, which employs estrangement to fight habitual looking and a certain "perceptual numbness" and make people look at familiar things with a fresh eye (Jameson 1998, 39).

26. The staging of violence may be typical for US culture but is certainly not unique to it. A striking example of staged and recorded violence from outside the United States that comes to mind are the videotaped kidnappings and beheadings of victims in Iraq as "a media tool for exerting asymmetric pressure on various states" (Appadurai 2006, 12).

27. In a dialogue with Lisa Wolford entitled "The Mindfields of Dystopia: The Pervasive Effects of 9/11," Gómez-Peña points out that even the meaning of terms like "transgressive," "radical," "extreme," or "revolutionary" is changing. This is partly due to the American culture of excess, in which there seems to be nothing left to transgress. But it is also due to the fact that these terms have been invested "with the demonizing meanings of the Bush doctrine and the Patriot Act." After 9/11, terms like "transgressive" or "extreme" are associated with terrorism. As a result, artists are forced to "tone down" their vocabulary and images so that they don't "'offend' American patriots" (Gómez-Peña 2005, 273). Gómez-Peña tries to reclaim these concepts for his artistic practices.

28. Benjamin's principle in German reads: "Immer radikal, niemals konsequent." Benjamin wrote this in a letter to Gershom Scholem on May 29, 1926 (Benjamin 1978, 425).

References

Achcar, Gilbert. 2006. *The Clash of Barbarisms: The Making of the New World Disorder*. Translated by Peter Drucker. Boulder, CO: Paradigm.

Adorno, Theodor W. 1970. *Ästhetische Theorie*. Frankfurt am Main: Suhrkamp.

Adorno, Theodor W., and Max Horkheimer. (1947) 1988. *Dialektik der Aufklärung: Philosophische Fragmente*. Reprint, Frankfurt am Main: Fischer Verlag.

———. (1947) 2002. *The Dialectic of Enlightenment*. Edited by Gunzelin Schmid Noerr. Translated by Edmund Jephcott. Reprint, Stanford, CA: Stanford University Press.

Agamben, Giorgio. 1998. *Homo Sacer: Sovereign Power and Bare Life*. Translated by Daniel Heller-Roazen. Stanford, CA: Stanford University Press.

———. 2002. *The Open: Man and Animal*. Translated by Kevin Attell. Stanford, CA: Stanford University Press.

Althusser, Louis. 1969. "Marxism and Humanism." In *For Marx*, translated by Ben Brewster, 219–47. London: Penguin.

———. 1984. "Ideology and Ideological State Apparatuses (Notes towards an Investigation)." In *Essays on Ideology*, 1–60. London: Verso.

Amossy, Ruth, and Therese Heidingsfeld. 1984. "Stereotypes and Representation in Fiction." *Poetics Today* 5 (4): 689–700.

Appadurai, Arjun. 2006. *Fear of Small Numbers: An Essay on the Geography of Anger*. Durham, NC: Duke University Press.

Arendt, Hannah. 1999. Introduction to *Illuminations: Essays and Reflections*, by Walter Benjamin, 7–58. Edited by Hannah Arendt. Translated by Harry Zohn. London: Pimlico.

Armitage, John. 2003. "On Ernst Jünger's 'Total Mobilization': A Re-evaluation in the Era of the War on Terrorism." *Body and Society* 9 (4): 191–213.

Arnold, Matthew. (1869) 1966. *Culture and Anarchy*. Edited by J. Dover Wilson. Reprint, Cambridge: Cambridge University Press.

Attridge, Derek. 2004. *J. M. Coetzee and the Ethics of Reading*. Chicago: University of Chicago Press.

———. 2009. "On Knowing Works of Art." In *Inside Knowledge: (Un)doing*

Ways of Knowing in the Humanities, edited by Carolyn Birdsall, Maria Boletsi, Itay Sapir, and Pieter Verstraete, 17–34. Newcastle upon Tyne, UK: Cambridge Scholars Publishing.

Atwell, David. 1990. "The Problem of History in the Fiction of J. M. Coetzee." *Poetics Today* 11 (3): 579–615.

Austin, J. L. (1962) 1980. *How to Do Things with Words*. Edited by J. O. Urmson and Marina Sbisà. Reprint, Oxford: Oxford University Press.

Bacon, Helen H. 1961. *Barbarians in Greek Tragedy*. New Haven, CT: Yale University Press.

Baer, Ulrich. 2001. *Remnants of Song: Trauma and the Experience of Modernity in Charles Baudelaire and Paul Celan*. Stanford, CA: Stanford University Press.

Bal, Mieke. 1991. *Reading Rembrandt: Beyond the Word-Image Opposition*. Cambridge: Cambridge University Press.

———. 1999. *Quoting Caravaggio: Contemporary Art, Preposterous History*. Chicago: University of Chicago Press.

———. 2002. *Travelling Concepts in the Humanities: A Rough Guide*. Toronto: University of Toronto Press.

———. 2011. *Of What One Cannot Speak: Doris Salcedo's Political Art*. Chicago: University of Chicago Press, 2011.

Barnavi, Élie. 2006. *Les religions meurtrières*. Paris: Flammarion.

Barthes, Roland. 1957. *Mythologies*. Paris: Editions du Seuil.

———. 1981. "The Discourse of History." In *Comparative Criticism: A Yearbook*, edited by E. S. Shaffer, translated by Stephen Bann, 3:3–20. Cambridge: Cambridge University Press.

Bauman, Zygmunt. 1991. *Modernity and Ambivalence*. Ithaca, NY: Cornell University Press.

Benhabib, Seyla. 2002. *The Claims of Culture: Equality and Diversity in the Global Era*. Princeton: Princeton University Press.

Benjamin, Andrew. 1989. *Translation and the Nature of Philosophy: A New Theory of Words*. London: Routledge.

Benjamin, Andrew, and Peter Osborne. 1994a. Introduction to *Walter Benjamin's Philosophy: Destruction and Experience*, edited by Andrew Benjamin and Peter Osborne, x–xiii. London: Routledge.

———, eds. 1994b. *Walter Benjamin's Philosophy: Destruction and Experience*. Edited by Andrew Benjamin and Peter Osborne. London: Routledge.

Benjamin, Walter. 1978. *Briefe*. Edited by Gershom Scholem and Theodor W. Adorno. 2 vols. Frankfurt am Main: Suhrkamp.

———. 1985. *The Origin of German Tragic Drama*. Translated by John Osborne. London: Verso.

———. 1991. *Gesammelte Schriften*. Edited by Rolf Tiedermann. 7 vols. Frankfurt am Main: Suhrkamp.

———. 1994. *The Correspondence of Walter Benjamin, 1910–1940*. Edited by Gershom Scholem and Theodor W. Adorno. Translated by Manfred R. Jacobson and Evelyn M. Jacobson. Chicago: University of Chicago Press.

———. 1999a. *The Arcades Project*. Translated by Howard Eiland and Kevin McLaughlin. Cambridge, MA: Harvard University Press.

———. 1999b. *Illuminations*. Edited by Hannah Arendt. Translated by Harry Zohn. London: Pimlico.

———. 2004. *Walter Benjamin: Selected Writings*. Vol. 1, *1913–1926*. Edited by Marcus Bullock and Michael W. Jennings. Cambridge, MA: Harvard University Press.

———. 2005a. *Walter Benjamin: Selected Writings*. Vol. 2, bk. 1, *1927–1930*. Edited by Michael W. Jennings, Howard Eiland, and Gary Smith. Cambridge, MA: Harvard University Press.

———. 2005b. *Walter Benjamin: Selected Writings*. Vol. 2, bk. 2, *1931–1934*. Edited by Michael W. Jennings, Howard Eiland, and Gary Smith. Cambridge, MA: Harvard University Press.

———. 2006a. *Walter Benjamin: Selected Writings*. Vol. 3, *1935–1938*. Edited by Howard Eiland and Michael W. Jennings. Cambridge, MA: Harvard University Press.

———. 2006b. *Walter Benjamin: Selected Writings*. Vol. 4, *1938–1940*. Edited by Howard Eiland and Michael W. Jennings. Cambridge, MA: Harvard University Press.

Bennett, Jane. 1996. "'How is it, then that we still remain barbarians?': Foucault, Schiller, and the Aestheticization of Ethics." *Political Theory* 24 (4): 653–72.

Bennett, Jill. 2005. *Empathic Vision: Affect, Trauma, and Contemporary Art*. Stanford, CA: Stanford University Press, 2005.

Bennett, Tony, Lawrence Grossberg, and Meaghan Morris, eds. 2005. *New Keywords: A Revised Vocabulary of Culture and Society*. Malden, UK: Blackwell Publishing.

Bensmaïa, Réda. 1986. Foreword to *Kafka: Toward a Minor Literature*, by Gilles Deleuze and Felix Guattari, ix–xxi. Minneapolis: University of Minnesota Press.

Benveniste, Émile. 1966. *Problèmes de linguistique générale*. Paris: Gallimard.

Bernal, Martin. 1987. *Black Athena: The Afroasiatic Roots of Classical Civilization*. New Brunswick, NJ: Rutgers University Press.

Bernheimer, Richard. 1952. *Wild Men in the Middle Ages: A Study in Art, Sentiment and Demonology*. Cambridge, MA: Harvard University Press.

Bernstein, Richard J. 2005. *The Abuse of Evil: The Corruption of Politics and Religion since 9/11*. Cambridge, MA: Polity.

Bérubé, Michael. 2005. "Relativism." In Bennett, Grossberg, and Morris, *New Keywords*, 304–6.

Bhabha, Homi K. 1994. *The Location of Culture.* London: Routledge.

Boer, Inge E. 2004. *Disorienting Vision: Rereading Stereotypes in French Orientalist Texts and Images.* Edited by Mieke Bal. Amsterdam: Rodopi.

Booth, Wayne. 1961. *The Rhetoric of Fiction.* Chicago: University of Chicago Press.

Bourriaud, Nicolas. 2002. *Relational Aesthetics.* Translated by Simon Pleasance and Fronza Woods. Dijon: Les presses du réel.

Bourriaud, Nicolas, Daniel Buren, and Kendell Geers. 2005. "With the Effectiveness of a Tank: A Conversation between Nicolas Bourriaud, Kendell Geers and Daniel Buren." In *Next Flag: The African Sniper Reader,* edited by F. Alvim, Heike Munder, and Ulf Wuggenig, 146–61. Zurich: Migros Museum.

Bracken, Christopher. 2002. "The Language of Things: Walter Benjamin's Primitive Thought." *Semiotica* 138 (1/4): 321–49.

Bronner, Stephen Eric. 1999. *Ideas in Action: Political Tradition in the Twentieth Century.* Lanham, MD: Rowman and Littlefield.

Brown, Wendy. 2001. *Politics out of History.* Princeton: Princeton University Press.

———. 2006. *Regulating Aversion: Tolerance in the Age of Identity and Empire.* Princeton: Princeton University Press.

———. 2010. *Walled States, Waning Sovereignty.* New York: Zone Books.

Bryson, Norman. 1983. *Vision and Painting: The Logic of the Gaze.* London: Macmillan.

Buckley, Sandra. 2002. "Gaijin." In *Encyclopedia of Contemporary Japanese Culture,* edited by Sandra Buckley, 161–62. London: Routledge.

Bush, George W. 2003. *We Will Prevail: President George W. Bush on War, Terrorism, and Freedom.* London: Continuum.

Butler, Judith. 1993. *Bodies That Matter: On the Discursive Limits of "Sex."* New York: Routledge.

———. 1997a. *Excitable Speech: A Politics of the Performative.* New York: Routledge.

———. 1997b. *The Psychic Life of Power: Theories in Subjection.* Stanford, CA: Stanford University Press, 1997.

———. 2000. "Competing Universalities." In *Contingency, Hegemony, Universality: Contemporary Dialogues on the Left,* by Judith Butler, Ernesto Laclau, and Slavoj Žižek, 136–81. London: Verso.

Butler, Judith, John Guillory, and Kendall Thomas. 2000. Preface to *What's Left of Theory? New Work on the Politics of Literary Theory,* viii–xii. Edited by Judith Butler, John Guillory, and Kendall Thomas. New York: Routledge.

Cadava, Eduardo. 1997. *Words of Light: Theses on the Photography of History.* Princeton: Princeton University Press.

Cameron, Nigel. 1970. *Barbarians and Mandarins: Thirteen Centuries of Western Travelers in China.* New York: Walker/Weatherhill.

Caro, Anthony. 2002. *The Barbarians*. New York: Mitchell-Innes and Nash; London: Annely Juda Fine Art.

Cavafy, C. P. 1992. *Collected Poems (Revised Edition)*. Edited by George Savidis. Translated by Edmund Keeley and Philip Sherrard. Princeton: Princeton University Press.

Césaire, Aimé. (1955) 2000. *Discourse on Colonialism*. Translated by Joan Pinkham. Reprint, New York: Monthly Review Press.

Clark, Gillian. 1999. "Translate into Greek: Porphyry of Tyre on the New Barbarians." In *Constructing Identities in Late Antiquity*, edited by Richard Miles, 112–32. London: Routledge.

Clark, T. J. 2006. *The Sight of Death: An Experiment in Art Writing*. New Haven, CT: Yale University Press.

Clifford, James. 1989. "Notes on Travel and Theory." *Inscriptions* 5:177–88. http://culturalstudies.ucsc.edu/PUBS/Inscriptions/vol_5/clifford.html.

Coetzee, J. M. (1980) 2000. *Waiting for the Barbarians*. Reprint, London: Vintage.

———. 1988. "The Novel Today." *Upstream* 6:2–5.

Cohn, Dorrit. 1999. *The Distinction of Fiction*. Baltimore: Johns Hopkins University Press.

Colebrook, Claire. 2002. *Gilles Deleuze*. London: Routledge.

Colvin, S. 1999. *Dialect in Aristophanes: The Politics of Language in Ancient Greek Literature*. Oxford: Oxford University Press.

Constantinou, Marios. 1998. "The Cavafian Poetics of Diasporic Constitutionalism: Toward a Neo-Hellenistic Decentering of the Kyp(riot)ic Experience." In *Cyprus and Its People: Nation, Identity, and Experience in an Unimaginable Community, 1955–1997*, edited by Vangelis Calotychos, 171–204. Boulder, CO: Westview Press.

Corngold, Stanley. 2002. "Kafka's Later Stories and Aphorisms." In *The Cambridge Companion to Kafka*, edited by Julian Preece, 95–110. Cambridge: Cambridge University Press.

Culler, Jonathan. 2000. "Philosophy and Literature: The Fortunes of the Performative." *Poetics Today* 21 (3): 503–19.

Curtis, David Ames. 1992. Foreword to *Political and Social Writings: 1961–1979: Recommencing the Revolution: From Socialism to the Autonomous Society*, by Cornelius Castoriadis, vii–xiv. Translated by David Ames Curtis. Minneapolis: University of Minnesota Press.

Damian, Carol. 2005. "Solo Show: Graciela Sacco." *ArtNexus* 57 (August). www.artnexus.com/Notice_View.aspx?DocumentID=15076.

Davis, Colin. 2005. "États présent: Hauntology, Spectres and Phantoms." *French Studies* 59 (3): 373–79.

Deleuze, Gilles. 2004. "Nomadic Thought." In *Desert Islands and Other Texts (1953–1974)*, 252–61. Los Angeles: Semiotext(e).

Deleuze, Gilles, and Félix Guattari. (1972) 1984. *Anti-Oedipus: Capitalism and*

Schizophrenia. Translated by Robert Hurley et al. Reprint, London: Athlone.

———. (1975) 1986. *Kafka: Toward a Minor Literature.* Translated by Dana Polan. Reprint, Minneapolis: University of Minnesota Press.

———. 1987. *A Thousand Plateaus: Capitalism and Schizophrenia.* Translated by Brian Massumi. London: Continuum.

———. 1994. *What Is Philosophy?* Translated by G. Burchell and H. Tomlinson. London: Verso.

de Man, Paul. 1979. *Allegories of Reading: Figural Language in Rousseau, Nietzsche, Rilke, and Proust.* New Haven, CT: Yale University Press.

Derrida, Jacques. (1972) 1982. "Signature, Event, Context." In *Margins of Philosophy*, translated by Alan Bass, 307–30. Reprint, Brighton, UK: Harvester Press.

———. (1972) 2004. *Dissemination.* Translated by Barbara Johnson. Reprint, London: Continuum.

———. 1985. "Des tours de Babel." In *Difference in Translation*, edited and translated by Joseph F. Graham, 165–207. Ithaca, NY: Cornell University Press.

———. 1988. *Limited Inc.* Translated by Samuel Weber and Jeffrey Mehlman. Evanston, IL: Northwestern University Press.

———. 1992. "This Strange Institution Called Literature: An Interview with Jacques Derrida." In *Acts of Literature*, by Jacques Derrida, 33–75. Edited by Derek Attridge. Translated by Geoffrey Bennington and Rachel Bowldy. London: Routledge.

———. 1994. *Specters of Marx: The State of the Debt, the Work of Mourning, and the New International.* Translated by Peggy Kamuf. London: Routledge.

de Vries, Hent. 2002. *Religion and Violence: Philosophical Perspectives from Kant to Derrida.* Baltimore: Johns Hopkins University Press.

Diamond, Stanley. 1974. *In Search of the Primitive: A Critique of Civilization.* New Brunswick, NJ: Transaction.

Dries, Manuel. 2010. "On the Logic of Values." *Journal of Nietzsche Studies* 39:30–50.

Droit, Roger-Pol. 2007. *Généalogie des barbares.* Paris: Odile Jacob.

Düttmann, Alexander García. 1994. "Tradition and Destruction: Walter Benjamin's Politics of Language." Translated by Debbie Keates. In Benjamin and Osborne, *Walter Benjamin's Philosophy*, 32–57.

Eagleton, Terry. 2009. *Reason, Faith, and Revolution.* New Haven, CT: Yale University Press.

Echevarría, Roberto González. 2003. Introduction to *Facundo: Civilization and Barbarism*, by Domingo Faustino Sarmiento, 1–16. Translated by Kathleen Ross. Berkeley: University of California Press.

Elias, Norbert. (1939) 2000. *The Civilizing Process: Sociogenetic and Psychogenetic Investigations.* Translated by Edmund Jephcott. Reprint, Malden: Blackwell Publishing.

Enwezor, Okwui. 1997. "Altered States: Die Kunst des Kendell Geers." In *Inklusion-Exklusion*, 202–5. Köln: DuMont. [Exhibition catalog]

Ertür, Başak, and Müge Gürsoy Sökmen, eds. 2008. *Waiting for the Barbarians: A Tribute to Edward W. Said.* London: Verso.

Fabian, Johannes. 1983. *Time and the Other: How Anthropology Makes Its Object.* New York: Columbia University Press.

———. 2001. "Culture with an Attitude." In *Anthropology with an Attitude: Critical Essays*, 87–100. Stanford, CA: Stanford University Press.

Felman, Shoshana. (1980) 2003. *The Scandal of the Speaking Body: Don Juan with J. L. Austin, or Seduction in Two Languages.* Translated by Catherine Porter. Reprint, Stanford, CA: Stanford University Press.

———. 1987. *Jacques Lacan and the Adventure of Insight: Psychoanalysis in Contemporary Culture.* Cambridge, MA: Harvard University Press, 1987.

Ferguson, Niall, ed. 1997. *Virtual History: Alternatives and Counterfactuals.* London: Macmillan.

Fish, Stanley. 2002. "Don't Blame Relativism." *Responsive Community* 12 (3): 27–31.

Flaubert, Gustave. 2006. "Lettre à Sainte-Beuve (Paris, 23–24 décembre 1862)." In *Gustave Flaubert: Mémoire de la critique*, edited by Didier Philippot, 233–42. Paris: Presses de l'Université Paris-Sorbonne.

Flèche, Betsy. 1999. "The Art of Survival: The Translation of Walter Benjamin." *SubStance* 28 (2): 95–109.

Foster, Stephen C., and Rudolf Kuenzli, eds. 1979. *Dada Spectrum: The Dialectics of Revolt.* Madison, WI: Coda Press.

Foucault, Michel. (1966) 2002. *The Order of Things: An Archaeology of the Human Sciences.* Translated by Alan Sheridan. Reprint, London: Routledge.

———. 1972. "The Formation of Objects." In *The Archaeology of Knowledge*, 40–49. Translated by A. M. Sheridan Smith. New York: Pantheon.

———. 1975. *The Birth of the Clinic: An Archaeology of Medical Perception.* New York: Vintage.

———. (1975) 1995. *Discipline and Punish: The Birth of the Prison.* Translated by Alan Sheridan. Reprint, New York: Vintage.

———. 2000. "On the Archaeology of the Sciences: Response to the Epistemology Circle." In *Aesthetics, Method, and Epistemology*, vol. 2, *Essential Works of Foucault 1954–1984*, edited by James Faubion, 297–333. Translated by Robert Hurley et al. London: Penguin.

Freud, Sigmund. (1915) 1985. "Thoughts for the Times on War and Death." In *Civilization, Society and Religion*, 61–89. Translated by James Strachey. Reprint, Harmondsworth, UK: Penguin.

———. (1921) 1959. *Group Psychology and the Analysis of the Ego.* Translated by James Strachey. Reprint, New York: Norton.

————. (1930) 1962. *Civilization and Its Discontents*. Translated by James Strachey. Reprint, New York: Norton.

Frost, Robert. (1914) 2004. *North of Boston*. Reprint, Kila, MT: Kessinger Publishing.

Früchtl, Joseph. 2008. *Our Enlightened Barbarian Modernity and the Project of a Critical Theory of Culture*. Inaugural lecture. Amsterdam: Amsterdam University Press.

Garland-Thomson, Rosemarie. 2006. "Ways of Staring." *Journal of Visual Culture* 5 (2): 173–92.

————. 2009. *Staring: How We Look*. Oxford: Oxford University Press.

Gibbon, Edward. (1788) 1912. *The History of the Decline and Fall of the Roman Empire*. Vol. 4. Edited by J. B. Bury. Reprint, London: Methuen.

Goffart, Walter. 1981. "Rome, Constantinople and the Barbarians." *American Historical Review* 86:275–306.

Gómez-Peña, Guillermo. 1992–93. "The New World (B)order: A Work in Progress." *Third Text* 21 (6): 71–79.

————. 1996. *The New World Border: Prophecies, Poems & Loqueras for the End of the Century*. San Francisco: City Lights.

————. 2000. *Dangerous Border Crossers: The Artist Talks Back*. New York: Routledge.

————. 2005. *Ethno-Techno: Writings on Performance, Activism, and Pedagogy*. New York: Routledge.

Gómez-Peña, Guillermo, Ramon Treves, James McCaffrey, et al. 2006. "'The New Barbarians': A Photo-Performance Portfolio." *Journal of Visual Culture* 5 (1): 17–27.

Gong, Gerrit W. 1984. *The Standard of "Civilization" in International Society*. Oxford: Clarendon Press.

Gourgouris, Stathis. 2003. *Does Literature Think? Literature as Theory for an Antimythical Era*. Stanford, CA: Stanford University Press.

Grinde, Donald A., and Bruce E. Johansen. 1991. *Exemplar of Liberty: Native America and the Evolution of Democracy*. Los Angeles: American Indian Studies Center.

Groys, Boris. 2008. *Art Power*. Cambridge, MA: MIT Press.

Haas, Diana. 1982. "Cavafy's Reading Notes on Gibbon's *Decline and Fall*." *Folia Neohellenica* 4:25–96.

Hall, Edith. 1989. *Inventing the Barbarian: Greek Self-Definition through Tragedy*. Oxford: Clarendon Press.

Hall, Jonathan M. 1995. "The Role of Language in Greek Ethnicities." *PCPS* 41: 83–100.

————. 2002. *Hellenicity: Between Ethnicity and Culture*. Chicago: University of Chicago Press.

Hall, Stuart. 1982. "The Rediscovery of 'Ideology': Return of the Repressed in Media Studies." In *Culture, Society and the Media*, edited by Tony Bennett, James Curran, Michael Gurevitch, and Janet Wollacott, 56–90. New York: Routledge.

Hallward, Peter. 2001. *Absolutely Postcolonial: Writing between the Singular and the Specific*. Manchester, UK: Manchester University Press.

Hardt, Michael, and Antonio Negri. 2000. *Empire*. Cambridge, MA: Harvard University Press.

Hartog, François. 2001. *Memories of Odysseus: Frontier Tales from Ancient Greece*. Translated by Janet Lloyd. Edinburgh: Edinburgh University Press.

Hayward, Malcolm. 1994. "Genre Recognition of History and Fiction." *Poetics* 22:409–21.

Heather, Peter. 1999. "The Barbarian in Late Antiquity: Image, Reality, and Transformation." In *Constructing Identities in Late Antiquity*, edited by Richard Miles, 234–58. London: Routledge.

Hegel, G. W. Friedrich. 2004. *The Philosophy of History*. Translated by J. Sibree. New York: Barnes and Noble.

Heidegger, Martin. (1947) 1998. "Letter on 'Humanism.'" Translated by Frank A. Capuzzi. In *Pathmarks*, edited by William McNeill, 239–77. Reprint, Cambridge: Cambridge University Press.

———. 1962. *Kants These über das Sein*. Frankfurt: Klostermann.

Herrnstein Smith, Barbara. 1978. *On the Margins of Discourse*. Chicago: University of Chicago Press.

Hindess, Barry. 2005. "Nation." In Bennett, Grossberg, and Morris, *New Keywords*, 232–35.

Huntington, Samuel. 1993. "The Clash of Civilizations?" *Foreign Affairs* 72 (3): 23–49.

———. 1996. *The Clash of Civilizations and the Remaking of World Order*. New York: Simon and Schuster.

Isaac, Benjamin H. 2006. *The Invention of Racism in Classical Antiquity*. Princeton: Princeton University Press.

Isin, Engin Fahri. 2002. *Being Political: Genealogies of Citizenship*. Minneapolis: University of Minnesota Press.

Jacobs, Carol. 1993. *Telling Time: Levi-Strauss, Ford, Lessing, Benjamin, de Man, Wordsworth, Rilke*. Baltimore: Johns Hopkins University Press.

———. 1999. *In the Language of Walter Benjamin*. Baltimore: Johns Hopkins University Press.

Jahoda, Gustav. 1999. *Images of Savages: Ancient Roots of Modern Prejudice in Western Culture*. New York: Routledge.

Jakobson, Roman. 1971. "On Linguistic Aspects of Translation." In *Selected Writings*, vol. 2, *Word and Language*, 260–66. The Hague: Mouton.

Jameson, Fredric. 1998. *Brecht and Method*. London: Verso.

———. 1999. "Marx's Purloined Letter." In *Ghostly Demarcations: A Symposium on Jacques Derrida's "Specters of Marx,"* edited by Michael Sprinker, 26–67. London: Verso.

Jones, W. R. 1971. "The Image of the Barbarian in Medieval Europe." *Comparative Studies in Society and History* 13 (4): 376–407.

Jünger, Ernst. 1932. *Der Arbeiter: Herrschaft und Gestalt*. Hamburg: Hanseatische Verlagsanstalt.

———. 1993. "Total Mobilization." In *The Heidegger Controversy*, edited by Richard Wolin, 119–39. Cambridge, MA: MIT Press.

Kafka, Franz. 1930. "Beim Bau der chinesischen Mauer." *Der Morgen* 6 (3): 219–31.

———. 1961. *Parables and Paradoxes*. New York: Schocken.

———. 1970. *Sämtliche Erzälungen*. Edited by Paul Raabe. Frankfurt am Main: Fischer Verlag.

———. 1999. *The Complete Short Stories of Franz Kafka*. Edited by Nahum N. Glatzer. London: Vintage.

———. 2006. *The Zürau Aphorisms*. Translated by Michael Hofmann. New York: Schocken.

Karaoglou, Ch. L. 1978. "Ena 'simeio stixis' sta poiimata tou K. P. Kavafi" [A "punctuation mark" in the poems of C. P. Cavafy]. In *Afieroma ston Kathigiti Lino Politi* [A tribute to Professor Linos Politis], 297–312. Thessaloniki.

Kartofel, Graciela. 2006. "Solo Show: Graciela Sacco." *Art Nexus* 60 (April). www.artnexus.com/Notice_View.aspx?DocumentID=16236.

Keeley, Edmund. 1976. *Cavafy's Alexandria: Study of a Myth in Progress*. Cambridge, MA: Harvard University Press.

Kelley, Robin D. G. 2000. "A Poetics of Anticolonialism." Introduction to *Discourse on Colonialism*, by Aimé Césaire, 7–28. Translated by Joan Pinkham. New York: Monthly Review Press.

Kerkham, Ruth. 2000. "There's a Bomb in This Exhibition: Kendell Geers Charged." *Parachute* 99:30–40.

Kossew, Sue. 1996. *A Post-colonial Reading of J. M. Coetzee and André Brink*. Amsterdam: Rodopi.

Krell, Alan. 2002. *The Devil's Rope: A Cultural History of Barbed Wire*. London: Reaktion.

Kreuter, Eric Anton. 2006. *Victim Vulnerability: An Existential-Humanistic Interpretation of a Single Case Study*. New York: Nova Science Publishers.

Kristeva, Julia. 1991. *Strangers to Ourselves*. Translated by Leon S. Roudiez. New York: Columbia University Press.

Krost, Peta. 1998. "Interview with Kendell Geers." *Saturday Star*, January 24. http://members.tripod.com/e_race/peta.htm.

Lamarque, Peter, and Stein Haugom Olsen. 1994. *Truth, Fiction, and Literature.* Oxford: Clarendon Press.

Large, Duncan. 2010. "A Note on the Term 'Umwerthung.'" *Journal of Nietzsche Studies* 39:5–11.

Lattimore, Owen. 1962. *Inner Asian Frontiers of China.* Boston: Beacon Press.

Lecercle, Jean-Jacques. 1990. *The Violence of Language.* London: Routledge.

Lechonitis, G. 1977. *Kavafika autoscholia* [Cavafian self-comments]. Athens: Denise Harvey.

Levin, Thomas Y. 1988. "Walter Benjamin and the Theory of Art History." *October* 47 (Winter): 77–83.

Levine, Michael G. 2008. "'A Place So Insanely Enchanting': Kafka and the Poetics of Suspension." *MLN* 123:1039–67.

Lévy, Bernard-Henri. 1979. *Barbarism with a Human Face.* Translated by George Holoch. New York: Harper and Row.

———. 2008. *Left in Dark Times: A Stand against the New Barbarism.* Translated by Benjamin Moser. New York: Random House.

Lewis, Bernard. 1990. "The Roots of Muslim Rage." *Atlantic* (September): 47–60.

Liddell, H. G., and R. Scott. 1996. *Greek-English Lexicon.* Oxford: Clarendon Press.

Long, Timothy. 1986. *Barbarians in Greek Comedy.* Carbondale: Southern Illinois University Press.

Mackridge, Peter. 2007. Introduction to *C. P. Cavafy: The Collected Poems*, edited by Anthony Hirst, xi–xxxiii. Translated by Evangelos Sachperoglou. Oxford: Oxford University Press.

———. 2008. "Stichourgia kai noima ston Kavafi" [Versification and meaning in Cavafy]. In *Ekmageia tis poiisis: Solomos, Kavafis, Seferis* [Imagines of poetry: Solomos, Cavafy, Seferis], 261–91. Athens: Estia.

Mamdani, Mahmood. 2004. *Good Muslim/Bad Muslim: America, the Cold War, and the Roots of Terror.* New York: Pantheon.

Maronitis, D. M. 1999. *Omirika megathemata: Polemos, omilia, nostos* [Major Homeric themes: War, speech, homecoming]. Athens: Kedros.

Marx, Karl. 1988. "Estranged Labor." In *The "Economic and Philosophic Manuscripts of 1844" and the "Communist Manifesto,"* 69–84. Translated by Martin Milligan. New York: Prometheus Books.

Matthews, J. H. 1991. *The Surrealist Mind.* Cranbury, NJ: Associated University Press.

McClintock, Anne. 1995. *Imperial Leather: Race, Gender, and Sexuality in the Colonial Contest.* New York: Routledge.

McCole, John. 1993. *Walter Benjamin and the Antinomies of Tradition.* Ithaca, NY: Cornell University Press.

McKinsey, Martin. 2000. "Anazitontas tous varvarous" [Searching for the barbarians]. In *I poiisi tou kramatos: Monternismos kai diapolitismikotita sto ergo toy Kavafi* [The poetry of alloy: Modernism and interculturality in the work of Cavafy], edited by Michalis Pieris, 37–48. Heraklion: Crete University Press.

McLaughlin, Kevin. 2006. "Benjamin's Barbarism." *Germanic Review* 81 (1): 4–20.

Meek, Ronald L. 1976. *Social Science and the Ignoble Savage.* New York: Cambridge University Press.

Melas, Natalie. 2007. *All the Difference in the World: Postcoloniality and the Ends of Comparison.* Stanford, CA: Stanford University Press.

Menninghaus, Winfried. 1980. *Walter Benjamins Theorie der Sprachmagie.* Frankfurt am Main: Suhrkamp.

Mignolo, Walter. 1998. "Globalization, Civilization Processes, and the Relocation of Languages and Cultures." In *The Cultures of Globalization,* edited by Fredric Jameson and Masao Miyoshi, 32–53. Durham, NC: Duke University Press.

———. 2005. *The Idea of Latin America.* Oxford: Blackwell.

Miles, Richard. 1999. Introduction to *Constructing Identities in Late Antiquity,* edited by Richard Miles, 1–15. New York: Routledge.

Miller, John J. 2006. "From Pen to Sword: Robert E. Howard's Conan." *Wall Street Journal,* December 13. http://online.wsj.com/article/SB116596848576148273.html.

Mills, Charles W. 1997. *The Racial Contract.* Ithaca, NY: Cornell University Press.

Montaigne, Michel de. 1958. "On Cannibals." In *Essays,* 105–19. Translated by J. M. Cohen. London: Penguin.

Montesquieu. *Persian Letters.* (1721) 1993. Translated by C. J. Betts. Reprint, London: Penguin.

Moore-Gilbert, Bart. 1997. "Homi Bhabha: 'The Babelian Performance.'" In *Postcolonial Theory: Contexts, Practices, Politics,* 114–51. London: Verso.

Morris, Meaghan, and Naoki Sakai. 2005. "The West." In Bennett, Grossberg, and Morris, *New Keywords,* 372–74.

Morton, Stephen. 2003. *Gayatri Chakravorty Spivak.* London: Routledge.

Moses, Michael Valdez. 1993. "The Mark of Empire: Writing, History and Torture in Coetzee's *Waiting for the Barbarians.*" *Kenyon Review* 15 (1): 115–27.

Mouffe, Chantal. 2005. *On the Political.* Abingdon, UK: Routledge.

Munson, Rosaria Vignolo. 2005. *Black Doves Speak: Herodotus and the Languages of Barbarians.* Cambridge, MA: Harvard University Press.

Murji, Karim. 2005. "Ethnicity." In Bennett, Grossberg, and Morris, *New Keywords,* 112–14.

Neilson, Brett. 1999. "Barbarism/Modernity: Notes on Barbarism." *Textual Practice* 13 (1): 79–95.

Netz, Reviel. 2004. *Barbed Wire: An Ecology of Modernity.* Middletown, CT: Wesleyan University Press.

Neumaier, Otto. 2001. "Kratzen, wo es nicht juckt" [Scratching where it does not itch]. *Frame* 6 (March/April): 94–99.

Newman, Jay. 1982. *Foundations of Religious Tolerance*. Toronto: University of Toronto Press.

The New Testament for English Readers. 1865. Edited by Henry Alford. London: Rivingtons Publishing.

Nietzsche, Friedrich. (1874) 2008. *On the Use and Abuse of History for Life*. Translated by Adrian Collins. Reprint, Gloucester, UK: Dodo Press.

———. (1885) 1994. *Also Sprach Zarathustra*. Reprint, Stuttgart: Reclam.

———. (1885) 2008. *Thus Spake Zarathustra*. Reprint, Radford, VA: Wilder Publications.

———. (1901) 1968. *The Will to Power: An Attempt at a Revaluation of All Values*. Edited by Walter Kaufmann. Translated by Walter Kaufmann and R. J. Hollingdale. Reprint, New York: Vintage.

O'Connell, Richard. 2008. "Parallel Texts." *C. P. Cavafy Forum*, University of Michigan, Department of Modern Greek. www.lsa.umich.edu/UMICH/modgreek/Home/_TOPNAV_WTGC/C.P.%20Cavafy%20Forum/Waiting_for_the_Terrorists_Oconnel.pdf.

Perryer, Sophie. 2002. "Kendell Geers." *Artthrob* 58 (June). www.artthrob.co.za/02jun/artbio.html.

Plato. 2009. *The Dialogues of Plato*. Vol. 4. Translated by Benjamin Jowett. Charleston, SC: BiblioBazaar.

Poggioli, Renato. 1959. "Qualis Artifex Pereo! or Barbarism and Decadence." *Harvard Library Bulletin* 13 (2): 135–59.

Rancière, Jacques. 1999. *Disagreement: Politics and Philosophy*. Translated by Julie Rose. Minneapolis: University of Minnesota Press.

Rawson, Claude. 2001. *God, Gulliver, and Genocide: Barbarism and the European Imagination, 1492–1945*. New York: Oxford University Press.

Razac, Olivier. 2003. *Barbed Wire: A Political History*. Translated by Jonathan Kneight. New York: New Press.

Rickels, Laurence A. 1987. "Kafka and the Aero-Trace." In *Franz Kafka and the Contemporary Critical Performance: Centenary Readings*, edited by Alan Udoff, 11–27. Bloomington: Indiana University Press.

Robinson, Cedric. 1983. *Black Marxism*. London: Zed.

Román, Ediberto. 2010. *Citizenship and Its Exclusions: A Classical, Constitutional, and Critical Race Critique*. New York: NYU Press.

Rose, Steven. 2005. "Evolution." In Bennett, Grossberg, and Morris, *New Keywords*, 117–21.

Rosello, Mireille. 1998. *Declining the Stereotype: Ethnicity and Representation in French Cultures*. Hanover, NH: University Press of New England.

Ross, Kathleen. 2003. Translator's introduction to *Facundo: Civilization and Barbarism*, by Domingo Faustino Sarmiento, 17–26. Translated by Kathleen Ross. Berkeley: University of California Press.

Rousseau, Jean-Jacques. 1966. "Essay on the Origin of Languages." Translated by John H. Moran. In *On the Origin of Language*, edited by John H. Moran and Alexander Gode, 5–83. Chicago: University of Chicago Press.

Rugoff, Ralph, ed. 1997. *Scene of the Crime*. Cambridge, MA: MIT Press.

Rutherford, Danilyn. 2001. "The Foreignness of Power: Alterity and Subversion in Kafka's 'In the Penal Colony' and Beyond." *Modernism/Modernity* 8 (2): 303–13.

Ryan, Marie-Laure. 2002. "Fiction and Its Other: How Trespassers Help Defend the Border." *Semiotica* 138 (1): 351–69.

Sacco, Graciela. 1994. *Escrituras solares: La heliografía en el campo artístico* [Sun writings: Heliography in the artistic field]. Rosario, Argentina: Talleres Gráficos del Colegio Salesiano San José.

Said, Edward. (1978) 2003. *Orientalism*. London: Penguin.

———. 1983. "Travelling Theory." In *The World, the Text and the Critic*, 226–47. Cambridge, MA: Harvard University Press.

———. 1993. *Culture and Imperialism*. New York: Random House.

Salter, Mark B. 2002. *Barbarians and Civilization in International Relations*. London: Pluto Press.

Sans, Jérôme, and Kendell Geers. 2000. "Landmines in the Gallery: Interview with Jérôme Sans." *Trans>arts.cultures.media* 8:268–74.

Sarmiento, Domingo Faustino. (1845) 2003. *Facundo: Civilization and Barbarism*. Translated by Kathleen Ross. Reprint, Berkeley: University of California Press.

Sartre, Jean-Paul. (1943) 2001. *Being and Nothingness*. Reprint, New York: Citadel Press.

Saunders, Rebecca. 2001. "The Agony and the Allegory: The Concept of the Foreign, the Language of Apartheid, and the Fiction of J. M. Coetzee." *Cultural Critique* 47:215–64.

Savidis, G. P. 1985. *Mikra kavafika* [Short studies on Cavafy]. Vol. 1. Athens: Hermis.

Schiller, Friedrich. 1995. "Letters on the Aesthetic Education of Man." In *Essays*, edited by Walter Hinderer and Daniel O. Dahlstrom, 86–134. New York: Continuum.

Schulz, Hans, and Otto Basler. 1997. *Deutsches Fremdwörterbuch* [German dictionary of foreign words]. Vol. 3. Berlin: Walter de Gruyter.

Scott, Joan. 1991. "The Evidence of Experience." *Critical Inquiry* 17 (4): 773–79.

Seferis, Giorgos. 1974. *Dokimes* [Essays]. Vol. 1. Athens: Ikaros.

Shohat, Ella, and Robert Stam. 1994. *Unthinking Eurocentrism: Multiculturalism and the Media*. London: Routledge.

Silverman, Kaja. 1996. *The Threshold of the Visible World*. New York: Routledge.

Sorensen Goodrich, Diana. 1996. *Facundo and the Construction of Argentine Culture*. Austin: University of Texas Press.

Spariosu, Mihai. 2006. *Remapping Knowledge: Intercultural Studies for a Global Age*. Oxford: Berghahn.

Spivak, Gayatri Chakravorty. 1992. "Acting Bits/Identity Talk." *Critical Inquiry* 12 (4): 770–803.

———. 1993. *Outside in the Teaching Machine*. London: Routledge.

———. 1996. "Subaltern Studies: Deconstructing Historiography." In *The Spivak Reader*, edited by Donna Landry and Gerald Maclean, 203–36. London: Routledge.

———. 2003. *Death of a Discipline*. New York: Columbia University Press.

Staten, Henry. 1984. *Wittgenstein and Derrida*. Lincoln: University of Nebraska Press.

Steiner, George. 1975. *After Babel: Aspects of Language and Translation*. London: Oxford University Press.

Stoler, Ann Laura. 1995. *Race and the Education of Desire: Foucault's History of Sexuality and the Colonial Order of Things*. Durham, NC: Duke University Press.

Theisen, Bianca. 2006. "Simultaneity of Media: Kafka's Literary Screen." *MLN* 121 (3): 543–50.

Todorov, Tzvetan. 1984. *The Conquest of America: The Question of the Other*. Translated by Richard Howard. New York: Harper and Row.

———. 2008. *La peur des barbares: Au-delà du choc des civilizations*. Paris: Robert Laffont.

———. 2010. *The Fear of Barbarians: Beyond the Clash of Civilizations*. Translated by Andrew Brown. Chicago: Chicago University Press.

Traverso, Enzo. 2003. *The Origins of Nazi Violence*. Translated by Janet Lloyd. New York: New Press.

Tsing, Anna, and Gail Hershatter. 2005. "Civilization." In Bennett, Grossberg, and Morris, *New Keywords*, 35–39.

Tsirkas, Stratis. 1971. *O politikos Kavafis* [The political Cavafy]. Athens: Kedros.

Tziovas, Dimitris. 1986. "Cavafy's Barbarians and Their Western Genealogy." *Byzantine and Modern Greek Studies* 10:161–78.

Vagenas, Nasos, ed. 2000. *Sinomilontas me ton Kavafi: Anthologia xenon kavafogenon poiimaton* [Conversing with Cavafy: Anthology of foreign poems inspired by Cavafy]. Thessaloniki: Kentro Ellinikis Glossas, 2000.

van Alphen, Ernst. 2005. *Art in Mind: How Contemporary Images Shape Thought*. Chicago: University of Chicago Press.

———. 2007. "Configurations of Self: Modernism and Distraction." In *Modernism*, edited by Astradur Eysteinsson and Vivian Liska, 339–46. Amsterdam: John Benjamins.

———. 2008. "Affective Operations of Art and Literature." *Res: Anthropology and Aesthetics* 53/54 (Spring/Autumn): 20–30.

Vaneigem, Raoul. 1999. *A Cavalier History of Surrealism*. Translated by Donald Nicholson-Smith. Edinburgh: AK Press.

Venuti, Lawrence. 1994. "Translation and the Formation of Cultural Identities." *Current Issues in Language and Society* 1:214–15.

———. 1995. *The Translator's Invisibility: A History of Translation*. London: Routledge.

———. 1996a. "Translation, Heterogeneity, Linguistics." *TTR: Traduction, Terminologie, Rédaction* 9 (1): 91–115.

———. 1996b. "Translation, Philosophy, Materialism." *Radical Philosophy* 79:24–35.

Warner, Jamie. 2008. "Tyranny of the Dichotomy: Prophetic Dualism, Irony, and *The Onion*." *ejc/rec: The Electronic Journal of Communication/La Revue Electronique de Communication* 18 (2, 3, 4). www.cios.org/www/ejc/EJCPUBLIC/018/2/01841.html.

Wasserstein, Bernard. *Barbarism and Civilization: A History of Europe in Our Time*. Oxford: Oxford University Press, 2007.

Weber, Max. (1905) 1999. "The Spirit of Capitalism and the Iron Cage." In *Social Theory: The Multicultural and Classic Readings*, edited by Charles Lemert, 100–104. Reprint, Boulder, CO: Perseus-Westview.

Weber, Samuel. 1997. "Wartime." In *Violence, Identity and Self-Determination*, edited by Hent de Vries and Samuel Weber, 80–105. Stanford, CA: Stanford University Press.

Wenzel, Jennifer. 1996. "Keys to the Labyrinth: Writing, Torture, and Coetzee's Barbarian Girl." *Tulsa Studies in Women's Literature* 15 (1): 61–71.

Werneburg, Brigitte, and Christopher Phillips. 1992. "Ernst Jünger and the Transformed World." *October* 62:42–64.

White, Hayden. 1972. "The Forms of Wildness: Archaeology of an Idea." In *The Wild Man Within: An Image in Western Thought from the Renaissance to Romanticism*, edited by Edward Dudley and Maximillian E. Novak, 3–38. Pittsburgh: University of Pittsburgh Press.

———. 1973. *Metahistory: The Historical Imagination in Nineteenth-Century Europe*. Baltimore: Johns Hopkins University Press.

———. 1978. *Tropics of Discourse: Essays in Cultural Criticism*. Baltimore: Johns Hopkins University Press.

———. 1987. *The Content of the Form: Narrative Discourse and Historical Representation*. Baltimore: Johns Hopkins University Press.

Williams, Raymond. 1985. *Keywords: A Vocabulary of Culture and Society (Revised Edition)*. New York: Oxford University Press.

Winkelmann, Jan. 2001. "'Waiting for the Barbarians'—Kendell Geers." Translated by Andrea Scrima. In *Skulptur-Biennale Münsterland, Cat. Kreis Steinfurt*. Berlin: Vice Versa Verlag. www.jnwnklmnn.de/geers_e.htm. [Exhibition catalog]

Wohlfarth, Irving. 1994. "No-Man's-Land. On Walter Benjamin's Destructive Character." In Benjamin and Osborne, *Walter Benjamin's Philosophy*, 155–81.

Wood, Michael. 1996. "Kafka's China and the Parable of Parables." *Philosophy and Literature* 20 (2): 325–37.

Žižek, Slavoj. (1991) 2002. *For They Know Not What They Do: Enjoyment as a Political Factor*. Reprint, London: Verso.

———. 2005. *Iraq: The Borrowed Kettle*. London: Verso.

———. 2009. *Violence*. London: Profile.

Žižek, Slavoj, and Glyn Daly. 2004. *Conversations with Žižek*. Cambridge, MA: Polity Press.

Index

Cultural Memory | *in the Present*